DOING
EMOTIONS
HISTORY

HISTORY OF EMOTIONS

Editors
Susan J. Matt
Peter N. Stearns

DOING
EMOTIONS
HISTORY

Edited by
SUSAN J. MATT
and PETER N.
STEARNS

UNIVERSITY OF ILLINOIS PRESS
Urbana, Chicago, and Springfield

∞ This book is printed on acid-free paper.

Library of Congress Cataloging-in-Publication Data
Doing emotions history / edited by
Susan J. Matt and Peter N. Stearns.
pages cm. — (The history of emotions)
Includes bibliographical references and index.
ISBN 978-0-252-03805-1 (hardback)
ISBN 978-0-252-07955-9 (paper)
ISBN 978-0-252-09532-0 (ebook)
1. Emotions—Sociological aspects.
2. Emotions—Social aspects—History.
3. Ethnopsychology.
I. Matt, Susan J. (Susan Jipson), 1967–
II. Stearns, Peter N.
HM1033.D65   2014
152.4—dc23   2013024439

CONTENTS

INTRODUCTION

SUSAN J. MATT AND
PETER N. STEARNS

Why did early modern Europeans believe the world to be a vale of tears? In contrast, how and when did Americans come to be so cheerful? Why did homicidal husbands in the eighteenth century kill their wives out of anger, while husbands in the nineteenth were more likely to claim they murdered out of jealousy? How did Americans learn to manage their anger to increase productivity and profits?[1] These questions, and others like them, are topics that historians of the emotions have been raising for the last several decades. While concerned with the most personal of subjects—human feelings—their investigations have demonstrated that emotions have larger social and political implications and can shape public realities.

Rather than examining merely the external behaviors of individuals—the traditional subject of history—scholars of the emotions explore the anger, the envy, the love, and the greed that prompted such behaviors. They strive to know how history felt to those who lived through it.[2] This represents a fundamentally new direction in history, for as one scholar of the emotions has noted, "history began as the servant of political developments. Despite a generation's worth of social and cultural history, the discipline has never quite lost its attraction to hard, rational things. Emotions have seemed tangential (if not fundamentally opposed) to the historical enterprise."[3] That the history of emotions has overcome such traditions and prejudices and become a flourishing and rapidly expanding field shows just how worthwhile an approach it has proved to be. By studying feelings, historians are uncovering the worldviews and the most fundamental assumptions about life, culture, and personality that people in the past carried in their heads.

These investigations have shifted the discourse of history—away from the construct of the rational actor, whose behavior supposedly reflected only calculating self-interest. Self-interest was always a catch phrase, always vaguely defined, but was presumed to be a mental category devoid of "irrational," emotional content.[4] In questioning such concepts, and bringing emotions back into the story, historians have enriched what were fairly impoverished explanations of human motivation and offered more nuanced discussions of why men and women in other eras did what they did. As a result of such labors, they have demonstrated not only that emotions shaped history but that emotions themselves have a history.

This idea—that emotions have a history—was once controversial. It has been gaining ground over the last several decades, as historians, anthropologists, sociologists, psychologists, and at least some cognitive scientists have come to recognize the role that culture has in shaping feeling. Few in these disciplines would argue that emotions are constant across space and time. Instead, there is an emerging consensus that emotions have both biological and cultural components and that societies influence the expression, repression, and meaning of feelings by giving them names and assigning values to some and not others. For instance, marital love, which many once regarded as a fairly constant emotion in human history, actually shows great variability in different contexts. Some classicists contend that in ancient Greece, there was no romantic jealousy between partners, for the ideal of a love-based marriage did not yet exist. Love, however, could be found in friendships. The ideal of romantic, love-based marriages emerged haltingly, evident in some places in the Western world by the seventeenth century, spreading rapidly in the eighteenth, and becoming deeply rooted in the nineteenth. So for instance, while many colonial New England couples loved each other, they tried not to do so excessively, lest they put earthly joys ahead of their love of God. Nineteenth-century Americans shed such worries and came to idealize the love-based marriage, seeing it as an instantiation of the sacred. Twentieth-century Americans celebrated it as well, but discovered gaps between the ideal of romantic love and the often more prosaic forms of actual relationships. In fact, love became such a powerful ideal that it supplanted all other rationales for marriage; its absence in a marriage justified the dissolution of the partnership, leading one historian to conclude that in the late twentieth century, love had essentially killed marriage.[5]

Scholars have come to recognize that such transformations in emotional standards shape not only family relationships but also work life, class relations and identity, religious devotion, and political expression. As the significance of the field has become apparent, interest in it has grown, so much so that in 2010, a scholar announced that the field of history had taken an "emotional turn."[6] Once a small subfield, the history of the emotions is suddenly quite popular. From studies of the emotions in ancient Rome to explorations of sentiment in modern China, feelings seem to be everywhere. Even more significantly, historians of many stripes who did not think of themselves as students of the emotions are nevertheless beginning to incorporate them into their analysis of more traditional topics. As a result, the history of business, politics, science, and religion are being examined from the standpoint of feelings.

This volume obviously reflects many of the achievements of this new and important field. But *Doing Emotions History* ventures beyond a sampling and a celebration. The intent is to focus on some leading issues and opportunities in the field, to spur further discussion, and advance what is already exciting scholarship to even greater heights.

ORIGINS

Although the field has gained momentum only relatively recently, it is based on almost a century of exploration. Among early scholars to broach the subject were Johan Huizinga, who in his 1919 book, *The Waning of the Middle Ages*, examined the emotional climate of the fourteenth and fifteenth centuries, and Norbert Elias, whose classic 1939 work, *The Civilizing Process*, took up the subject of emotional control. The scholar most credited for first launching the field, however, was Lucien Febvre, who, in a series of essays first published in the 1930s and 1940s, called on historians to see human psychology not as universal and constant but as fluid and historically contingent. He told historians that their goal should be "to establish a detailed inventory of the mental equipment of the men of the time." From there, "by dint of great learning, but also of imagination," they would be able to "reconstitute the whole physical, intellectual and moral universe of each preceding generation."[7]

Febvre was part of the *Annales School*, which emphasized the *longue durée*, the slow rhythms of change that altered daily life and social structure. Beginning in the 1940s, and continuing to this day, Annales historians, including Marc Bloch and Fernand Braudel, Philippe Ariès, and, more recently, Roger Chartier, have studied the history of daily activity, private life, and the *mentalités* of earlier generations. They pioneered the historical investigation of emotions.

The field took root more slowly in the United States. In the 1960s, American scholars began to take up some of the Annales School's concerns, in an effort to write history from the "bottom up." Rather than focusing on political debates and leaders, the new social history looked instead at everyday men and women. Scholars first turned to the history of the working class, then to questions of race and gender, and finally to the exchanges, practices, and habits of daily life. They endeavored to write the history of the family, the body, food, hygiene, and sex. In the 1980s, a few scholars extended this research agenda and began to investigate the emotions.

These historians started by exploring the emotional codes and standards of past societies in order to understand the rules that shaped subjective life. This focus on what Peter and Carol Zisowitz Stearns called *emotionology* yielded an impressive array of works on particular emotions, ranging from anger to sadness to jealousy. These studies explored how social norms about emotional expression changed in reaction to transformations in family life and law, economic growth, and political upheaval. They relied upon advice guides, sermons, editorials, child-rearing manuals, and other forms of prescriptive literature that offered instructions on how and when to display or suppress emotions. While the Stearnses encouraged their fellow historians to take up the study of these emotional standards and rules, they also discussed the problems of such inquiries, writing, "Clearly, a history of the perception of tantrums, though significant, is not likely to be identical to that of [actual] childish behavior." Their point was that the study of emotional standards had its limitations, for such studies could not capture actual experience, nor could they describe the perceptions of those outside the literate culture that consumed such advice.[8] Yet, nevertheless, the Stearnses suggested that while emotional rules could not tell the whole history of an emotion, they could point to important social conventions and make clear how individuals conformed or deviated from these mores. Building on their work, other historians joined the fray, and the field grew rapidly in the 1990s and early twenty-first century. Today there are dozens of works exploring topics as far-flung as the history of friendship and the history of grief. Many of these works have incorporated a study of emotional standards but have complemented them with explorations of how individuals coped with, expressed, and repressed their feelings, sometimes following, sometimes flouting social norms.

This large and growing body of research has suggested that modes of emotional expression can reveal attitudes about political, social, and economic values. For instance, in the years leading up to the French Revolution, many who found the emotional codes of the ancien régime confining expressed their ideological distance from the French court by embracing a more sentimental style. Likewise, those who openly envied in the late nineteenth century flouted religious rules and cultural norms; in so doing they also showed their discomfort with prevailing social hierarchies and long-standing class divisions.[9] Choosing to express or repress a feeling, choosing to obey or ignore social conventions about feelings, can be an explicitly political act.[10] Emotions history, in other words, can be explored for its own sake—because emotions themselves are intriguing and important—or for what emotions reveal about broader facets of the human experience and social patterns.

SOME CORE ISSUES

Any relatively new field, like emotions history, generates or reflects some complex tensions. Four are particularly interesting and challenging and inform many of the essays that follow—without, however, being definitively resolved. The problem of social class has already been discussed but deserves explicit attention. Issues of causation loom large: what prompts changes in emotional formulation and are there any patterns, and what in turn do such emotional shifts cause? The question of audience, and the related selection of problems, constitutes a third area: is emotions history best directed toward other historians, offering new takes on established historical problems, or is there a scholarly audience, interdisciplinary in scope, that can and should take emotions history seriously? And finally: what about geography? The history of emotions so far has been mainly, but not exclusively Western, and usually focused on particular regions within this cultural tradition—but how and what kinds of geographical contours should the field accept?

The emotional history of "articulate" groups, open to the most widely publicized standards, is clearly easier to do than work on groups—social classes, religious subcultures, even age cohorts—that less actively consume any formal literature. Some pioneering work does show the potential of a history that expands across a wide social and cultural spectrum—beyond the articulate groups that most commonly author and attend to formal emotional advice. Philip Greven, for example, charted the emotional characteristics of a Protestant evangelical subculture in the United States and demonstrated that many of these traits endured well into the twentieth century.[11] Scholars have also probed the expressions and rituals of grief in the African American community and the evolution of uses of fear in American Catholicism. Historians have likewise turned their attention to emotions and work, examining, for instance, managerial efforts to manipulate lower-middle-class emotions in order to create superficially cheerful sales clerks. That emotional environment often stood in stark contrast to working-class emotional culture on the job. Despite these studies, it is clear that we need more consistent attention to divergences in emotional cultures and experiences in complex societies. There is also room for more work on how emotional standards shape interactions among groups and social classes. In the late nineteenth century, courts of law in several American states allowed middle-class women to sue for divorce on grounds of mental cruelty but barred this argument for working-class women on grounds that their feelings were not delicate enough to be abused. Emotional differentiations fuel social relationships, not always in pleasant ways.

A second challenge in the history of emotions involves causation, a vital but complicated topic in historical analysis of any sort. Since emotions history highlights change, the question arises as to whether there are any consistent or recurrent patterns in the factors that spur change. Why did romantic love gain new valuation in the eighteenth and nineteenth centuries? New ideas were clearly involved, from novels and popularized philosophy, but were there other sources? Did the shift, as some historians of Europe suggested, translate an increasingly competitive economic environment into the emotional realm,[12] where individuals needed a new image of familial affection to compensate for troubling, and novel, economic pressures? In the twentieth century, efforts to moderate grief in the United States surely reflected the massive shifts in actual mortality rates, particularly for children, where fighting death, rather than grieving for it, now seemed most essential. In cases of this sort, larger structural changes—in the economy, in demography—led to substantial alterations in emotional standards, and presumably to some extent at least in ensuing experience, and reshaped personal and familial reality. The need for historians to work systematically on sources of change more generally adds an important, but intriguing component to historical analysis in the whole subfield. Emotional change does not simply happen, and it is not usually the work of a breed of self-proclaimed experts alone. It is caused, and sometimes deliberately manipulated, by various economic and political interests.[13]

Causation also, of course, runs in the other direction as well. Emotional changes prompt wider shifts—for example, in the ways parents treat children, or at least think they should, or in arguments that prove acceptable in courts of law. American husbands, for instance, who tried to use nineteenth-century arguments to explain why they killed their wives amid uncontrollable passion found courts rejecting the pleas by the 1930s because standards of jealousy had substantially changed. Shifts in emotional standards and behaviors have wideranging effects, and this is a legitimate subject for analysis as well.

This links to the wider question of audience, another challenge in the history of the emotions. Most historians seek to connect their work to other efforts to understand the past, and this applies to much of the work in emotions history as well. Thus emotions history can contribute to innovative treatments of the American or French revolutions, or to explorations of the characteristics of the Renaissance. The goals are a better understanding of particular moments in the past, and the connection of emotions research to recognizable disciplinary topics with a history-interested audience in mind. But emotions history can also link to research on feeling conducted by other disciplines, like social psychology, where history nurtures a better grasp of the dimensions of change but where the focus on the past for its own sake is less intense. Much work in emotions history, of course, can inform both historical research and interdisciplinary inquiry. But where researchers really want to draw in, say, their colleagues in sociology, not naturally inclined to consider historical complexities in any event, or where they hope to use recent changes in emotional experience to help directly illuminate present patterns, it may be necessary to downplay some of the detailed connections to standard historical topics. Emotions history can aspire to a serious place among the core disciplines devoted to assessing human affect, but the relationships are not yet firmly established. The field can serve various kinds of analytical targets but not always all at the same time. Here is a tension visible in several of the essays in this collection and in the probable future of emotions history more generally.

Finally, there is the question of geography—of the regional bases for work on past emotional patterns and changes—a topic directly addressed in *Doing Emotions History*. As a subject, history is place-specific, and most work on the history of emotions has focused on particular nations or regions. The pioneering efforts have not always, however, defined the regional culture or its boundaries explicitly—assuming rather than demonstrating coherence. Even more rarely have they explored a region's distinctiveness through any real kind of comparative analysis against another regional case.[14] The field of emotions history has arguably advanced enough to warrant more explicit assessment of regional factors, including the revealing, if demanding, attempt to do comparative work. Finally, though this involves descriptive range more than analysis per se, it is clearly essential to move beyond the heretofore standard reliance on cases from Western European and North American experience. Emotions history needs to catch up with the increasingly global dimensions of the larger historical domain. In several ways, then, the field is poised for more fruitful encounters with issues of place and region. Here is another area where *Doing Emotions History* hopes to lay the groundwork for future work.

Indeed, the essays in this volume push forward, directly and indirectly, all four of the issues just discussed. While geography is particularly addressed in Part II, the regional analysis section, John Corrigan's essay in Part IV, which focuses on emotion and religion, shows the wide geographic compass possible when emotional experience, and not conventional cultural narratives is the topic. Discussions of specific emotions (Part III) but also the study of emotion and politics, religion, and media (Part IV) inevitably raise issues of social class: how did new emotional standards spread, for example, to help motivate new political arguments and behaviors across some social lines? Collectively, the essays also illustrate the challenge of audience: some case studies may appeal most directly to historians, but other essays, ranging more widely over religion or modernity, clearly invite interaction with other disciplines that deal with emotion. Brent Malin's discussion of modern media deliberately invokes interdisciplinary inquiry. And virtually all of the essays, in discussing patterns of change, raise questions about causation and consequence, where historical work has particularly great potential in connecting emotions to other developments.

DEBATES AND DISCOVERIES

Besides addressing core issues in emotions history, the essays in *Doing Emotions History* also engage with intense existing debates within the discipline. For example, as the field has evolved, some scholars argue that rather than hunt for a single emotional code that governs a society, historians should be attentive to the multiple sets of standards that exist at any time. Medievalist Barbara Rosenwein, for instance, suggests that in all societies there are "emotional communities," and she proposes that in the course of a day, individuals may move through a range of them—from churches to taverns to parlors—each of which require different affective styles.[15] Other scholars have offered alternative theories. William Reddy, in his study of French political culture in the eighteenth and nineteenth centuries, writes, for instance, of "emotional regimes," which spread and enforce dominant emotional norms, and "emotional refuges," in which individuals can seek emotional release and freedom from such regimes.[16]

Scholars of the emotions pick and choose between these theories or construct their own, but they have used them in innovative ways that rewrite many of the conventional narratives of history. In 1941, Lucien Febvre predicted that the history of emotions would revolutionize traditional views of the past when he observed, "So many people go around despairing at every turn—there is, they say, nothing left to discover, or so it seems, in regions that have been too well explored. All they need to do is plunge into the darkness where psychology wrestles with history—they would soon get back their appetite for discovery."[17] Although it took time, his prediction has been borne out. For instance, historians of religion are showing that theological debates have been not just about abstract ideas of faith and works but also about affective style. Early Protestantism differentiated itself from Catholicism not only in its ideas about salvation but in its attitudes about how one should best show and experience religion emotionally.[18]

Historians of the American and French Revolution have likewise demonstrated that in addition to being based on philosophies of natural rights and consent, the revolutionary movements were built upon theories of sentiment and particular emotional states.[19] Scholars of capitalism, for whom rational actors have traditionally dominated the stage, have shown instead that economic behavior was often based on emotion, and that the ability to engage in "getting and spending," to be acquisitive, desiring, and individualistic was dependent on changes in emotional life and style.[20] Those who study the history of marriage and the family have discovered that it was not just legal codes and religious doctrine that shaped power relations in households but that emotional norms could as well. For instance, when couples began to celebrate romantic love in the nineteenth century, women's informal status in marriage often improved, even if their legal status did not.[21] Such discoveries suggest that looking at history from the standpoint of feelings yields new narratives that differ in timing, in emphasis, and in the cast of characters from more conventional histories.

This volume seeks to sort through the new themes and trends emerging in emotions history and understand where the field is going. It builds upon the dozens of books and hundreds of articles that have been published in the field, bringing together the latest research. It does not offer an emotional history of all regions, nor does it cover all epochs. Instead, it uses case studies to explore concepts and issues that run across the discipline, and that all students of the emotions must confront. It examines key conceptual questions: How can one locate emotion in the past? How much does it change over time? What role do media and technology have in shaping emotional culture?

Collectively and individually, the essays in this book take up such fundamental subjects in emotion history as methodology and periodization. As contemporary historians have begun to tackle the history of emotions, many have had to first define for themselves what emotion is. By the very nature of their inquiry, historians concur that while there may be some basic emotions that exist in all people, how they are expressed and what they mean varies dramatically across cultures and centuries. But that is where the agreement ends, for there are ongoing debates about whether emotions can be separated from the language and culture used to describe them. Some have proposed, for instance, that the very act of naming and describing a feeling gives it a shape and fixity that it otherwise would not have.[22] Others wonder about the lack of words to describe an emotion—does a feeling exist if there is no name for it? Given these difficulties, how should historians regard written records of the emotions? What other sources do they have at their disposal, and how should these be used? Susan Matt's essay examines these debates over the central theoretical and methodological assumptions of the field.

The book also explores the lively and ongoing debates over timing. One contentious issue for historians is the extent to which modernity changed emotional life, particularly in Europe and America. The topic is hotly debated, with many historians of the modern era suggesting that a profound change occurred at the end of the medieval period, as new standards of emotional expression and control emerged. Some argue that in the modern period, families became more loving, particularly toward their offspring; others focus on the rise of a new set of emotional rules that taught self-consciousness, embarrassment, and self-control. In contrast, many medieval scholars contend that these are overgeneralizations at best, and that there were a variety of emotional rules and norms, rather than a single model of familial love during the Middle Ages; further, they maintain that many communities demonstrated the same patterns of familial relations evident in later centuries. Peter Stearns explores the debates over continuity and change in emotional culture, focusing particularly on the effects of modernity on sentiment. This discussion of timing also links the history of emotions to questions about how economic change and shifting modes of production or whole systems like capitalism affect emotional life.

Place as well as timing shapes history. As we have noted, scholars of the emotions have focused largely and primarily on Western Europe and the United States. There is new work emerging on other regions, however. Mark Steinberg's essay on Eastern Europe examines a regional emotional culture and how it shaped attitudes about religion, morality, catastrophe, and loss; Norman Kutcher examines issues of continuity and distinctiveness in China. Kutcher emphasizes the complexities of traditional Chinese approaches, whereas Steinberg focuses more on recent themes. Both rely on a mixture of evidence—from intellectual formulations to architectural design to humor. Both emphasize the importance of avoiding widely held stereotypes, but both believe that it is possible and important to identify vital elements of a regional emotional culture. Together, these essays not only advance the field of emotions history beyond its initial Western heartland; they also begin to project the kind of comparative analysis that must advance historical and interdisciplinary understanding in the future.

Darrin McMahon and Pam Epstein offer focused studies of two particular emotions, sketching both their histories and their historiography. McMahon examines why joy and other positive emotions have largely been neglected by scholars, while suggesting clearly that there are rich opportunities for greater historical understanding in this realm. He is able to identify some particular moments in the past when examinations of joy are particularly revealing, leaving the further task of more systematically exploring wider changes and regional diversities as challenges for the future. Pamela Epstein's work on love touches on topics that historians have tackled before but offers new insights—and types of evidence—for patterns of change associated with modern urbanization. Essays in this section invite further work. Many of the advances of emotions history to date have come from explorations of particular emotions, from anger to nostalgia. McMahon urges a broader palette, open to the study of yet additional feelings and especially more positive ones. Epstein, in some contrast, shows how a fairly well-established historical category, in this case love, is open to additional assessment through the use of innovative sources.

The final essays demonstrate the potential that emotions history has for rewriting traditional narratives through exploration of wider social relationships. Nicole Eustace's work examines how political history is reshaped by attention to the emotions. She explores how sentiment undergirded political identities and allegiances and how emotion shaped civic memory and consciousness in revolutionary and early-nineteenth-century America. She also considers why emotions have been excluded from traditional political narratives. John Corrigan's sweeping examination of religion and emotion shows the varied possibilities for mutual relationships, including common developments in different religious settings as well as important patterns of change. Emotion obviously affects religious meaning, but Corrigan urges an even broader inquiry into this complex relationship. Finally, Brent Malin, in his examination of early-twentieth-century media, explores the particular concerns that emerged about these new technologies' emotional implications. All three of these essays illustrate the advantages of examining social and emotional changes in tandem.

• • •

Through these essays, *Doing Emotions History* brings together examples of the latest research on the emotions, an assessment of the field as a whole, and a sense of new directions to pursue. The goal is to illustrate key issues, without pretending to provide comprehensive coverage. Thus questions about change and periodization, about probing regional cultures with at least some comparative sense, about how to explore individual emotions and open new territory, and finally about linking emotions history to wider facets of the social past—all receive attention, along with explicit methodological problems. The analytical examples, as well as the specific findings, can help make the next generation of emotions research more intentional and systematic than the pioneering studies of the past few decades. The central goal is to bring additional students and scholars to the field so that we may improve our grasp of how emotions develop socially and find expression amid historical change.

NOTES

1. Carol Z. Stearns, "'Lord Help Me Walk Humbly': Anger and Sadness in England and America, 1570–1750," in *Emotion and Social Change: Toward a New Psychohistory*, ed. Carol Z. Stearns and Peter N. Stearns (New York: Holmes and Meier, 1988); Christina Kotchemidova, "From Good Cheer to 'Drive-By Smiling': A Social History of Cheerfulness," *Journal of Social History* 39 (2005), 5–37; Dawn Keetley, "From Anger to Jealousy: Explaining Domestic Homicide in Antebellum America," *Journal of Social History* 42 (2008), 269–297; Peter N. Stearns, *American Cool: Constructing a Twentieth-Century Emotional Style* (New York: New York University Press, 1994); Carol Z. Stearns and Peter N. Stearns, *Anger: The Struggle for Emotional Control in America's History* (Chicago: University of Chicago Press, 1986).

2. Peter N. Stearns and Jan Lewis, Introduction, in *An Emotional History of the United States*, ed. Jan Lewis and Peter N. Stearns (New York: New York University Press, 1998), 1.

3. Barbara H. Rosenwein, "Worrying about Emotions in History," *American Historical Review* 107 (June 2002), 821.

4. Jan Plamper, "The History of Emotions: An Interview with William Reddy, Barbara Rosenwein, and Peter Stearns," *History and Theory* 49 (May 2010), 238.

5. David Konstan, *The Emotions of the Ancient Greeks: Studies in Aristotle and Classical Literature* (Toronto: University of Toronto Press, 2006); Laurel Thatcher Ulrich, *Good Wives: Image and Reality in the Lives of Women in Northern New England, 1650–1750* (New York: Knopf, 1982); Edmund Morgan, *The Puritan Family: Religion & Domestic Relations in 17th Century New England*, rev. ed. (New York: Harper Perennial, 1966); Ann Swidler, *Talk of Love: How Culture Matters* (Chicago: University of Chicago Press, 2000); Stephanie Coontz, *Marriage, A History: How Love Conquered Marriage* (New York: Penguin, 2006).

6. Plamper, "The History of Emotions."

7. Lucien Febvre, "History and Psychology," in *A New Kind of History: From the Writings of Febvre*, ed. Peter Burke, trans. K. Folca, (New York: Harper and Row, 1973), 5, 9.

8. Peter N. Stearns and Carol Z. Stearns, "Emotionology: Clarifying the History of Emotions and Emotional Standards," *American Historical Review* 90 (October 1985), 813–836, 827.

9. William M. Reddy, *The Navigation of Feeling: A Framework for the History of Emotions* (Cambridge: Cambridge University Press, 2001), 145–146; Susan J. Matt, *Keeping Up with*

the Joneses: Envy in American Consumer Society, 1890–1930 (Philadelphia: University of Pennsylvania Press, 2003).

10. Nicole Eustace, *Passion Is the Gale: Emotion, Power, and the Coming of the American Revolution* (Chapel Hill: University of North Carolina Press, 2008), 11; Reddy, *Navigation of Feeling*, 124–125.

11. Philip Greven, *The Protestant Temperament: Patterns of Child-Rearing, Religious Experience, and the Self in Early America* (Chicago: University of Chicago Press, 1978); Arlie Russell Hochschild, *The Managed Heart: Commercialization of Human Feeling, Twentieth Anniversary Edition* (Berkeley: University of California Press, 2003); Lewis and Stearns, *Emotional History of the United States*.

12. Edmund Leites, ed., *Conscience and Casuistry in Early Modern Europe* (Cambridge: Cambridge University Press, 2002).

13. Stearns, *American Cool*.

14. Joanna Bourke, *Fear: A Cultural History* (London: Virago Press, 2005).

15. Rosenwein, "Worrying about Emotions in History"; Barbara Rosenwein, *Emotional Communities in the Early Middle Ages* (Ithaca, N.Y.: Cornell University Press, 2006).

16. Reddy, *Navigation of Feeling*, 124–129.

17. Febvre, "Sensibility and History: How to Reconstitute the Emotional Life of the Past," in *New Kind of History*, 12.

18. Susan Karant-Nunn, *The Reformation of Feeling: Shaping the Religious Emotions in Early Modern Germany* (New York: Oxford University Press, 2010).

19. Sarah Knott, *Sensibility and the American Revolution* (Chapel Hill: University of North Carolina Press for the Omohundro Institute of Early American History and Culture, 2009); Andrew Burstein, *Sentimental Democracy: The Evolution of America's Romantic Self-Image* (New York: Hill and Wang, 1999); Eustace, *Passion is the Gale*; Reddy, *Navigation of Feeling*.

20. Matt, *Keeping Up with the Joneses*.

21. Karen Lystra, *Searching the Heart: Women, Men, and Romantic Love in Nineteenth-Century America* (New York: Oxford University Press, 1989).

22. See, for instance, Jean Starobinski, "The Idea of Nostalgia," *Diogenes* 54 (Summer 1966), 81; Reddy, *Navigation of Feeling*, 104, 105, 129.

PART I

BASIC ISSUES

ASSESSING CHANGE

CHAPTER 1

MODERN PATTERNS
IN EMOTIONS HISTORY

PETER N. STEARNS

After thirty to forty years of serious, informative work on emotions history, scholars have not clearly answered what would seem a vital and timely question: do emotions and emotional standards change when a society moves toward modernity? This essay seeks to explore the current status of the issue, to indicate promising lines for renewed attention, and to urge greater priority for analysis and discussion.

Current indecision (at best) or neglect results from three factors. First, modernity itself is a contested notion. Most would agree that industrial, urban societies differ from agricultural ones, but how widely this spills over onto areas like politics and culture is hardly a settled item. Second, emotions history raises some particular challenges for inquiries into change, because emotions have some biological and psychological basis that resist even powerful transforming forces, and because all societies, premodern or modern, need some regulatory efforts in some negative emotional areas. Modern change may, as we will argue, be real, but it is not going to involve sweeping contrasts.

But it's the third constraint that really invites the most urgent attention: current analysis is deeply shaped by excessive scholarly oscillations over the past thirty years.

There is no question that some earlier efforts to characterize modern emotions, primarily in the Western context, oversimplified to the point of being well off the mark; this was initially true of efforts to describe premodern families as lacking love and affection—the catch phrase was "about as much emotion as one would expect to find in a bird's nest," but it extended also to claims about unregulated anger.[1] Overgeneralizations about premodern fear or grief have also stirred rebuttals. On the other hand, the key issues have been subsequently unduly displaced by medievalist critiques. It is worth reopening questions about emotional concomitants to modern progresses like industrialization or urbanization. The goal here is to relaunch a discussion, inviting contributions from both premodern and modern sides and with a special plea for work—still unusual—that bridges between the two. We should look at some of the claims that have been offered, a few of which have needlessly fallen from view, and, of course, to remind ourselves of the many problems that have been noted. Above all, we need to examine the emotional implications of some key modern structures themselves—the piece that, it seems to me, has been notably absent in many of the discussions to date.

There is precedent for a relaunch of this sort from work in the history of childhood. Here too, initial claims about the modern were clearly excessive, provoking an (arguably equally excessive) backlash from premodernists; this in turn generated some years of needless confusion or silence but ultimately yielded the opportunity for a more sophisticated discussion of change and continuity. The childhood debate began with claims by Philippe Ariès, sometimes enhanced by subsequent exaggerations from other historians, that premodern Western society had not recognized childhood as a clearly separate stage in life, which might in turn have promoted various forms of inattention or ill treatment. The hypothesis did spur important research in what had been a neglected field. Fairly quickly, however, it led to counterthrusts by medievalists and early modernists, bent on showing that people in their cherished periods did value children and (in some extreme counterclaims) should not be differentiated as parents from their modern counterparts. The resultant stalemate actually slowed research for a time—after all, if there were no real distinctions why *do* history, particularly amid such contested interpretations. It turns out, of course, that some valid lines can be drawn between premodern and modern childhoods—for example, in the move from predominant work to predominant schooling—without claiming total differentiation or some systematic premodern severity. And historians working on other regions, such as Japan, actually have found some premodern-modern differences in childhood recognizability that are not totally different from those posited by Ariès.[2]

On a broadly similar basis, there is no reason that some careful claims about modernity in emotion need rouse premodernists to battle. The claims can be fully compatible with acknowledging emotional complexities and nuances in premodern periods—including recognition of the common humanity involved. They do not have to assume uniformity or stagnation in premodern emotions—all sorts of change and variety are possible within the long framework of agricultural societies. At the same time, a careful assertion of claims about modern change must acknowledge important continuities, both because the modern-premodern line is never rigid in any area of endeavor and because of the biopsychological basics that no historical periodization will erase. Invoking care is not the same thing, however, as ignoring modern factors altogether, which (as with childhood earlier) some premodernists have come close to contending. It should not promote emotions history as a series of pointillist inquiries without the possibility of some larger dynamics—among other things because the result might essentially remove history from participation in interdisciplinary inquiry on grounds of excessive detail and caution. Again, it's time for some new approaches to what a modern framework for emotional change might entail.[3]

Before proposing a partially new tack, however, it's important to review the current state of play, including modernist assertions that have been made to date and ensuing rebuttals, because the combination establishes a few points that need not be lost, and certainly a number of initial cautions.

It's vital, of course, to approach the topic with some notion of what "the modern" is all about. A new Oxford University Press series marks 1500 as the point at which the modern begins, though it is hard to know why. To be sure, Western society after 1500 became more commercial and launched its long process of colonial expansion. Most studies of the modern, however, would wait at least another two centuries, when the rise of science, some political systemization, and some of the beginnings of industrialization mark a more decisive set of changes—first Western, but ultimately global. For emotions history, key initial questions involve whether any emotional changes accompanied the onset of greater modernity, and certainly what emotional shifts the changing economic and social structures would generate.

While serious work on the issue of modern emotions began virtually at the same time as Lucien Febvre's famous appeal for opening the field as a whole, as noted in the Introduction, it was only in the 1980s that an initial picture began to emerge. By this point, several historians were staking claims about discrete emotions, offering analyses that can still be usefully plumbed. But it was the revival of an earlier, more sweeping theoretical framework that spurred the greatest interest, stimulating additional research but also calling forth a devastating critique that spilled beyond the initial target. Reassessing this debate and diversion is an essential preliminary to any new advance.

PETER N. STEARNS

THE CIVILIZING DISTRACTION

The most ambitious response to the challenge of emotional modernity derived from the intriguing work of Norbert Elias (who built in turn on observations of scholars like Johan Huizinga).[4] The key notion was a "civilizing process" that progressively curbed raw emotional spontaneity as well as crude somatic impulses. Elements of the Elias findings are compatible with some of the more specific early work in emotions history—particularly around anger—but the two approaches are decidedly not identical. Indeed, the clearer and more ambitious theoretical structure around the Elias formulation has often obscured the other set of options, arguably more empirically grounded, prompting as well some of the more strident critiques. The result is a combination that may well have miscast the debate around the modern much as the Ariès claims long bedeviled the history of modern childhood. For there are significant and distinctive features of the Elias theory in its own right, beginning for our purposes with the real possibility that the civilizing process framework, while certainly warranting scrutiny, is not so much a statement about modern emotional patterns as an interesting gloss on premodern adjustments on the eve of modernity.

The idea of a civilizing process, presumably beginning with the Renaissance, extending with the development of royal courts in other parts of Europe and ultimately trickling down to other social classes, focuses more on manners than on emotions per se, but there is unquestionable overlap. To meet new standards of polite society, people were encouraged to become more restrained, whether the focus was on physical manifestations, like belching, or emotional outbursts, such as open displays of anger. The sweep and ambition of the Elias theory have attracted a great deal of enthusiasm, and many historians and social scientists have found the approach congenial. A major study of manners in nineteenth-century America, for example, directly uses the civilizing process theory to talk about how an aspiring urban middle class sought to shake off frontier habits and simultaneously distinguish itself from immigrant and working-class elements in the growing cities.[5] New levels of emotional control were a vital part of the evolution. On another front, historians looking specifically at anger have plugged into the theory, noting for example that the word *tantrum*, to designate an unacceptably wild and, it was ultimately decided, childish display of this emotion—and through this to formulate new levels of disapproval for this particular lack of emotional control—emerged for the first time in the later eighteenth century.

In its own right, but even more as a statement of modern frameworks for emotional standards and experience, the civilizing process approach has some important limitations, even aside from the criticisms it has engendered from historians of premodern emotion. Geographically, it is explicitly Western, which doesn't undermine the theory—after all, Elias intended a comment on the Western experience—but which may suggest some liabilities in terms of characterizing a more widely applicable set of modern factors. More important, its chronological focus raises some knotty problems for any explicit consideration of the modern. Tensions over chronology have already loomed large—even aside from the outright critiques of the whole approach. Is it plausible, amid all the developments associated with modernity, that an emotional culture and associated physical etiquette launched amid the Renaissance upper classes would almost uniquely maintain a hold on modern patterns five centuries later? Seizing on the Renaissance as the beginning of a new behavioral and emotional etiquette may be quite accurate, but it hardly identifies the civilizing process with the emergence of modern European society: the inception is too early in a situation where even the most ardent proponents of modernization do not seriously venture before the late seventeenth century and the rise of science. Elias, in other words, may be quite right, but his findings are orthogonal to any full discussion of the interrelationship between modern conditions and emotional change. His process may spill over into the modern, or at least its first stages, but not necessarily through any structural link. Here in turn lies one of the reasons that the most ardent Elias partisans—disproportionately located among Dutch historians and sociologists—have had to struggle so mightily to find continuity in his process into identifiably modern times. Connections may survive into nineteenth-century middle-class culture, as John Kasson agrees, linking newly restrictive manners in the United States to a civilizing offensive imported from Europe—but they risk running aground in the fiercely anti-Victorian mood of the twentieth century. Use of civilized restraint to distinguish respectable from unrespectable groups did not disappear, but the emphasis shifted considerably toward greater inclusiveness (or less de facto tolerance). Further, a variety of overt reactions against nineteenth-century Victorian formulas called for far less repression and reticence. There are several core mismatches between the theory and a more comprehensive focus on modern change.

The strong suggestion is, then, to disentangle any ongoing assessment of the civilizing process approach from a discussion of modernity and emotion. In Western history, tendencies toward greater restraint deserve attention as part of early modern adjustments, and they may have contributed to a rather short-lived Victorian culture as well. But they don't describe a modern framework—any more than an assessment of changes in monarchy, however important for the immediate premodern centuries spilling into the nineteenth century, helps much with modern Western political trends. And this distinction returns us ultimately to the question of what, independent of the Elias model, we know about modern emotional change. But first we need briefly to acknowledge the medievalists' counterattacks and the implications that often extend well beyond Elias's findings.

THE COMPLEXITIES OF PREMODERN EMOTION

Led tirelessly by Barbara Rosenwein, who deserves great credit for both empirical and theoretical correctives to the first generation of work in Western emotions history, medievalists (and others interested in premodern emotion) have lambasted the Elias approach and in the process have introduced a number of indisputable points applicable to emotions history (evidence permitting) in any time or place.[6] Most fundamentally, we must be aware how unlikely it is that any organized society can ever afford to be as impulsive or unrestrained as Huizinga or Elias tended to represent for the medieval West. Rosenwein properly warns of the weaknesses of what she calls the hydraulic model of emotion, in which a cauldron of feelings may swirl without cognitive input or constraint.[7] This is not how emotion works, which means, of course, that a modern/premodern divide based on an introduction of impulse control is, by definition, off the mark. While some evidence may suggest higher rates of per capita violence in the Middle Ages than later on (Rosenwein perhaps shies away from this issue more than she should), there is no reason to assume that any society will ever seek or manage to avoid some definite rules on responsibilities for control. Earlier visions of the Middle Ages lacked an adequate range of evidence and were distorted by a smug modernist sense of progress and teleology inaccurately applied to the realm of emotion. The baseline for the idea of civilizing change was wildly distorted—and so the theory cannot represent any full process of change. Whether the whole theory must be rejected—we've already noted some of its difficulties on the modern end—or subjected to much more nuanced scrutiny as a passage from the complexities of the Middle Ages through the early modern centuries, may still warrant some discussion, and it's worth remembering that medievalists themselves have divided over this point. At the least, the counterattacks by medievalist-revisionists make it clear that any restatement will face formidable obstacles.*

---

* A full disclosure note here: Rosenwein's comments have included disputes with my own earlier work, particularly concerning anger. She correctly notes that I naively accepted the Huizinga-Elias notion of a more openly angry medieval past, though she also distorts some of my analysis, widening the gap beyond necessity.

The critique, however, spills beyond the Elias approach, or even the welcome opening of medieval emotion to serious and varied scrutiny (now pursued by a number of scholars, often inspired by Rosenwein's intellectual leadership). Rosenwein sees important connections between the flaws she finds in the civilizing process view of the Middle Ages and other, more bounded comments on emotions like love or fear. These issues, too, must be addressed in any revived analysis of modern change. Whether virtually all previous emotions work that sought to identify modern change was tainted by the same simplistic approach to medieval impulsiveness as was Elias's work is genuinely debatable, and even Rosenwein's sweeping correctives have left a few statements either undisputed or untouched. Clearly, however, the urgent understanding that there is no simple emotional society to be found that can then be replaced by modern restraints or depths constitutes a new challenge for statements of change. The corresponding need to look carefully at both sides of any turning points, rather than offering premodern straw men, complicates—though hopefully ultimately offers to improve—any process of analysis.

Rosenwein, however, goes even further than this, in at least two respects.** First, she urges focus on the different emotional communities available in any complex society, whether modern or premodern, and demonstrates (with colleagues) the range of alternatives available even in the early Middle Ages. And surely here too she scores: we know that modern people, certainly, pass through different emotional options—from spectator activities to work to family, for example—so the idea makes sense. Quite possibly, changes in the range and availability of emotional communities may prove to be one way to discuss emotions history more generally, always recognizing that there will be variety in any period. Where the approach becomes problematic, however, is when it risks obscuring larger cultural systems, and Rosenwein is quite candid about her skepticism concerning the identifiability of such systems, working instead on the use of emotional communities to trace change and continuity from premodern to modern—an ambitious project. But the caution she has encouraged prompts other scholars to settle for narrower topics and less analytical challenge. Some attention to the interplay between larger emotional patterns and particular emotional communities and subgroups offers an essential counterbalance. Too much focus on variety at any point in time may well distract from bigger changes, as well as providing more complexity and detail

** It is also worth noting that a focus in the Middle Ages in not the only test of "premodernity." Work on evolutions in the classical period suggests some vigorous contrast with modernity, a complication Rosenwein largely ignores.

than is desirable where historical work on emotion encounters the concerns and interests of other relevant disciplines. The point here is not to dispute possible gains available from the focus on communities, but to argue that it should not preempt other analytical targets, as well as opportunities to link historical findings about emotional change to the interests of, say, sociologists or social psychologists.

The second problem is more direct: like many revisionists before her, Rosen-wein sometimes presses her critique to the point of arguing that there may be no serious differences, in terms of emotional standards and behaviors, between the medieval and the modern. Medieval parents sometimes used fear with their children? What about the horror fiction available in the nineteenth or twentieth centuries? More broadly, since both medieval and modern societies host a great variety of emotional communities, there may be no sharp gaps between the two eras; or possibly the best approach is to posit a whole series of chronologi-cal changes that break the past millennium plus into a multiplicity of complex periods. Not surprisingly, Rosenwein finds herself at some points "querying the very idea of modernity."[8] As we will note, her hesitancy is not consistent: she does at times grant some important modern emotional innovations, as with an open interest in happiness.

To the extent that this kind of critique places new burdens of proof on mod-ernists to show carefully that modern conditions either generated or depended on some significant emotional change, so much the better. Again, we can all agree that some of the pioneers assumed too-easy a contrast. But the critique risks more in potentially discouraging a larger compass in favor of safer narrow probes. In fact, the evidence of the past decade plus suggests that the discour-agement has been real: while the range of empirical efforts in emotions history has widened on both sides of the premodern-modern divide, conversations about patterns of change that might span the divide have dimmed. And this is precisely why it is important to suggest that the critique has gone too far. It is time to assimilate its valid lessons, accept greater complexity—but return to more active inquiry into the emotional conditions of modernity. Figuring out the relationship between modernity and emotion is vital toward both elements of the equation—the notion of modern society and emotional context alike.

THREE PATHS

If the premise—that it is time for renewed analysis of emotional modernity— is granted, then there are at least three approaches to consider. Not mutually exclusive, we will take them up in turn. The first involves recapitulating earlier work that did highlight important shifts beginning with the eighteenth century that may point the way to parallel studies or larger syntheses. Granted, some of this work can be linked to some of the same flaws that have crippled the civilizing offensive, but there can be more subtle reworkings that preserve important findings and hypotheses. Second, and this has been less commonly done, we can take some of the known innovations of modern society—such as massive demographic change—and probe the emotional causes and consequences involved. Here is a rich field for further inquiry. And third, building on both of the initial options, we can probe premodern-to-modern transitions in comparative terms, broadening beyond the Western experience, to suggest both the variety in emotional styles (and perhaps communities) that are compatible with modernity but also some possible commonalities. Without pretending that we've proved some modern patterns of change in advance, there are exciting possibilities in reopening the subject.

FROM LOVE TO GUILT, THROUGH GOOD CHEER

We already know quite a bit about modern changes in emotion, and what we know, in some cases suitably reshaped in light of critiques, offers models for additional work and fodder for additional analysis.

Largely independent of the Elias approach, the first explicit sorties into premodern-to-modern emotions history occurred within the framework of more comprehensive treatments of developments in the family. This included attention to the somewhat unexpected impacts of Protestantism in pushing for a warmer familial environment but also the implications of an increasingly commercial economy in intensifying compensatory family relationships.[9] We must repeat: some of this initial work was overdone, neglecting evidence about strong emotional ties before the eighteenth century and irresponsibly ignoring the shared biology-psychology between premodern and modern people. Although the idea of rising affection was not ensnared in the civilizing process model, it did initially assume the same kind of stark contrast, in this case with an assumed coldness in traditional families; and the critics have quite rightly seized on this stereotype. Correcting, and complicating, the understanding of the changes involved in the growing recognition of romantic love does not mean that all notions of modern change need be thrown out with the oversimplified bath.

It still remains indisputable, to take one example, that romantic expectations for marriage began to increase in the eighteenth century, playing some role in courtship practices and mate selection (always granted that, as a skeptic long ago pointed out, most modern people manage to fall in love with someone in their socioeconomic bracket). Changes led to reconsideration of arranged marriages and a fascinating tension between romantic love and sexual restraint in middle-class respectability. Almost certainly, by the later nineteenth century, this ongoing shift promoted new disillusionments and marital collapses because of the gap between emotional hopes and emotional realities: there's real, if complex, impact here. Simultaneous with the development of new commitments to romantic love, the rhetoric around maternal emotional responsibilities began to shift. Again, a modernist must not claim that somehow mothers were loveless before: but the new explicitness and growing currency of the idea of active maternal emotional commitment certainly altered discussions of family life and may well have touched behavior. Mothers became responsible for new aspects of family emotions, including temper control. How much these changes affected actual emotional experience can obviously be questioned—emotions historians always face the problem of tracing the impact of definable shifts in standards. And we need to insist on the emotional complexities of family life before the shifts—again, no one reasonably now posits a loveless premodern/loving modern dichotomy. But a certain degree of adjustment can still be granted, based at least on new ideas and literary conceits and probably on some new emotional needs as well in an increasingly commercial economic environment; and the findings can guide further research into modern emotional consequences and the relationship between new standards (and their class and gender implications) and actual experience.[10]

Indeed, it was precisely the subject of love that inspired one of the initial efforts to apply greater sophistication to the whole premodern to modern transition, before the onslaught of the larger critiques and the resulting analytical paralysis. John Gillis, in his study of the history of marriage, persuasively argued against any idea of some complete gulf between conjugal experiences of love before modern times and those since, while also explicitly acknowledging a significant cultural shift beginning in the seventeenth century that began to give such love unprecedented social validation.[11] Gillis notes that many couples found what we would still identify as love before modern times, if often after wedlock rather than before, while he also highlights the frequent gaps between modern ideals and actual, marital emotional experience. The result: less change in actual emotions than might be imagined (and certainly less than the first generation of marriage historians hypothesized), but definite, significant change nevertheless. The very fact of massively altered social expectations shifted emotional experience considerably. By dealing directly both with (late) premodern and modern evidence, the Gillis study directly treats the issues of transition, change, and continuity in a way that should be more routinely incorporated into this aspect of emotions history. The work, though issued before the full distraction of the counterattack on emotional modernism, provides a real model for approaches that can make use of the valid warnings of the committed pre-modernists, without being incapacitated by them.

We don't have comparable gold standards in other emotional areas, but the conclusions about love hardly exhaust the available list. Indeed, attention to love itself spilled over into several other emotional categories—possibly incautiously, but with some claims that deserve renewed attention.

Grief is a case in point, though work here developed somewhat separately, and with a slightly different modern chronology, from that on love. After all, as many nineteenth-century marriage writers suggested, a family more consciously aware of affectionate expectations might also shift its ideas about grief, and possibly its real experiences with the emotion. There were, as with love, some initial oversimplifications. Several early family historians, obviously awed by the high infant death rates in premodern times yet also attracted by the misleading impression of lovelessness, assumed a casualness about death that would, of course, be replaced by high emotion in the modern period. Here was another area where more careful work, for example with letters and diaries, has produced a much more nuanced understanding of premodern reactions. The death of a child, even amid a large brood and with full awareness that children often expired, could be a searing event for both parents. It is however true that some of the symbolism and rhetoric surrounding the death of a child, or of a mother in childbirth, did shift in the nineteenth century. One study finds for example that a significant recasting of male emotion concerning maternal mortality in the American South, between the eighteenth and nineteenth centuries, helped revise family birth-control policies, as husbands gained greater emotional awareness of possible loss. More generally, responses to a child's death became more ceremonially elaborate and more overtly apologetic. A new tone even entered into military reactions, as parents exerted unprecedented efforts in the American Civil War to identify and memorialize the remains of soldier-sons—granted that this was also an unusually bloody and internal conflict. Modern changes in grief are unquestionably complex, but there are possibilities open to further inquiry.[12]

Studies of the rise of new emotional expectations within the family also claimed implications for anger. Several scholars dealing with the eighteenth-century family noted a new concern—again, at least at the rhetorical level—about expressions of anger in the family, even with regard to servants. Correspondingly, marriage and child-rearing manuals in the Victorian nineteenth century devoted a great deal of attention to anger restraint as part of appropriate family life. Men, in the common middle-class formula, were urged to preserve a capacity for anger as motivation in public life, but to hold it back in the family, while more systematic temper control became a key part of respectable femininity. Elements of the shifting emotional formula would even enter into law in places like the United States in the later nineteenth century, through the novel concept of mental cruelty. This is, however, an area where claims of change encounter the more recent findings about awareness of the need for anger restraint in many premodern emotional communities. Capturing the transitions into new anger standards with modernity poses an obvious challenge for further work, though it is at least possible to formulate some hypotheses.[13]

Several other emotional areas have also been explored in terms of modernity, less closely connected to family frameworks. Most, however, thus far involve sketches rather than full portraiture.

Fear is an interesting case in point, though it has become snarled not only by the medievalist critique but by sweeping claims about more recent patterns. The French scholar who opened this vital aspect of emotions history, Jean Delumeau, claimed a pervasiveness of fear in both family and community life prior to modern times, followed by Enlightenment efforts to cut into this emotional pattern through more secular and scientific arguments. It is also true that child-rearing guidelines in the nineteenth century began to pay more explicit attention to the need to avoid fear in discipline, suggesting a related change in intent. Delumeau was however not a modern historian, and his hypotheses about a lessening of fear (to be followed, however, in the twentieth century by new anxieties about degenerative disease) do not reflect systematic research—quite apart from the challenge of revisiting exaggerations about medieval fears. A topic has been staked out, and there are some available findings, but the subject is open for more serious exploration.[14]

The same applies to guilt and shame. Some colonial American experts have explored a shift away from shame by the early nineteenth century, both in the treatment of criminals and in the discipline of children. Shaming in schools, for example, though yielding slowly and incompletely, became increasingly unfashionable in a campaign in the Western world that continues to this day. It is possible that some combination of declining community cohesion (weakening the context for shame) and new ideas about guilt-based individual controls did generate modern change. Even more than with fear, however, we have at most a very preliminary model, with some scattered eighteenth-to-nineteenth-century evidence in its favor. Current psychological work on the importance of shame suggests complexities that historians have yet to try to tackle.[15]

Three final categories point more decisively toward a distinctive modern development. All reflect recent research that has at least partially explored the premodern baseline for change as well as change itself. All have also been largely immune, so far, to the kinds of criticism premodernists have aimed at hypotheses concerning love, fear, or anger.

The idea of a new humanitarian sentiment, beginning to take shape in the eighteenth century and directed toward passionate concern for the conditions of people distant in space and in culture, seems well established. This initially emerged in the unprecedented multinational campaigns against the slave trade but would ultimately identify a wider range of targets and philanthropic responses. It was not just a matter of emotion: substantial changes in philosophy and religion undergirded the emergence of modern humanitarianism. But there was, or could be, an important emotional component, a fervent sense of connection with the sufferings of strangers. Here, clearly, new kinds of emotional expression built on earlier channels within more traditional religious affiliation and charitable sentiments, and we don't yet know enough about the process of adjustment or the extent of continuity that remained involved. Where, for example, did Quaker emotion come from, so prominent in so many global efforts over the past two centuries, compared to earlier Christian emotional expression?[16]

Even more interesting, where additional modern claims have been staked around a roughly congruent eighteenth- to early-nineteenth-century divide in the Western experience, is the arrival of cheerfulness.[17] A new valuation and definition of happiness at the intellectual level, as part of the Enlightenment, was clearly matched, if more gradually, by new emphasis on the importance of cheerfulness in conveying appropriate personal disposition and demeanor. The change occurred against a contrasting premodern valuation placed on a more melancholic approach, with the attendant need to apologize for any overindulgence in mirth. The innovation seems clear, in terms of the advice books and ultimately a growing social premium placed on smiling in a variety of contexts. As with humanitarianism, once launched, the trajectory would simply expand over time, in terms of Western standards and expectations. Here too, however, we lack adequate premodern work, aside from attention to pervasive melancholia in the seventeenth century: no one should neglect the many signs of jollity in premodern art, along admittedly with some predilection for more somber representations in formal portraiture. Revealingly, a new word, *sulky*, emerged in 1744 to describe people, including children, who did not measure up to the new norms.

Finally, there is the case of nostalgia. The word itself was coined by a Swiss medical student in 1688, suggesting a direct link to modern conditions. Increasing global travel and new patterns of migration—modern patterns of displacement, in short—almost certainly contributed to a heightened experience of nostalgia; they certainly called new attention to it from the later eighteenth century onward. Even here we need to figure out the emotional differences between this new category and older, perhaps vaguer, yearnings for past times. Modern nostalgia itself is not a constant: sometimes it refers to invented pasts, sometimes it responds more directly to upheavals like revolutions, sometimes it may even reflect new practices in work and consumerism. But access to the emotion, and explicit labeling, do strongly suggest an emotional characteristic of modernity.[18]

Existing, and impressively varied, work on emotions history that posits a real if complex transition between the early modern and the modern sets a partial agenda for a larger return to the analysis of emotional change in the modern Western world. A host of gaps remain. Few if any of the areas have been adequately fleshed out—romantic love comes closest—and in most cases there is serious need to revisit claims in light of the premodernist critiques. The modern patterns themselves are too often unconnected in terms of mutual relationships or shared causation. (What, for example, might nostalgia have to do with modern emphasis on love?) Too many claims, also, apply more clearly to some groups than to others, a common weakness of much emotions history to date. Too often, though understandably, modern turns out to mean middle class. Gender has been better served, with explicit attention to male/female differentiations from the nineteenth century onward, but there are opportunities for further assessment here as well. The available menu is well worth scrutiny, as it mixes obvious challenges, solid findings, and plausible hypotheses. Here is one set of guidelines toward next steps.

The findings about modern change do tie together around a shared link to modernity; they are not random historical accidents. Nostalgia reflects accelerating change, a modern quintessential. New emphasis on love picked up on a need to introduce new functions for family, as the family as economic unit began its devolution, and arguably a need as well for essential alternatives to the harshness of an increasingly commercial, competitive economy.[19] Changes in grief linked to modern demography, a point to which we will return. Reconsideration of shame involved alterations in the reliance on traditional community structures. Several of the modern emotional trends also touched base with broader cultural changes—such as the idea of children as innocent blank slates, to be protected from fearsome discipline, rather than slaves of original sin—which in turn helped translate larger modern shifts into personal and emotional standards. Correspondingly, further juxtapositions of existing findings and explorations of other encounters between emotional configurations and modern conditions promise additional knowledge in the future.

MODERN PROCESSES AND EMOTIONAL CHANGE

A second path in exploring the nature and limits of emotional modernity involves working from known shifts in social and political conditions to their emotional preconditions and consequences. This approach is less familiar in emotions history, though it can build on connections suggested by historians in fields seemingly as distant as demography. The approach involves some fairly certain findings but even more research questions that can amplify the next stage of inquiry and ultimately link back to the utilization of existing work in emotions history more narrowly construed.

The approach also suggests some larger assumptions about relationships between emotions and wider social structures. At what points do shifts in emotional standards and experience help translate larger patterns into daily life? How does emotional change relate to historical innovations such as capitalism? At what points might emotional shifts help *cause* larger phenomena; at what points do they *mediate* between developments otherwise-caused and ordinary experience; and at what points are they simply the *results* of structural alterations? We are not in a position to sort out the options as yet, but explicit attention to the relationships between modern change and modern emotional change provides opportunities for firmer understanding.

Three brief cases will hopefully suggest some larger possibilities, and indeed interested emotions historians might join other historians and social scientists in probing additional relevant aspects of a modern agenda. All three show important links between incontestable modern developments and emotional change, and if they do not by themselves definitively establish the utility of the modern as a category, they certainly point strongly in that direction.

Modern consumerism, we now know, began to take shape in the Western world in the eighteenth century, and whatever the complexities in its historical definition, it certainly qualifies as a durable, accelerating modern phenomenon. While there is no single pattern of consumerism—at least by the twentieth century, the American embrace was not fully characteristic even of the West—the commitment to individual acquisition as a criterion of the successful life or the successful society has had wide ramifications. And the phenomenon, though building on some earlier, global precedents, began its ascent about two and a half centuries ago.

As consumerism developed, a number of connections with emotions history can be or have been suggested. Causation is one. An important interpretation of consumerism's origins, by Colin Campbell, points to close links between eighteenth-century consumerism and the broader turn toward romantic love (and possibly greater familial affection more generally). The same kind of expressive individualism was involved, and key facets of early consumerism, particularly the attraction of new, more vivid clothing styles, related directly to the more explicit pursuit of romance in courtship. Consumerism's other main eighteenth-century targets, in the areas of home furnishings, table settings, and products such as tea and sugar, linked more broadly to new kinds of exchanges within the family, in which new acquisitions might both facilitate and demonstrate tighter family bonds. At least in Western society, consumerism and emotional change may have been wedded early on.[20]

Beyond this, the rise of consumerism certainly raises important questions about shifts in emotionality—though at this point without the ability to specify cause or effect. The fact is that consumerism, even short of its American extreme, involves pouring emotional attachments into objects of purchase and the process of acquisition in novel ways. How this developed—and the notion of a serious link to the broader turn toward more affectionate expectations may be a valid start—is a crucial issue. During the eighteenth century itself, some early consumerists allocated household items in their wills, suggesting a vivid connection between objects and emotional meaning: giving a chest of drawers to Cousin Lucy was a new way to express love. By the nineteenth century, and certainly today, avid consumers readily write of the equivalence between their purchases and interactions with lovers or otherwise suggest the emotional release that consumerism provides. Specific features of modern consumerism—whether the crowd emotions of spectator sports or the intriguing emotional attachments aimed at pets—translate the connections in other ways. Ultimately, ascending consumerism would also prompt sharp redefinitions of envy, another way to track the emotional contexts for modern behavior and the impacts of emotional change.[21] Finally, again from the eighteenth century onward, consumerism inspired a more explicit emotional experience of boredom—the absence of sufficient consumer delights—than any premodern society had defined.[22]

The points are clear: consumerism is, among other things, a facet of modern emotions history; it illustrates important emotional innovations, though we need to learn more about how the transition took place and what earlier emotions were replaced or modified; and its evolution invites further commentary about connections with other aspects of emotional expression. There are great opportunities here for cross-fertilization between emotions history and one of the most characteristic popular outcroppings of modernity.

Links between modern demography and emotional change are at present even more diffuse, though some particular junctures have been identified. Culturally sensitive demographic historians began to ask several decades ago about the motives—and we can add, emotional motives included—that might have contributed to family decisions to reduce birth rates. Of course, there were economic spurs in many cases, as children's work opportunities changed, but new affectionate ties may have been involved as well in what was clearly a new pattern of family expectation and behavior. Even more obviously: what kinds of emotional change, if any, did modern birth-rate levels generate? Answering this question does not involve repeating earlier mistakes about traditional family coldness. But with fewer children, did emotional investments in the individual child go up, and what impacts did this have on the various parties involved? We know that by the late nineteenth century, economic valuations of children (for example, in insurance policies) went up, even though children were actually more useless than they had been when work regimes predominated. This is at least suggestive of a higher emotional investment. Other questions surface: as sibling sets dwindled, how did children relocate emotional ties to other family members, including parents, but also to nonfamily peers? Here, as with consumerism, novel demographic processes involve clear emotional implications, inviting focused historical inquiry.[23]

The same applies obviously to the advent of modern mortality patterns, around the turn of the twentieth century. Fewer infant deaths might also encourage changes in familial emotional attachments. Advancing longevity, at least by the twentieth century and along with other changes, seems to have encouraged some redefinition of emotional ties to grandparents. But it's the impact on grief that invites particular comment. As noted, we know that grief around the death of a child or a young adult was hardly unknown before modern times. Yet modern demography has surely redefined the emotional landscape in several important ways. It makes the rare death that still occurs more emotionally unendurable than had been true before. For some parents, it may actually heighten anxieties around seeking to prevent such an unspeakable emotional horror. Above all, it may surround premature death, certainly in the family and sometimes in society more generally, with a characteristically modern amalgam of grief and guilt. As death became rarer before later age (and ultimately, sometimes even in later age itself), it became harder to avoid a sense of fault when against modern odds the reaper did strike. Hints of this change—away from more traditional grief alone—began to emerge in the mid–nineteenth century in commentary on maternal responsibility for what should be preventable levels of morality; and the connections have arguably cascaded ever since.[24]

Finally, modern levels of urbanization also invite inquiry about impacts on emotional experience. Pamela Epstein's essay, later in this volume, suggests that the expanding cities and in-migration required new emotional strategies for interacting with strangers and finding love in the city—even as romantic standards were themselves evolving. It will be important to use case studies of this sort to build fuller comparisons of the emotional consequences of urbanization in different regions. Are there some common modern components involved?

In sum, we have a clear formula for the generation of research hypotheses: identify important facets of modernity—like increased encounters with strangers[25]—and look for both emotional preconditions and emotional consequences. The accelerated pace of life, for example, surely has abundant emotional connections. Established emotions will register effects, but historical work in more novel areas, like transformations in impatience and reactions to impatience, will bear fruit as well.

The main point here is to suggest the importance of an emotional lens on modernity as a means of deepening the meaning of what key modern changes have entailed in various facets of life, while confirming an understanding of modernity's significance in emotions history itself. Some linkages add to the list of established findings. More suggest questions for further research. The opportunities have only been glimpsed thus far.

COMPARING MODERNITIES

A third path—barely evoked to date—involves using the development of modern emotions as a framework for comparison. The goal is both to provide additional evidence for understanding some of modernity's standard connections to changes in emotional standards and behaviors, and to demonstrate that modernity permits a variety of emotional patterns (whether traditional or novel).

On the diversity side: inclusion of Japan as a modern society obviously complicates any impulse to associate a decline in the use of shame with standard emotional modernity. The kind of new scrutiny applied to shame, as the West entered modernity, simply did not develop in the equally modern but more group-oriented Japanese case. Modern conditions may impose some kinds of changes in emotional discipline across cultural lines, but the results are at the least complex, with multiple patterns resulting in some key cases.

On the commonalities side: modern demography with its smaller family size, combined with emotional influences from the West and elsewhere, may well generate increased attention to familial affection, including romantic love, despite varied traditional precedents, as part of modernity regardless of place. There are strong suggestions of this kind of overlap in contemporary China, for instance.

Then there is some possible middle ground. Modernity (again, including global influences) may increase attention to cheerfulness, but this occurs against varied cultural backdrops. Modern, including foreign-owned, work environments encourage a more cheerful demeanor among Russian service workers than had prevailed in Soviet times, but it hardly makes Russians as eager to smile as their American counterparts. Indeed a national adage still holds that someone who smiles a lot is either a fool or an American. Regional patterns can generate variants even around some common patterns of change. Although the examples of regional analysis in this volume don't fully tackle the issue of modernity, they begin to develop the level of precision that can be applied to a regional/periodization combination.

At this point, pretty obviously, we have a host of potential comparative questions, with few guiding examples of completed analysis. As the geographical range of emotions history expands, and as an interest in charting the relationship between modernity and emotional change resumes, comparison will be crucial to further understanding. The invitation is exciting.

CONCLUSION

Working on transitions to modern emotional contexts is hardly the complete agenda for the field of emotions history, though it is a relevant priority. Many premodernists will continue to be eager to explore particular facets of their area or period, or work on regional or community comparisons that have nothing to do with the advent of modern conditions, or explore patterns of change before the modern heaves into view. Particular linkages, like the interaction between emotion and religion, may not generate uniform distinctions between modern and premodern experience—John Corrigan refers to this complexity in his essay in this volume. It's abundantly clear as well that there are diverse topics available as well for modernists, beyond the changes from premodern to modern emotional patterns. Even where the move into modernity is of interest, modernists need to spend some time (in this area, as in others) figuring out its precise chronology, for example in dealing with complex relationships between Victorian and more recent standards and experiences.

Some crucial emotions may not have a distinctively modern history (just as in history more generally, not all social fields respond to modern contexts).

Certainly, given the tentativeness of research thus far, anger must be viewed as a problematic candidate, though the desirability of renewed examination is real as well. Fear is intriguing. The one big effort to discuss a premodern-to-modern transition in the West, including the effort to reduce fear in child discipline, now seems somewhat problematic, though not without a suggestive potential. At the same time, a variety of modernists, headed by Joanna Bourke, make a point of referring to fear as the "dominant" modern emotion—without, however, actually tracing its emergence (and ascent?) from premodern patterns.[26] There's an obvious challenge here, along with some solid work on subperiods and regions, but a dearth of relevant analysis.

It should go without saying also that any approach to modern emotion must take care not to assume any systematic superiority. There are lots of drawbacks in the newer norms, such as the compulsory qualities of cheerfulness, some of which even help explain some modern emotional illnesses, like the increase in depression.[27] Change need not be complicated by glib implications of progress.

The need for caution deserves modest reemphasis. We know how easy it is to oversimplify in generalizing about modern change. Emotions historians need to work with other social scientists, understandably impatient with too much nuance, to avoid misleading generalizations about modern emotional characteristics. The conversations will be facilitated if at the same time we can share a commitment to further exploration of what modern emotional contexts do entail, and a realization that some important statements are already possible.

There is room as well, however, for a return to bold hypotheses that balance the complexities recent critics have highlighted with a willingness to explore. What, for example, might a premodern-to-modern history of jealousy look like? We know that in the premodern West, jealousy was a disputed emotion: some argued that it was an inevitable and desirable companion to love, others that it spoiled what should be a purer emotion. Jealous defense of honor won praise in some communities, but by the seventeenth century, women were more likely to claim jealousy than men in defense of aggressive acts. Even in advance of desirably detailed research, then, we know that this was a socially complex emotion. On the modern side, after a few decades jealousy would come in for new, and more systematically reproving, attention, both in recommended emotional behaviors and in courts of law. As we should expect, both cultural shifts and modern structural innovations contributed to change. The newer cultural definitions of romantic love on the whole urged freedom from possessiveness; and the equation of jealousy with admirable zeal in the cause of honor virtually disappeared. To be sure, different regional cultures handled jealousy differently even within Western society overall, and a modified legacy of honor-based codes remained in some cases. But more general modern factors played in strongly. First, the defensibility of honor declined with the advent of more commercial motivations and virtues, with clear application to emotions like jealousy. Second, over time the increasing modern imperative for a greater public mixing of genders required more systematic attention to jealousy restraint. Legal codes, among other things, adjusted accordingly, rejecting jealous justification for crimes, despite prior courtroom tradition. Finally, jealousy issues in modern societies may also have been partially redefined by new emotional tensions amid small sibling sets.[28] These are, admittedly, big claims, and they are hypotheses at this point in advance of fuller study. One complication is obvious simply from the Western experience: the acceptability of jealousy can go up in initial adjustments to modernity, as successful legal defenses in a few mid-nineteenth-century murder cases demonstrated. It would take a few more decades for this surge not just to recede but to be explicitly countered. If a general trend can be legitimately identified, it must, of course, also be tested against other cultural cases undergoing modern change. Here, the point is not to claim confirmation in advance of data, but to suggest the availability at least of a plausible hypothesis.

The main point is to reengage with issues of modernity and emotion, to urge a renewal in research and analysis mindful of prior gains and pitfalls. Established findings already set some guidelines while inviting further testing, and additional hypotheses and opportunities abound. The field is inherently challenging, because it cuts across normal chronological specialties: we badly need more examples of bridging work, dealing with premodern patterns but also subsequent transitions and outcomes. How did particular societies, communities and even personalities generate or react to change, and what differentials were involved amid common modern pressures?[29] Focused analysis will, of course, generate additional examples of complexities and outright continuities: the agenda must be open. Scholars can address the subject through particular emotions, through connections with other topics—for example, in religious or political history—or through teasing out emotional components of more familiar modern developments—this last involving the particular opportunities for comparative work. We do not know yet how significant modern contexts will prove to be in helping to organize the history of emotion. Some connections, however, are already clear, and additional plausibilities invite attention. Precisely because, even in the West, modernity is a recent arrival, still being assimilated and shaped, the desirability of exploring its emotional contours and limitations offers unusual promise.

Renewed commitment to using modernity as a key category in generating further research on emotions history adds a vital dimension to our understanding of how the changes associated with modernity are implemented and experienced. It suggests connections among otherwise discrete projects in emotions history, including linkages with other developments as in religion or politics. Use of modernity offers huge potential in guiding comparative work—a vital next step in the field, always acknowledging a balance between common patterns and diverse responses. It also serves as a basis for wider interdisciplinary discussions, with historical understanding improving social science formulations around a shared interest in exploring ambitious analytical frames. The gains for further scholarship are several, and they are within reach.

NOTES

A version of this paper was presented at a conference inaugurating the Center for Research on the History of Emotions, University of Western Australia, June 2011. I benefited from counsel by the group.

1. Edward Shorter, *The Making of the Modern Family* (New York: Basic Books, 1975); Lawrence Stone, *The Family, Sex and Marriage in England, 1500–1800*, abr. ed. (New York: Harper Perennial, 1983).

2. Phillip Ariès, *Centuries of Childhood: A Social History of Family Life* (New York: Vintage, 1962); Linda Pollock, *Forgotten Children: Parent-Child Relations from 1500 to 1900* (Cambridge, U.K.: Cambridge University Press, 1983); Peter N. Stearns, *Childhood in World History*, 2nd ed. (New York: Routledge, 2010).

3. William Reddy, *The Navigation of Feeling: A Framework for the History of Emotions* (Cambridge, U.K.: Cambridge University Press, 2001).

4. Norbert Elias, *The Civilizing Process: Sociogenetic and Psychogenetic Investigations*, rev. ed. (Oxford, U.K.: Blackwell Publishing, 2000).

5. John F. Kasson, *Rudeness and Civility: Manners in Nineteenth-Century Urban America* (New York: Hill and Wang Publishing, 1990).

6. For a recent summary, see Jan Plamper, "The History of Emotions: An Interview with William Reddy, Barbara Rosenwein and Peter Stearns," *History and Theory* 49 (May 2010), 237–265; see also Barbara Rosenwein, "Worrying about Emotions in History," *American Historical Review* 107, no. 3 (June 2002), 821–845.

7. See also other critiques of Elias, notably C. Stephen Jaeger, *Ennobling Love: In Search of a Lost Sensibility* (Philadelphia: University of Pennsylvania Press, 1999).

8. Plamper, "The History of Emotions," 250.

9. Edmund Leites, *Educating the Audience: Addison, Steele & Eighteenth-Century Culture* (Los Angeles: UCLA William Andrews Clark Memorial Library, 1984).

10. Elisabeth Badinter, *Mother Love* (New York: Macmillan Publishing Co., 1982); Peter

N. Stearns, *American Cool: Constructing a Twentieth-Century Emotional Style* (New York: NYU Press, 1994); Ellen Rothman, *Hands and Hearts: A History of Courtship in America* (Cambridge, Mass.: Harvard University Press, 1987); Karen Lystra, *Searching the Heart: Women, Men, and Romantic Love in Nineteenth-Century America* (New York: Oxford University Press, 1989); Robert Griswold, *Adultery and Divorce in Victorian America 1800–1900* (Madison: Institute for Legal Studies, University of Wisconsin-Madison Law School, 1986).

11. John R. Gillis, *For Better, For Worse, British Marriages 1600 to the Present* (New York: Oxford University Press, 1985).

12. Paul Rosenblatt, *Bitter Bitter Tears* (Minneapolis: University of Minnesota Press, 1983); Jan Lewis, *The Pursuit of Happiness: Family and Values in Jefferson's Virginia* (Cambridge, U.K.: Cambridge University Press, 1983); Drew Faust, *This Republic of Suffering: Death and the American Civil War* (New York: Vintage, 2008); Peter N. Stearns, *Revolutions in Sorrow: The American Experience of Death in Global Perspective* (Boulder, Colo.: Paradigm Publishers, 2007).

13. Peter N. Stearns and Carol Z. Stearns, *Anger: The Struggle for Emotional Control in American History* (Chicago: University of Chicago Press, 1986).

14. Jean Delumeau, *La Peur en Occident* (Paris: Hachette, 1978).

15. Phillip Greven, *The Protestant Temperament: Patterns of Child-Rearing, Religious Experience, and the Self in Early America* (Chicago: University of Chicago Press, 1988). Contemporary psychologists talk about effective uses of shame in the United States, suggesting continuities with earlier patterns; but of course they also ignore historical change. Additional references on the subject include June Tangney, *Shame and Guilt* (New York: The Guilford Press, 2002); and John Demos, "Shame and Guilt in Early New England in *Emotion and Social Change*, ed. Carol Z. Stearns and Peter N. Stearns, (New York: Holmes and Meier, 1988).

16. Thomas L. Haskell, "Capitalism and the Origins of the Humanitarian Sensibility, Part I," *American Historical Review* 90, no. 2 (April 1985), 339–361; Thomas L. Haskell and Richard F. Teichgraeber, eds., *The Culture of the Market: Historical Essays* (Cambridge, U.K.: Cambridge University Press, 1993).

17. Darrin McMahon, *Happiness: A History* (New York: Grove Press, 2006); Christina Kotchemidova, "From Good Cheer to 'Drive-By Smiling': A Social History of Cheerfulness," *Journal of Social History* 39, no. 1 (Fall 2005), 5–37; Peter N. Stearns, "Defining Happy Childhoods: Assessing a Recent Change," *Journal of the History of Childhood and Youth* 3, no. 2 (Spring 2010), 165–186.

18. Christopher Shaw and Malcolm Chase, *The Imagined Past: History and Nostalgia* (Manchester, U.K.: Manchester University Press, 1989); Nicolas Dames, *Amnesiac Selves: Nostalgia, Forgetting, and British Fiction, 1810–1870* (New York: Oxford University Press, 2001), Stephanie Coontz, *The Way We Never Were: American Families and the Nostalgia Trip*, rev. ed. (New York: Basic Books, 2000); Susan Matt, *Homesickness: An American History* (New York: Oxford University Press, 2011).

19. A powerful recent study on the link between modernity and love is Jennifer Cole

and Lynn Thomas, eds., *Love in Africa* (Chicago: University of Chicago Press, 2009); see also Eliza Ferguson, *Gender and Justice: Violence, Intimacy, and Community in Fin-de-Siècle Paris* (Baltimore: The Johns Hopkins University Press, 2010).

20. Colin Campbell, *The Romantic Ethic and the Spirit of Modern Consumerism*, 3rd ed. (London: WritersPrintShop, 2005); John Brewer and Roy Porter, *Consumption and the World of Goods* (London: Routledge, 1994); Gary Cross, *An All-Consuming Century* (New York: Columbia University Press, 2002).

21. Susan Matt, *Keeping Up with the Joneses: Envy in American Consumer Society, 1890–1930* (Philadelphia: University of Pennsylvania Press, 2002).

22. Patricia Meyer Spacks, *Boredom: The Literary History of a State of Mind* (Chicago: The University of Chicago Press, 1995).

23. Robert V. Wells, "Family Size and Fertility Control in Eighteenth-Century America: A Study of Quaker Families," *Population Studies* 25 (1971), 73–82; Viviana A. Zelizer, *Pricing the Priceless Child: The Changing Social Value of Children* (Princeton, N.J.: Princeton University Press, 1994).

24. Peter N. Stearns, *Anxious Parents: A History of Modern Childrearing in America* (New York: New York University Press, 2003); and *Revolutions in Sorrow*.

25. Recent work on sincerity, for example, suggests important changes in the nineteenth century as social hierarchies shifted; thus letter writing conventions began to shift from "Your Obedient Servant" to the more egalitarian reference "Sincerely." See R. Jay Magill, *Sincerity: How a Moral Ideal Born Five Hundred Years Ago Inspired Religious Wars, Modern Art, Hipster Chic and the Curious Notion that We All Have Something to Say (No Matter How Dull)* (New York: W. W. Norton and Company, 2012).

26. Joanna Bourke, *Fear: A Cultural History* (London: Little Brown Hardbacks, 2005).

27. Peter N. Stearns, *Satisfaction Not Guaranteed: Dilemmas of Progress in Modern Society* (New York: NYU Press, 2012).

28. Peter Salovey, ed., *The Psychology of Jealousy and Envy* (New York: Guilford Press, 1991); Peter N. Stearns, *Jealousy: The Evolution of an Emotion in American History* (New York: NYU Press, 1990).

29. Exploration of social groups and communities in terms of responses to modernity will reveal important variety but also instances of conversion even with disparate chronologies (as with American Catholicism's belated—1950s—adaptation of mainstream Protestant views on disciplinary fear). It will also reveal the formation of new emotional communities, as in late-eighteenth-century America, or later with the flowering of various modern recreational cultures. See Timothy and Joseph Kelly's essay, "American Catholics and the Discourse of Fear," in *Emotional History of the United States* (New York: New York University Press, 1998); Philip J. Greven, *The Protestant Temperament* (Chicago: University of Chicago Press, 1977); Allan Guttmann, *Sports Spectators* (New York: Columbia University Press, 1986).

CHAPTER 2

RECOVERING THE INVISIBLE

METHODS FOR THE HISTORICAL STUDY OF THE EMOTIONS

SUSAN J. MATT

From the very beginning, those who have studied the history of the emotions have realized the difficulties they faced. In 1941, Lucien Febvre, the first scholar to call for such investigations, wrote that the undertaking would be fraught with challenges. He observed, "Any attempt to reconstitute the emotional life of a given period is a task that is at one and the same time extremely attractive and frightfully difficult."[1] Febvre suggested that emotions of other eras and societies were so very different from those of the present day that their recovery required the scholar to abandon preconceived ideas about the human psyche and to recognize that contemporary categories and experiences of emotions were not identical to those of earlier times.

Febvre's insights, offered nearly seventy-five years ago, describe well the field of emotions research today. His fundamental assumption—that human feelings are influenced by cultural and social life—serves as the basis of modern historical explorations. His belief that such explorations would be methodologically challenging has been borne out as well, for historians who study the emotions face an array of challenges as they try to pinpoint both what they are studying and how to study it. When they decide to examine the history of an emotion, how will they get at it? The feeling itself is long gone. So too is the person who experienced it. While a neuroscientist might argue that it therefore would be impossible to study an emotion of the past because it is an evanescent impulse, vanished and untrackable, historians think differently and look for a feeling's traces years after it is has been experienced.

Finding and interpreting these traces is difficult, and is the subject of this essay, which sketches some of the methods and sources that scholars use to reconstruct the history of the emotions. It first will briefly examine the contested connection between feelings and words. Then, it will turn its attention to an equally thorny issue—the relationship between emotional norms and individual emotional experience. Finally, it will consider the sources that scholars have available to them, and the creative ways that historians—including contributors to this volume—use them to understand the past.

WORDS AND THEIR LIMITS

Generally, the traces of emotional life that remain for the scholar to study are words or symbols left behind, and most often historians have gravitated toward words. These are not the same as emotions, but they bear a relation to them. That relation, however, is somewhat unclear.

Indeed, so tricky is the relationship between words and emotion that even the term *emotion* itself is now recognized as being vague in its meaning. According to historian Thomas Dixon, the word entered the English language in the seventeenth century, but "it did not become established as the name for a category of mental states that might be systematically studied until the mid–nineteenth century." Dixon suggests that in the early nineteenth century, the Scottish philosopher Thomas Brown was central to establishing it as a new "theoretical category in mental science," but even Brown himself was somewhat unclear about what the term connoted: "The exact meaning of the term emotion . . . is difficult to state in any form of words." Those who tried to offer a concrete definition would struggle for years to come. An author in 1859 claimed that "emotion is the name here used to comprehend all that is understood by feelings, pleasures, pains, passions, sentiments, affections." As Dixon makes clear, from the moment of its introduction into the English language, *emotion* was a vague catchall term, historically contingent and fuzzily defined. No wonder that it continues to be so today.[2] Historians may say they know an emotion when they see one, but in fact there is imprecision built into the very nature of their research.

Linguistic and analytical problems plague historians not just in thinking about the whole category of emotion but also crop up as they try to understand individual feelings. A number of historians have argued that feelings cannot exist completely independently of language, and that words give shape to emotion. By choosing to identify and name one's feelings in one way rather than another, individuals define their emotions in the process of expressing them. William Reddy has written that verbal expressions of emotions "are themselves instruments for directly changing, building, hiding, intensifying emotions, instruments that may be more or less successful."[3]

Other historians have shared this perspective. In his pathbreaking study of nostalgia, for instance, Jean Starobinski noted, "It is not, then, the emotion itself which comes before us; only that part which has passed into a given form of expression can be of interest to the historian." As he wrote about the epidemic of nostalgia that broke out across Europe after that word was coined in the late seventeenth century, he continued, "Emotion is not a word, but it can only be spread abroad through words." All that was traceable, he suggested, were the changing terms men and women had used to describe their feelings, and their waxing and waning popularity. Starobinski maintained that words and feelings were not entirely separate, writing that "the verbalization of emotion is intertwined with the structure of that which is experienced." As a result, he concluded, "the history of emotions, then, cannot be anything other than the history of those words in which the emotion is expressed."

Words shape the emotions of those who lived in the past, marking the limits of the possible and the recognized. Likewise, our own vocabularies limit how we in the present understand the emotions of other eras. Starobinski wisely pointed out that historians must take care when they study the words of earlier generations, and resist imposing modern meanings and connotations on to cultures of the past, which had their own historically specific vocabularies. His cautions continue to resonate with modern researchers, for the issue of words is a live one. *Nostalgia* is a case in point. The word, created in 1688, originally was a formal medical term for what we now term homesickness. (That latter term did not itself enter the English language until the 1750s.) Only in the early twentieth century did nostalgia take on the meaning of a diffuse longing for the past and for lost times. To speak of men and women being nostalgic—in either sense—before 1688 is anachronistic. To speak of them being so afterward requires the careful delineation of meaning, if one strives to use the word as the historical actors themselves used it.[4] This problem of shifting meanings is not limited to the case of nostalgia, but is endemic to the field.

There are then obvious difficulties in studying words to understand emotions. We do not know quite what an emotion is, nor do we know what the words to describe particular feelings meant to earlier generations. We may have different words or no words for emotions and concepts that earlier cultures thought central, and vice versa. And even within a single society, at a given moment, the meaning of those words and the feelings they describe may be understood differently by different individuals.

Then, too, there is the issue of reportage. Even in firsthand accounts of sentiments, attitudes, and emotions, nothing is raw or unfiltered. Personal declarations of feelings reflect both broad cultural categories as well as individual choices and conscious or unconscious efforts at self-fashioning. Writers craft their journals, letters, and memoirs, presenting their feelings with an eye to prevailing conventions or rules about feelings. Sometimes they strive to fit these norms; other times they write in defiance of them, but always they refer to them.

In the end, there is a gap between what people felt and what historians can know about those feelings, yet there is nevertheless a value to be found in recovering these faint traces of past generations' sensibilities. Jean Starobinski suggested that as historians dealt with the problem of language, they should realize that "we can never recapture the subjective experiences of an eighteenth-century man as they were. We can only try not to attribute our problems and our 'complexes' to him too unknowingly. We can kindly grant him the attention due to a foreigner, to an inhabitant of a distant country whose customs and language are different and must be learned patiently."[5]

EMOTIONAL RULES

Central to understanding that foreign culture of the past is grasping the emotional conventions or rules of the era. At first, historical research focused primary attention on these rules, for they were relatively easy to uncover. Perhaps the most famous study to do so was Norbert Elias's *The Civilizing Process* (1939), which relied on etiquette guides, poems, and treatises such as those of Tannhäuser and Erasmus. Elias worked to demonstrate how new rules began to inculcate new standards of modesty and a new sense of shame. For instance, he cited the Wernigerode Court Regulations of 1570 to show how self-consciousness was inculcated. Those regulations spelled out that "one should not...relieve oneself without shame or reserve in front of ladies, or before the doors or windows of court chamber." Similar instructions came from the *Booke of Demeanor and the Allowance and Disallaowance of Certaine Misdemeanors in Companie.*

Let not they privy members be
Layd open to be view'd

it is most shameful and abhord
detestable and rude.[6]

Elias used such aphorisms and advice to argue that at the end of the medieval period, men and women began to exert more control over their bodies and feelings and came to develop a new sense of embarrassment and a corresponding system of etiquette. As the previous chapter demonstrated, his conclusions and his methods, though intriguing, have both been hotly debated, because the book offered little insight into how or whether people reacted to these new rules, and at times, it seemed that he mistook the rules for the reality of what people felt. More recent scholarship that seeks to use recommendations on manners to probe emotions and emotional change has encountered similar objections, though it also generates some fascinating hypotheses.[7]

Overall, the interest in social norms and conventions has not abated, because rules—explicit or implicit—are central to understanding how culture shapes emotion. Historians recognize that they are honored as much by their breach as by strict observance but contend that these rules nevertheless set the terms for emotional life and tell much about the cultures that created them. Indeed, when the historical study of the emotions took root in the United States in the 1980s, scholars such as Peter N. Stearns and Carol Z. Stearns called for a study of "emotionology"—the culturally determined rules that govern emotional life—arguing that this was a way to begin the study of emotions. More generally, they also acknowledged that inner experience and social rules often diverged. Uncovering regulations and ideals about feelings was not the same as uncovering actual emotional experience. Nevertheless, they maintained that the study of these codes offered a window onto the history of feelings. They wrote, "The distinction between emotionology and emotional experience suggests a clearer research strategy than most historians have so far pursued. Inquiry into love, anger, jealousy, and fear should begin with the emotionological context, which is more accessible than emotional experience and important in its own right.... In the second stage of inquiry historians should attempt to fathom emotional expressions across time, assuming a correspondence between these trends and those of emotionology but alert to the possibility of variance." They suggested, finally, that there was "a third task... which involves examining people's efforts to mediate between emotional standards and emotional experience."[8]

That research agenda, issued in 1985, presciently anticipated the paths historians have followed over the last three decades. First came those who looked at emotional ideals; later came historians who tried to reconstruct emotional experiences and the differences between conventions and individual feelings.

They were joined by those who suggested that there were many competing sets of expectations and rules within a single society, and that historians should strive to reconstruct the multiple "emotional communities" through which men and women traveled each day.[9] Gradually, a consensus emerged that although one could not study emotional life without understanding the social rules governing it, neither should one explore those rules without at least trying to assess individual reactions to them.

Contemporary scholars recognize that rules are a site of contest and controversy, and that they can reveal the fractures within a society; rules are signs of people struggling to control themselves and others. So, for instance, the emotional norms about envy and consumer desire in late-nineteenth- and early-twentieth-century America revealed assumptions about class and entitlement, as the upper classes tried to restrain the sometimes threatening envy of the lower orders. The wealthy might wear furs or silks, because they had the means to justify their tastes for luxuries, while the poor were seen as sinfully covetous for wanting the same things. Such emotional rules reinforced (or at least tried to reinforce) class hierarchy and applied differently to different groups. The middle classes' and working classes' reactions to and sometimes outright defiance of such conventions indicated that they had a different sense of entitlement and equality than elite rule makers either envisioned or desired. Here is a case where rules for emotional expression varied across a population, for they allowed some to express longing and required others to repress it.

In contrast, there are plentiful examples of an emotional convention that was widely shared across a society but that had vastly different meanings and implications for different parts of the population. A good example is cheerfulness, which began to be more valued in the eighteenth century. That valuation increased in the nineteenth, and, as a result, there was a growing expectation that Americans of all colors and classes would be cheerful. To many, it denoted optimism, initiative, and control. As Christina Kotchemidova has noted, "In a country built upon the assumption that everyone should pursue their happiness, failure to achieve that happiness lost one the respect of the others. . . . The individual was expected to triumph over the circumstances."[10] For free men and women, cheerfulness was a sign of success or, failing that, of aspirations for it. In contrast, cheerfulness, while widely expected of slaves during the nineteenth century, held a very different meaning for them. Nicole Eustace, in chapter 8, explains that during the colonial era, whites perceived their bondsmen as naturally morose. However, by the antebellum period, enslaved men and women were expected to hide their feelings and show pleasure in their condition. Former slave Elizabeth Keckley recalled that her master, Colonel

Burwell, did not like "to see one of his slaves wear a sorrowful face, and those who offended in this particular way were always punished. Alas! the sunny face of the slave is not always an indication of sunshine in the heart." Henry Watson, an escaped slave, recalled that "the slaveholder watches every movement of the slave, and if he is downcast or sad,—in fact, if they are in any mood but laughing or singing, and manifesting symptoms of perfect content at heart, they are said to have the devil in them . . . and they are often whipped or sold."[11] Slaves' cheerfulness and whites' cheerfulness were governed by different imperatives and reflected quite different realities. Whites' good cheer was supposed to indicate that they were in control of themselves and their futures. The forced cheerfulness of slaves, however, revealed the extent to which they were under the control of others. In exploring how such rules vary across populations, and the different ways that individuals reacted to them, historians can begin to understand some of the often subtle but fundamental connections between emotions and power.

A number of essays in this volume do just that. Among other things, Darrin M. McMahon explores the differing value that Catholics and Protestants accorded joy in daily life. Nicole Eustace looks at the way that changing rules and ideals about emotional expression affected Americans from the Revolution to the War of 1812. She explores how citizens' private emotions were marshaled to public and political ends and how central new emotional conventions were to an emerging sense of nationhood. Mark Steinberg, in his study of Eastern European emotional life, explores how Soviet leaders worked to create enthusiasm and optimism about their policies and how disillusioned citizens came to see expressions of unhappiness as potent signs of dissent.

SOURCES AND THEIR LIMITS

In an ideal world, scholars would have access to both prescriptive sources— which lay out the rules and norms—as well as firsthand accounts of men and women's emotional experiences and reactions to these norms. In reality, however, the direction their research actually takes depends not only on their theoretical framework but also on the sources available to them. In some cases, all that has been possible to find are the prescriptions governing emotional life. This is particularly true the further back in time one goes. For instance, many classicists rely on the philosophers of antiquity for evidence of emotional life in the ancient Mediterranean world. The texts that Plato, Aristotle, the Stoics, and Cicero left behind offer ideals for relationships and emotional comportment, but it is not always clear just how widespread such ideals were. In some cases, these studies rely on philosophy and philology to reveal psychology. As a result, they are frequently intellectual histories that trace the changing idea of an emotion over time. Those who try to understand emotional life during later eras generally have more sources with which to work, and these often allow them to conjoin the intellectual histories of emotions—the dominant ideals and ideas—with explorations of how such ideas were received or rejected, adopted or adapted, in social and cultural life.[12]

But where to find sources, both those detailing prescriptions and those describing lived experience? Taking their cues from Elias's *The Civilizing Process*, some scholars have probed the large body of advice about how to govern and display one's feelings that first proliferated during the Renaissance and that continues to be produced today. Manners books, advice manuals, sermons, and child-rearing literature offer a window onto the emotional conventions of the past. The explicit recommendations found in such guides—about how to manage love, anger, homesickness, or sadness in oneself or one's family—often lay bare the prevailing visions of the ideal individual in particular eras.

Other sources that historians have long availed themselves of are artistic representations of emotions. Like the prescriptions found in advice books, they do not capture the inner lives of ordinary men and women; instead they show the vision of particular artists. Nevertheless, their details often cast light on common emotional practices. Two of the earliest scholars of the emotions, Johan Huizinga and Norbert Elias, used tapestries, sepulchral art, and paintings as means of understanding the aesthetics and emotions of the medieval era. Elias used the fifteenth-century *Medieval House-Book*, with its depictions of gallows, marital spats, and couples bathing, to argue (controversially) that medieval Europeans lacked self-consciousness and emotional control. Of the scenes portrayed in the book, he wrote, "All these are expressions of a society in which people gave way to drives and feelings incomparably more easily, quickly, spontaneously, and openly than today, in which the emotions were less restrained . . . less evenly regulated and more liable to oscillate more violently between extremes."[13] Later historians have continued to turn to art for insight into emotion, whether it be the double portraits of the Renaissance that friends commissioned as a token of their strong bonds, or the late-nineteenth-century political cartoons designed to inflame the emotions of the American electorate.[14]

Popular literature has become a revealing source for understanding cultural ideals and models as well. For instance, William Reddy has used the essays of Voltaire and the novels of Balzac and Sand as a way to gauge the changing emotional mood in France.[15] The novels of Jane Austen similarly illustrate how new ideas about female friendship began to rise in the late eighteenth and early nineteenth centuries.[16] Literature can both reflect common emotional practices and serve as models for new styles of feeling and acting. For instance, some argue that Europeans and Americans learned the style and vocabulary of romantic love from eighteenth-century novels and plays and used these as templates for their own emotional lives.[17] Others have commented on the way that battle-weary soldiers during World War I adopted the words and clichés of journalists who had not been in battle to describe their own feelings about the combat that they themselves had experienced.[18]

All of these sources have the same limitations. They reveal much about how artists, writers, psychologists, and manners experts understood the world, but they cannot reveal whether such views and sentiments were widely shared. They also represent mostly elite perspectives, rather than those of everyday people. How did ordinary men and women receive the art, the advice, the novels? Did they see it as reflective of their own emotions or widely divergent from them? What of those who hailed from classes or groups that clearly did not follow elite conventions but also did not generate formal guides to the rules and styles they followed? For instance, in nineteenth-century New York, "Bowery boys" and "Bowery gals" displayed a style of clothing and an attitude that clearly flouted genteel conventions, but they were not prolific in describing the rules that influenced their behavior.[19] In short, it is hard to fully reconstruct all of the conventions that existed in a diverse society and even more difficult to know how people responded to them.

In an effort to redress these problems, to get a sense of the variety of emotional experience across the class spectrum, and to gauge the relationship between conventions and actual behavior, some have turned to journals, letters, and diaries, which more fully reveal how individuals themselves felt and expressed emotion. These sources allow scholars to write not just intellectual histories of emotions but social and cultural studies. For example, rich archival collections have allowed scholars to move beyond the patriotic speeches that exhorted soldiers to be brave in combat and to discover, instead, how men at war actually felt as they faced peril and death. One study of the Civil War traced the way that romantic ideals about battle and courage gradually eroded as terror and cynicism took over.[20] Similarly, the letters and journals written by men and women moving west in nineteenth-century America make it clear that the ideology of manifest destiny that sent waves of settlers across the Mississippi was often countered by powerful tides of homesickness that swept people east.[21] Although these archival sources give new complexity and nuance to traditional narratives, and bring in more of the voices of the middling classes, they do have their limitations, for they privilege those who had time, training, paper, and pen to write. Often left out are the voices of the poor, the illiterate, the enslaved. For this reason, far more is known about the emotional experiences of the upper and middle classes than about the working classes and the impoverished.

Scholars have looked elsewhere for sources that might bridge this divide. Some have turned to legal sources, for while these are clearly written sources, they often record the lives and deaths, divorces and disputes of those who could not write. For instance, wills and household inventories have proven useful as windows onto emotional life in the past. One study of wills from Tudor England traced the lineaments of familial affections and connections across generations, countering earlier notions that family love was less intense before the rise of capitalism and industrialism.[22] Natalie Zemon Davis has looked at pardon requests in sixteenth-century France as a way to understand questions of guilt and supplication, and in doing so, she has shed light on the differing emotional repertoires available to men and women in that era. She concluded that as they defended themselves on charges of murder, men and women described their murderous impulses differently. Men were more likely to explain their actions as the result of impulse, such as sudden anger or drunkenness, while women made recourse to a different array of excuses. Less likely to use the impulsive, "sudden anger" defense because it did not jibe with expectations of womanly behavior, many supplicants for pardon "were either silent about their feelings or many-tongued, bringing jealousy, despair, and guilt to the action, along with anger."[23] Likewise, divorce cases and criminal records reveal much about the texture of marital relationships and the emotional rewards and obligations they entailed, and these often offer insight into the experiences of a broad swath of society, including the poor and the illiterate. The benefits of legal analysis are visible in studies such as that of Dawn Keetley, which showed that American men who killed their wives in the eighteenth century justified their actions by claiming their spouses had made them angry, sometimes by their laziness, sometimes by their disobedience. A century later, murderous husbands explained their actions in terms of romantic jealousy—their wives had betrayed them and had come to love others, and this, in their minds, justified their homicidal actions. Such a change in legal defenses shows the growing centrality of romantic love in marriage over the course of the nineteenth century.[24]

Historians are becoming increasingly clever in examining material culture for signs of emotion, and many of the artifacts they study can illuminate the experience of broader swaths of the population. Some of the most enduring material symbols of emotion are related to death. A number of historians have studied gravestones and burial arrangements to reconstruct how earlier generations dealt with familial love and grief. Epitaphs from the fifth and sixth centuries in central Europe have been used to show the strong and loving connections between parents and children.[25] Similarly, the adjacent burials of friends from the medieval era have been used to demonstrate the centrality of friendship in the web of affectionate relationships.[26] Slaves in the colonial South often buried their dead with artifacts designed to help them on their supernatural journeys back to Africa, reflecting both their homesickness on earth, and their hopefulness about the hereafter.[27] More recent burial practices offer a way to gauge how fears about death have changed over time. In the nineteenth century, the fear of being buried alive was so widespread that people invented escape contraptions that might be deployed from within a coffin. In the twentieth century, both the apparatuses and the fears about being buried alive disappeared, replaced by new anxieties about the pain and suffering that the ill might feel this side of the grave.[28] In addition to the gravestones, the shared tombs, and the coffin escape mechanisms, several historians have explored executions and how both spectators and the condemned reacted to them in order to gauge changing attitudes toward sensibility, shame, cruelty, and mortality.[29]

Material culture also sheds light on less sober emotions—so for instance, one scholar has examined the convention of smiling in snapshots to better understand the development and cultivation of American cheerfulness.[30] Another has used consumer habits—from food purchases to TV watching—to better understand how people coped with homesickness.[31]

Scholars in this volume have been ingenious in discovering new ways to trace the emotions of past generations. Mark Steinberg, in his study of Eastern European emotional life, has cast a wide net, using material as diverse as jokes and political violence to illuminate emotional identities and values. John Corrigan shows the importance of ritual and architecture as evidence for the history of emotion and religion and urges new steps, including the exploration of digitized data, that hold great promise for future work. Pamela Epstein's essay shows the potential of research that looks to imaginative forms of expression, in this case newspaper classified ads; while Brent Malin uses scholarly debates as a way to investigate the emotional effects of modern media. The array of sources is diverse and, collectively, considerable—and the essays together demonstrate how scholars can use historical evidence innovatively to answer important questions about profound changes in emotional life and experience.

NOTES

1. Lucien Febvre, "Sensibility and History: How to Reconstitute the Emotional Life of the Past," in *A New Kind of History: From the Writings of Febvre*, ed. Peter Burke, trans. K. Folca (New York: Harper and Row, 1973), 19.

2. Thomas Dixon, "'Emotion': The History of a Keyword in Crisis," *Emotion Review* 4 (2012), 338–344.

3. William M. Reddy, *The Navigation of Feeling: A Framework for the History of Emotions* (Cambridge: Cambridge University Press, 2001), 105.

4. Jean Starobinski, "The Idea of Nostalgia," *Diogenes* 54 (Summer 1966), 81–83. Susan J. Matt, *Homesickness: An American History* (New York: Oxford University Press, 2011), 27.

5. Starobinski, "Idea of Nostalgia," 83.

6. Norbert Elias, *The Civilizing Process: The History of Manners*, trans. Edmund Jephcott (New York: Urizen Books, 1978), 131–132.

7. Cas Wouters, *Informalization: Manners and Emotions Since 1890* (Thousand Oaks, Calif.: Sage Publications, 2007).

8. Peter N. Stearns and Carol Z. Stearns, "Emotionology: Clarifying the History of Emotions and Emotional Standards," *American Historical Review* 90 (October 1985), 825.

9. Barbara Rosenwein, "Worrying about Emotions," *American Historical Review* 107 (2002), 821–845.

10. Christina Kotchemidova, "From Good Cheer to 'Drive-By Smiling': A Social History of Cheerfulness," *Journal of Social History* 39 (Fall 2005), 10.

11. Elizabeth Keckley, *Behind the Scenes; Or, Thirty Years a Slave and Four Years in the White House* (New York: G. W. Carleton and Co., 1868), 29; Henry Watson, *Narrative of Henry Watson, a Fugitive Slave*, 3rd ed. (Boston: Bela Marsh, 1850), 32–33; John Blassingame, *The Slave Community: Plantation Life in the Antebellum South* (New York: Oxford University Press, 1972), 161; Lawrence Levine discusses the fact that whites found slaves inscrutable, and that slaves found it necessary to hide their true emotions. See Lawrence W. Levine, *Black Culture and Black Consciousness: Afro-American Folk Thought from Slavery to Freedom* (New York: Oxford University Press, 1977), 99–101.

12. For a discussion of (among other things) the problem of sources, see the fine essay by Piroska Nagy, "Historians and Emotions: New Theories, New Questions," October 2008, http://emma.hypotheses.org/147 (accessed March 20, 2013).

13. Elias, *Civilizing Process*, 214. See also J. Huizinga, *The Waning of the Middle Ages: A Study of the Forms of Life, Thought and Art in France and the Netherlands in the Dawn of the Renaissance* (Garden City, N.Y.: Doubleday, 1954).

14. Carolyn James and Bill Kent, "Renaissance Friendships: Traditional Truths, New Dissenting Voices," in *Friendship: A History*, ed. Barbara Caine (London: Equinox, 2009), 110–164. Stefanie Schneider, "Stop Them Damned Pictures: Political Cartoons, the Study of Emotions, and the Construction of the Anglo-American relationship," in *Emotions in American History: An International Assessment*, ed. Jessica Gienow-Hecht, (New York: Bergahn Books, 2010).

15. Reddy, *Navigation of Feeling*, 242–249.

16. Barbara Caine, "Taking Up the Pen: Women and the Writing of Friendship," in *Friendship*, 215–222.

17. Ann Swidler, *Talk of Love: How Culture Matters* (Chicago: University of Chicago Press, 2001).

18. Starobinski, "The Idea of Nostalgia," 82.

19. Christine Stansell, *City of Women: Sex and Class in New York, 1789–1860* (Urbana: University of Illinois Press, 1987), 89–101.

20. Gerald F. Lindermam, *Embattled Courage: The Experience of Combat in the American Civil War* (New York: Free Press, 1987).

21. Matt, *Homesickness*.

22. Stephen Francis, "Brass Pots and Velvet Doublets: The Distribution of Material Wealth in Late Henrician England," presented at the Arizona Center for Medieval and Renaissance Studies, February 1999.

23. Natalie Zemon Davis, *Fiction in the Archives: Pardon Tales and Their Tellers in Sixteenth-Century France* (Palo Alto, Calif.: Stanford University Press, 1987), 36–37, 104–105.

24. Dawn Keetley, "From Anger to Jealousy: Explaining Domestic Homicide in Antebellum America," *Journal of Social History* 42.2 (2008), 269–297.

25. Barbara H. Rosenwein, *Emotional Communities in the Early Middle Ages* (Ithaca, N.Y.: Cornell University Press, 2006).

26. Constant J. Mews and Neville Chiavaroli, "The Latin West," in Caine, *Friendship*, 102–103.

27. Matt, *Homesickness*, 24–25. Philip Morgan, *Slave Counterpoint: Black Culture in the Eighteenth Century Chesapeake and Lowcountry* (Chapel Hill: University of North Carolina Press, 1998), 642.

28. Joanna Bourke, *Fear: A Cultural History* (Emeryville, Calif.: Shoemaker and Hoard, 2005), 50.

29. Sarah Knott, "Sensibility and the American War for Independence," *American Historical Review* 109 (2004), 19–40; Jurgen Martschukat, "A Horrifying Experience? Public Executions and the Emotional Spectator in the New Republic," in Gienow-Hecht, *Emotions in American History*, 181–200.

30. Christina Kotchemidova, "Why We Say 'Cheese': Producing the Smile in Snapshot Photography," *Critical Studies in Media Communication* 22 (March 2005), 2–25.

31. Matt, *Homesickness*, 155–157, 248–267.

PART II

REGIONAL
ANALYSIS

CHAPTER 3

THE SKEIN OF
CHINESE EMOTIONS
HISTORY

NORMAN KUTCHER

It would be impossible to begin a chapter on the history of emotions in China without at least making glancing reference to the stereotype of "the emotionless Chinese." This shibboleth is of uncomfortably long lineage. It began, most likely, with the coming of nineteenth-century Protestant missionaries to China, men and women who, shocked at the seeming impassivity of the Chinese they encountered, attributed their lack of affect to a kind of racial impermeability to pain and suffering. For these missionaries, it was not much of a leap to argue that once Chinese embraced Christ, among the most precious gifts they would receive was the gift of emotion. Christ's love would rescue the Chinese not just from paganism but also from unfeeling itself. This was the view of the biblical educator James Hastings, who in 1911 described missionaries who had been privileged to see the "hard, emotionless Chinese face as it has glowed with the joy that illumines him who knows that Christ is his Saviour."[1]

The perceptions of missionaries became part of the larger cultural view of China. Parishioners who, in their Sunday morning services heard stories of impassive Chinese, easily fell prey to popular depictions of them as cold and cruel. The Chinese villains in nineteenth- and early-twentieth-century American fiction were calculating men who showed no emotions when they tortured their innocent enemies. As Harold Isaacs demonstrated, these perceptions of cruel Chinese who were impervious to pain went directly from popular culture into the perceptions of cultural difference people used to understand historical events. By the early 1950s, when China was already "lost" to communism, the image of the cold and unfeeling Chinese was used to explain the human wave assaults of the Korean War.[2] When Chinese in massive numbers surged across the Yalu, with poor-quality clothing in the cold climate and vastly inferior weapons, it was indifference in the face of death that made them formidable, if barely human, opponents.

Such was the power of this particular Western view of China that it some-how persuaded not only Westerners but also Chinese themselves that lack of emotion had been at least partially responsible for China's unhappy fate. When the novelist Ba Jin wrote his masterpiece *Family* (*Jia*), it was in no small part to rail against the perceived emotional bankruptcy and hypocrisy of the tra-ditional family. And when the generation of May Fourth thinkers began their project to reform Chinese culture, one of their major sources of inspiration was Ibsen's *A Doll's House*. The moment in that play in which Nora, refusing to bear the hypocrisy of the loveless marriage, angrily slammed the door and left home became the rallying moment for those who sought to inject what they perceived to be real emotion into Chinese culture.[3]

This Western-inspired project to change Chinese emotions made its way into the reform agendas of the two major contenders for leadership in modern China: the Communists (CCP) and the Nationalists (GMD). Both sought to find a means of generating feelings among their supporters. When they called for patriotism, they used the term *aiguo*, to love one's country. In so doing, they were deploying a term of deepest emotion.[4] Soldiers in the Cultural Revolution, who were being viewed in the West as mindless automatons, at the same time were being told in China that they should *ri ai Mao Zedong*: warmly love Mao Zedong. Among Nationalists, perhaps no one went as far as Zhang Ji, who in 1927 wrote: "Our hope is to . . . go into the midst of the people, into this emo-tionless Chinese society . . . taking these unemotional bones, injecting some emotional joy."[5]

Perhaps because the issue of emotion has been so prominent in Chinese history, the study of it, particularly in recent years, has advanced considerably. Scholars such as Paolo Santangelo, Haiyan Lee, and Dorothy Ko (to mention just a few names) have written fascinating and important studies that have made sense of a once elusive topic. Add to these works others that have been done on the history of emotions in Chinese literature, and one has an astonishingly impressive array of scholarship at one's disposal.

My purpose here is not to survey this literature. Instead, I would like to draw out some common threads that run through it. For while the literature on emotion in Chinese history stretches over very wide time periods and very wide subjects, these three threads recur. By teasing them out, I hope not only to provide a perspective on past scholarship but also to suggest some directions for future research.[6]

Each of these threads seems at first rather self-evident—and indeed no more relevant to China than to the rest of the world. It is only as we examine these threads more carefully that we find qualities of emotions history that are distinctively Chinese. At this stage, however, we begin with a straightforward description of each. The first of these threads is *orthodoxy*. Specific Chinese traditions—and here Confucianism is the case in point—dictated the rules of proper behavior: these rules were considered to regulate even the emotions. Feeling correct emotions was indeed a kind of Confucian preoccupation. The second thread is *context*. Whether, or how, an emotion was expressed was a product of the venue (textual or otherwise) in which it was to be described or expressed. One could write about one's emotions differently in different genres, and one could express one's emotions differently in different outlets. The third thread is the role of the *formula* (or, the *formulaic*) in emotion and its expression. How do we understand professions and descriptions of emotion that are expressed via stock phrases? The three threads interweave considerably, but we will begin by addressing them individually.

ORTHODOXY

There is no word that goes with *orthodoxy* in China more frequently than *Confucian*. The Confucian school of thought was intensely concerned with telling people how they should lead their lives. Even more, because Confucian orthodoxy was adopted and promoted by the state, it came to have a power that dwarfed all other orthodoxies. Because this Confucian orthodoxy had much to say about the proper regulation of the emotions, it will greatly concern us here.

Ironically, when we look at the chief source of Confucius's own ideas, the *Analects* (*Lun yu*), we see that the fifth century B.C.E. philosopher's views on emotions were neither clear nor consistent. In the main, he appears as a man who used his learning to cultivate and ultimately master his emotions, so that late in life he could do whatever he wanted without violating the norms of proper behavior—that is, his emotions would be in perfect tune with his actions and he would therefore desire only what was correct. The paramount expression of this is one of the most famous quotations in the *Analects*:

> "At fifteen, I had my mind bent on learning. At thirty I stood firm. At forty, I had no doubts. At fifty, I knew the decrees of Heaven. At sixty, my ear was

an obedient organ for the reception of truth. At seventy, I could follow what my heart desired, without transgressing what was right." (*Analects* 2:4)

But Confucius also appears in the *Analects* as a man prone to emotion and even emotional outbursts. In these moments, he is unable to live up to his own standards and his own teachings. Confucius's best and most beloved disciple was Yan Hui. When the two men traveled to Kuang, they met with danger. Yan Hui fell behind, and Confucius was seized with fear that his disciple had been killed. When they met up, a relieved Confucius said, "I thought you had died." Yan Hui responded, "While you were alive, how should I presume to die?" (*Analects* 11:23). And yet, Yan Hui did predecease Confucius, in what precipitates the most emotion-laden moment in the *Analects*. On learning of Yan Hui's death, Confucius was so distraught that he cried out: "Alas, Heaven is destroying me! Heaven is destroying me!" (*Analects* 11:9). Confucius bewailed the loss of Yan Hui so greatly that his surviving disciples had to warn him that his grief was excessive (*Analects* 11:10).

The death of Yan Hui is so powerful in part because of the simple beauty of the relationship between these men—the disciple consoling his teacher by saying he would not dare to predecease him—and the poignancy of that favorite disciple's death. But when we look at the larger context, this moment becomes more meaningful still. When Confucius proclaims that heaven is destroying him, he is conjuring an image of heaven that runs directly counter to the other depictions of heaven in the *Analects*. Throughout the text, Confucius constructs an image of a benevolent but distant heaven, one that is a mechanism for order and virtue but which was essentially silent. In a rhetorical question posed to his disciple Zigong, Confucius asks: "Does Heaven speak? The four seasons pursue their courses and all things are continually being produced, but does Heaven say anything?" (*Analects* 17:19). But the grief and anger he felt at the loss of Yan Hui caused him, at least temporarily, to abandon that more impersonal view of heaven in favor of a view of a more interventionist, even malevolent one—else how could a benevolent heaven have taken his best disciple from him?

Moreover, when Confucius's disciples warn him that he is grieving excessively for Yan Hui, they are suggesting that their Master has deviated from his own principles. Their admonition needs to be understood in the larger context of Confucius's views of family relations. According to that view, the dictates of filial piety demanded that one have a greater duty to members of one's own family than to nonrelatives, and that the greatest duty one had was to one's parents.[7] Confucius's own emotions, in this instance, drag him outside the bounds of acceptable behavior: his grief is extreme at the loss of Yan Hui, but such extreme grief should be reserved for a son's grief for his father. In this case, he is wailing in the extreme for someone who is both younger and not a family member. The death of Yan Hui, then, causes Confucius to feel and express emotions that force him to contradict his most basic beliefs. And we the reader are left with a view of Confucius's attitude toward emotions as inconsistent.

It fell to subsequent Confucian thinkers to more carefully elucidate the Confucian attitude toward emotion. Mencius, who lived in the third century B.C.E. and was the most significant Confucian thinker to come on the scene after Confucius's death, made important contributions in this area. In particular, he is well known for clarifying Confucius's attitude about human nature. The Master himself had not spoken clearly or specifically on the issue of whether human nature was good or evil. In large part, this was because Confucius lived during an era in which human nature was not a major source of philosophical debate. Not so in Mencius's time, when the subject was hotly contested.

Mencius held that human nature was good. And most importantly for our purposes, he held that the essential goodness of human nature was proven by, and originated in, human emotions. There is no clearer evidence of this than an oft-quoted passage from the *Mencius*. In 2:6, Mencius describes the situation of a child about to fall into a well.

> If men suddenly see a child about to fall into a well, they will without exception experience a feeling of alarm and distress. They will feel so, not as a ground on which they may gain the favour of the child's parents, nor as a ground on which they may seek the praise of their neighbours and friends, nor from a dislike to the reputation of having been unmoved by such a thing. From this case we may perceive that the feeling of commiseration is essential to man . . . the feeling of commiseration is the principle of benevolence.

In other words, to Mencius, it was a human emotion that was both the origin and ultimate proof of the goodness of men—because they felt distress and alarm when they saw a child about to fall into a well. In this emotion lay the sprouts, as he called it, of the principle of human benevolence (*ren*), which was the matured outcome of the emotion.[8] Out of a sympathetic heart, one could develop a feeling of benevolence. Emotion, then, to Mencius, was good—evil came about because people failed to live up to the emotions with which they had been naturally endowed.

With the rise of Neo-Confucianism in the ninth century, we see further elaboration of the Confucian attitude toward emotion. The scholar Paolo Santangelo has done the most to elucidate the role of emotions in Neo-Confucianism. He quotes the philosopher Cheng Yi (1033–1107), who reconciled Mencius's ideas about the essential goodness of emotions with the Neo-Confucian view that they were harmful:

> [Man's] original nature is pure and tranquil. Before it is aroused, the five moral principles of his nature [identified by Mencius], called humanity, righteousness, propriety, wisdom, and faithfulness, are complete. As his physical form appears, it comes into contact with external things and is aroused from within. As it is aroused from within, the seven feelings, called pleasure, anger, sorrow, joy, love, hate, and desire, ensue. As feelings become strong and increasingly reckless, his nature becomes damaged. For this reason, the enlightened person controls his feelings so that they will be in accord with the mean. He rectifies his mind and nourishes his nature. This is therefore called turning the feelings into the [original] nature. The stupid person does not know how to control them. He lets them loose until they are depraved, fetter his nature, and destroy it. This is therefore called turning one's nature into feelings.[9]

For Cheng Yi, emotions came in good and bad forms. The emotions man was born with were the keys to his essential goodness. Bad emotions came later, and so by controlling them, one could retain, or return to, one's essential nature.

If Cheng Yi was one of the most important founders of Neo-Confucianism, Zhu Xi (1130–1200) was the synthetic philosopher who brought it to its mature Song-dynasty form. In his crystallization of Neo-Confucian thought, Zhu Xi integrated the ideas of Cheng Yi (and his brother, Cheng Hao), along with ideas of many of his predecessors. In his writings, Zhu Xi maintained and developed Cheng Yi's ideas about the connection between one's original nature and the emotions. In so doing, he too paid deference to Mencius. In Zhu Xi's view, when a child is on the brink of falling into a well, the operative principle is one of stimulus and response. The external stimulus of seeing the child about to fall into the well arouses the emotion of distress, which stimulates the emotion of compassion that was at the root of benevolence (*ren*).[10]

Zhu Xi, then, remains faithful to the Mencian view that emotions can be both good and bad. And yet, Neo-Confucianism, and the Neo-Confucianism of Zhu Xi himself, has in general a much less favorable view of emotions. While granting their power for good and their connection to the origins of human nature (as contained in Mencius), Zhu Xi stresses the negative view of emotion when connected with what he called the selfish desires (*si yu*). These were the desires that, simply put, aimed to benefit only the individual.[11] Specifically, he returns to the *Analects* to stress Confucius's emphasis on the need to restrain these selfish desires.[12] Selfish desires and feelings were, in this view, what led people off the moral path. Emotions, therefore, became something to be controlled and regulated.

Where exactly this new view of emotion came from is hard to say, but the origins of Neo-Confucianism may provide a clue. One major factor in the rise of Neo-Confucianism was the Buddhist challenge. Arriving in China in the first century C.E., Buddhism over the successive centuries developed a massive following. Confucians who sought to mount a response to Buddhism inevitably borrowed ideas from their adversary. Buddhism viewed emotions and desires as barriers to enlightenment, and Neo-Confucians may have borrowed that perspective. Another possibility has to do with the moral project of the Neo-Confucians. As social reformers, they sought to understand the origins of the moral decay they saw around them. In so doing, they may have come to focus on emotions such as greed and envy, which had led to a breakdown in society.

Whatever the origins of this more negative view of human emotions, Zhu Xi's view of the matter would be the dominant one for centuries—becoming enshrined in state orthodoxy. From there it was disseminated widely in society. Students who studied for the state-sponsored examinations were forced to master Zhu Xi's ideas. Perhaps just as significantly, Zhu Xi's ideas were popularized through his work *Family Rituals* (*Jia li*). This text, a kind of guide to family management, proliferated in popular editions, and evidence exists that many late imperial households held copies of it.[13]

The text is not purely a manual for the conduct of rituals—although that is certainly a major part of it. Much of the text deals with regulating the conduct of the members of the family. And it poses a clear argument against the selfish desires. The ritual sections are most interesting because they adhere to the basic Confucian notion that the emotions can be regulated by proper performance of rituals. The text, for example, provides not only step-by-step instructions on how to perform a funeral but also tells the mourner when to cry. To a Western reader, it seems remarkable that a text could dictate a function of the parasympathetic nervous system. But in the world of Neo-Confucianism, this is precisely the point: correct performance of ritual and observing the rules of propriety cultivates the person, so that he or she feels the proper emotion at the proper moment.[14] Because all members of an extended family were supposed to carry out the rituals, their effectiveness was supposed to spread beyond the bounds of the literate. Even nonliterate clan members could participate in—and be cultivated by—the rituals they practiced.

There were other ways, beyond the textual, that Zhu Xi's orthodoxy was spread through society. As Francesca Bray has observed, "Architecture played a key role in imposing and reproducing orthodoxy and social conventions in late imperial China."[15] In a discussion of the impact of *Family Rituals'* power to regulate emotion in the household, Bray shows how the main features of Zhu Xi's thought were inscribed on the structure of the house. The offering hall, placed as it was at the center of the house, ensured the emotion of respect that accompanied ancestral veneration; the separation between inner and outer ensured the maintenance of hierarchy and restrained the lusts. Thus, even non-literate members of a household could absorb Zhu Xi's ideas (which were built on tenets of thinkers who had preceded him).

CONTEXT

Confucianism played a powerful role in society, regulating the emotions one was supposed to feel and express. But what room was left to express emotions that did not conform to Confucian expectations? It is in this area that we see the importance of context. I use the term *context* here to stand for two specific things: first, *genre*, meaning that certain emotions can be expressed in certain textual venues; second, *compartmentalization*, meaning that people can experience life in a divided way, expressing some emotions in some contexts, other emotions in other contexts.

In premodern China, authors' writings were gathered into editions known as *bieji*, which followed largely standard formats. These would include their memorials to the throne, prefaces they had written for the works of others, letters, commemorative biographies, and poems.[16] Writers chose particular genres for the expression of particular emotions. A memorial to the throne, for example, would require dispassion, even when emotional issues, such as the sufferings of others, were at issue. Commemorative biographical essays also tended to be rather impassive given that they were written to memorialize a friend or associate. But in their poems, these writers could express the full range of human feeling—including, most importantly, those feelings that went against the dictates of strict Confucian orthodoxy.

The most moving example of this is the poems that people wrote to commemorate the deaths of children. In the Confucian view, love and duty in the society were hierarchical, and one carried out mourning for a senior, rather than for a junior. In the case of the death of a child, mourning and indeed the funeral itself was, depending on the age of the child, truncated or even not carried out. Despite these restrictions, those who lost a child felt intense pain. Though Confucian rituals sought to program emotions, they could not succeed in these extreme instances. And though an official could not acknowledge, let

alone describe, his loss in a memorial to the throne, he could do so in his poetry. The collected works of many officials contain the emotion-laden poems
of those who sought to come to terms with the death of a child. In contrast
with the public acts of mourning that accompanied the death of a parent, these
show the sorrow of a private heart alone with its grief.

Bian Gong (1476–1532), for example, was a Ming-dynasty official, whose
poems are filled with descriptions of boat-pullers, woodcutters, and others
of the nonelite classes. He also wrote a brief but moving poem in which he
remembers his dead son:

> Years ago, to the winding banks of this lake in spring
> I brought my son to play.
> The flowers greeted his jade-white skin with smiles;
> the clouds floated beside his patterned robe.
> He explored the bamboo on the shore across,
> and took out a boat to search for fish.
> Now I come alone, grieving in my heart;
> the misty moon at evening holds my sorrow.[17]

In describing "grieving in his heart," Bian Gong uses the conventional expression for feeling a loss that could not be expressed in formal mourning. The
genre of poetry allows him a space for its expression.

Once we move outside the bounds of a writer's collected works, we encounter literary genres that were generally not considered fully respectable. Here
two particular forms come to mind: the miscellany and the work of fiction.
The miscellany, or *biji*, was published in small numbers of copies and was often
distributed among friends. Because of its limited circulation, it provided the
writer more freedom to express emotion. Fiction was more widely disseminated, but on the other hand it was often written anonymously or pseudony-
mously. Such texts, which were written and read largely surreptitiously, helped
people deal with their emotions. Indeed, as David Hawkes notes, it was often
(and perhaps erroneously) presumed that fiction's real function was to help
people "blow off steam."[18]

That different emotions could be expressed in different genres reflects the
more general phenomenon of what we today call *compartmentalization*, meaning that people can express emotion differently in different contexts. Of course,
there was nothing unique to China in this phenomenon. But I would argue that
in premodern China compartmentalization was particularly acute: perhaps
because of the power of Confucianism to control at least some types of public

discourse, perhaps because of the power of the state to do so. Compartmentalization was also more greatly tolerated because of how religion was viewed. Those in the West are less tolerant of compartmentalization because of the exclusivist nature of Western religions.

One alternative context to Confucian orthodoxy was certainly Daoism. An old saying was a man could be a Confucian when in office and a Daoist when out. That is, when removed from the obligations of serving the state, he could retreat from Confucian orthodoxy to a kind of Daoist reclusion, where he had none of the same obligations, emotional or otherwise.[19] The texts of Daoism are filled with examples of people defying Confucian expectations. One well-known example occurs in the *Zhuangzi*. When Zhuangzi's wife dies, his friend comes to pay a formal condolence call and finds Zhuangzi singing and banging on a pot instead of observing mourning. When questioned, Zhuangzi says only that while he initially felt sadness, on reflection he realized his wife had merely returned to the nothingness from which she had come.[20]

Other contexts, too, were available for the expression of nonorthodox emotions. As Hung-tai Wang has demonstrated, for an elite male, one such context was his relationship with courtesans. In traditional China, a man could live with multiple women and could also have relationships outside the home with courtesans. His wife, almost always chosen by his parents, was considered his only official partner, and his relationship with her was the only one countenanced by Confucianism. This relationship, then, reproduced Confucian orthodoxy. He chose his other womenfolk based on his own feelings and desires. For that reason, it was routinely the case that in his relationship with his wife, he expressed his officially sanctioned, Confucian emotions, whereas in his relationship with his concubines and with courtesans outside the home, he expressed his nonorthodox passions. It was when he was outside his home and in the context of a commercial relationship that he could feel his most intense emotions, in a relationship with someone that was not about duty but was about feelings.[21]

The architecture of the home, too, allowed for the compartmentalization of emotion. As noted above, research by Francesca Bray demonstrates that the late imperial Chinese home, built in accordance with the rules contained in Zhu Xi's *Family Rituals*, became in effect a text for the reproduction of orthodox Confucian values. But Bray's work also shows that these same houses afforded the opportunity to express alternative and at times contradictory worldviews. The example she uses is geomancy: the set of beliefs according to which a house was sited on the land to bring wealth and prosperity to the descendants.[22] The house, then, in the end reproduced two very different worldviews: one, oriented on a North-South access and around the ancestral shrine, which functioned to serve the ancestors and the family line; and two, sited as it should be on the land, which functioned to bring wealth to the inhabitants.

The same form of compartmentalization applied in what was arguably the most emotion-laden ritual in Chinese society: the funeral. In *Family Rituals*, Zhu Xi portrays the funeral and mourning in exclusivist terms, as serving the orthodox Confucian needs of the society. He even warns specifically against the intrusion of Buddhist practices into the funeral. In fact, the funeral in all its aspects encompassed diverse and contradictory beliefs. While the funeral was Confucian in outline, Buddhist and Daoist professionals, each with their distinct views of death and the afterlife, were also called in to officiate. Geomancy, too, was an important part of the funeral and figured into the burial. The gravesite chosen for a body, and how that plot was sited on the land, became of prime importance in bringing wealth to the descendants.

This last example, the funeral, suggests the real way in which, despite the pressure to maintain Confucian values by regulating the emotions, a variety of emotions were in fact permitted. To a Westerner, perhaps, who is more accustomed to monotheistic religions and jealous gods who do not allow worship of other deities, the cacophony of permissible religious practices at a traditional Chinese funeral would seem odd. But in the Chinese worldview, religious beliefs can comfortably coexist. One can visit one temple to one god on one day, and another temple, to a very different god, on another. These different contexts allowed for the expression of very different emotions.

THE FORMULAIC

The place of the formulaic in the expression of emotions in China might just well be the aspect of it that seems most foreign to the Western observer, who tends to associate the sincere expression of emotion with originality. We expect, for example, that when we console someone over a death, we will offer some heartfelt words that transcend the banal. Even when we buy a condolence card, we expect that our careful selection of the card, and the words we write on it, will express something special, some specific connection we can build to the bereaved and perhaps the deceased.

This view of the world is very much at odds with that of premodern China, where the expression of correct emotions through strict adherence to a formula was considered the sincerest form of expression. From the death announcement, through condolence visits, through the mourning period itself, what was said (or written) was fully scripted. Even emotions themselves were scripted—a son, for example, would express the pain and guilt he felt over the death of his parent by use of the stock phrase, "Through my own neglect, my parent has died." To which the condolence caller would respond, "Matters of life and death are decreed by Heaven. Why speak of guilt and shame?"[23]

In literature, too, as David T. Roy noted in his study of the famous novel *The Plum in the Golden Vase (Jin ping mei)*, emotions were expressed in the text via repetition of well-known popular songs. When, for example, the character Pan Jinlian pines waiting for her lover Ximen Qing to come to her, the anonymous author conveys the painful blend of love and hatred she feels for him, not by a fresh description, but by inclusion of a what was probably a well-known song lyric: "The pain of heartache is hard to dispel." "In a sorrowful breast depression feeds on itself."[24] The characters' thoughts are expressed through what Roy describes as "a complex mosaic of borrowed language, comprising proverbial sayings, catch phrases, stock epithets and couplets, quotations from earlier poetry and song, and formulaic language of all kinds inherited from the literary tale as well as traditional vernacular fiction and drama."[25]

So central was the formulaic in the expression of emotion, that we find written and spoken Chinese to be replete with stock four-character expressions (*chengyu*) for the expression of emotions.[26] Such expressions have historical allusions embedded within them, which helps make them economical ways to express nuance. In the case of anger, the most well-known *chengyu* is "*nu fa chong guan*," literally, "so angry that one's hair lifts up one's hat." Its origin is in a story from the Warring States period, and it has long been used as a formulaic expression of rage. Other *chengyu* allow for descriptions of very particular sorts of anger. For example, "*nao xiu cheng nu*" is a *chengyu* that arose rather late—it appears first in the classic novel *Dream of the Red Chamber*. Its literal meaning is "the anger that arises from shame." More self-explanatory than other *chengyu*, it refers to the particular sort of anger that arises from resentment over having one's shameful predicament or previous actions exposed.

Besides conveying particular nuances of emotion, four-character phrases may also be shorthand ways of reinforcing Confucian orthodoxy. And as part of the spoken language, this reinforcement effect reached to the nonliterate people in society. For example, the *chengyu* for a dead friend is "*ai dao wang you*," literally, "to grieve for a lost friend." The words *ai dao* are meant to express feelings of grief that are emotional, but that also conform to the rules of propriety because the deceased was not a parent. As we noted in the first section, true mourning is reserved for an elder family member.

CONCLUSIONS

The three threads discussed above have made it difficult for the scholar who seeks to understand the history of emotion in China. How can one study a child's emotions toward his or her parents, when there was such intense societal pressure to express the norms of filial piety? Formulaicism, too, has made it difficult for the historian to discern emotion. How is one to judge real emotions, when they are expressed in stock phrases? Even the third thread, the role of context, can be of only limited help. Although it is true that one could express different emotions in different contexts, some of the most revealing contexts are not available from large segments of the society. Poetry, for example, is the best place to gain access to the direct emotional experience of the writer, but most people did not write poems, and many poems have not survived. And even poetry has its limits. I venture to say that poems expressing brute anger toward a parent would be next to impossible to find in premodern China.

The challenge of understanding the history of emotions in China may sometimes make it difficult to answer the most challenging question of all: whether emotions were, after all, simply different in premodern China than elsewhere. Those who have asked the question have generally come down somewhere in the middle, arguing that some emotions may, in part or in full, be socially constructed, while others are essential to the human experience. This is the position taken by Brian King, who argues that neglect of either of these perspectives will result in a mistaken understanding of Chinese emotion.[27] It is also the position of Halvor Eifring, who explores the issue through discussion of facial expression. He notes that in the novel *The Story of the Stone*, many if not most of the facial expressions would be familiar to a Westerner: for example, blushing out of embarrassment. Some, however, would be unfamiliar, such as sticking out the tongue when overwhelmed by fear. Expressions like the latter, he argues, are socially constructed and the product of learned behavior.[28]

One way of looking at the issue is that while underlying emotions in China were very similar to those in the West, their modes of expression were often different. This is the position taken by Nicolas Zufferey, who has written that "while the emotions might be universal, the method of expressing them and explaining them varies according to time and place."[29]

This matter relates to what Zuffery calls the social dimension of emotion. That is, that the outward expression of the emotion is just as significant, just as sincere, as its inner feeling, largely because it expresses values the society holds dear. Considerations such as this one obviate the need for separating "sincere" from insincere emotions, because it is the sincere adherence to orthodox values, expressed in professions of emotion, that the society valorizes. He uses the example of martial arts novels, in which it is normal for a hero to cry pitifully on the death of his parents—even if he has never met them. In this case, the "sincerity" of the emotion is manifest in the values reflected in the hero's tears. Zufferey goes on to connect the difference between emotion to the different places of religion in China and the West.[30]

In a fascinating essay, Christoph Harbsmeier pursues much the same line of thought. He differentiates usages of the two words for crying: "*ku*," which he translates as wailing; and "*qi*," which he translates as weeping. Tracing the usages of each of these terms in early texts, he shows that while they are often both translated as "crying," there are important and subtle differences between them. *Ku*, or wailing, is essentially reserved for crying that reflects the social dimension of emotion. It is done, for example, by a filial son at a parent's funeral. Weeping, on the other hand, is a much more personal and spontaneous expression of individual emotion. One does not need to weep as a public statement. But when one wails, it is to make a public profession of emotion. Weeping is also more often associated with children, and wailing with adults.[31]

By implication, Harbsmeier's argument also neatly draws together the three threads described in this chapter. Wailing, as a kind of public profession of emotion, is most frequently tied to orthodoxy. In the book *Family Rituals*, mourners are told when to wail. By wailing at the appropriate time, they demonstrate their adherence to orthodox values. And that wailing, properly speaking, is not "put on." Having cultivated the proper emotions during their life, it happens with no artificiality. Second, wailing and weeping are connected to proper context. One wails in the course of a parent's funeral but weeps in the context of a friend's funeral. To wail at the funeral of a nonrelative is to violate the norms of filial piety. Finally, wailing versus crying must be understood in the context of the formulaic. Wailing when properly performed is not meant to be spontaneous or to express some sort of original sentiment—it is not, in other words, supposed to be like tears in the West, which we take to be a sign of sincere emotions. Instead, it shows its sincerity by its adherence to the formulaic.[32]

Harbsmeier's argument is so persuasive because it is grounded in an exploration of language—and specifically in the differentiation of linguistic dyads. Indeed, some of the most interesting scholarship on emotion in Chinese history and literature may be found in the meaningful exploration of such dyads. Andrew Plaks, for example, is able to expose fascinating aspects of the emotions in the two great Chinese novels *The Plum in the Golden Vase* and *A Dream of*

Red Mansions (*Hong lou meng*) by focusing on the dyad *pian* (partiality) and *quan* (whole). In the latter work, in particular, he finds that these dyads leap off the page until the author's particular insight becomes abundantly clear: "that single-minded pursuit of individual gratification inevitably expands until the ego becomes a self[-]contained world unto itself, paradoxically rendering impossible the attainment of any degree of true wholeness."[33] Similarly, Dorothy Ko's remarkable exploration of the dyad *qing* (emotion) and *wen* (cultured) allows her to find insights into the feelings of the Confucian official Li Gong.[34]

If the exploration of such dyads presents a fruitful area of research, so too does the historian's traditional refuge: change over time. Orthodoxy, by its very definition, is supposed to be unchanging. And yet, a historian's scrupulous research may reveal that what was considered orthodox behavior was not always the same. One signpost of this change is instances in which individual writers advocate for change or debate what the actual orthodox position was. There were more than a few instances in which social changes in the society brought people and the skein of emotions as understood in China into conflict. At those moments, sensitive and articulate writers made bold arguments for reform in the system. Those moments have provided rich avenues for research, and will continue to do so in the future.

NOTES

1. James Hastings, *The Great Texts of the Bible* (New York: Charles Scribner's Sons, 1911), 60.

2. Harold R. Isaacs, *Scratches on Our Minds: American Images of China and India* (New York: John Day Co., 1958), 232–236.

3. Vera Schwarcz, *The Chinese Enlightenment: Intellectuals and the Legacy of the May Fourth Movement of 1919* (Berkeley: University of California Press, 1986), 114.

4. See Haiyan Lee, *Revolution of the Heart: A Genealogy of Love in China, 1900–1950* (Stanford, Calif.: Stanford University Press, 2007).

5. Michael G. Murdock, "Whose Modernity? Anti-Christianity and Educational Policy in Revolutionary China, 1924–1926," *Twentieth-Century China* 31, no. 1 (November 2005): 43.

6. My only caveat is that I will explore these threads in pre-twentieth-century China; that is, before the project to bring emotion to China really took hold. There have, however, been fascinating studies of emotion in the modern context. See Haiyan Lee, *Revolution of the Heart*; and Eugenia Lean, *Public Passions: The Trial of Shi Jianqiao and the Rise of Popular Sympathy in Republican China* (Berkeley: University of California Press, 2007).

7. T. Yijie, B. Bruya, and H. Wen, "Emotion in Pre-Qin Ruist Moral Theory: An Explanation of 'Dao Begins in Qing,'" *Philosophy East and West* (2003): 271–281, 273.

8. N. Zufferey, "Quelques réflexions sur la représentation des émotions en Chine et en chinois," *Social Science Information* 48, no. 3 (2009): 501–521; D. B. Wong, "Is There a Distinction between Reason and Emotion in Mencius?" *Philosophy East and West* 41, no. 1 (1991): 31–44; M. Im, "Emotional Control and Virtue in the 'Mencius,'" *Philosophy East and West* 49, no. 1 (1999): 1–27.

9. Paolo Santangelo, "Emotions and the Origin of Evil in Neo-Confucian Thought," in *Minds and Mentalities in Traditional Chinese Literature*, ed. Halvor Eifring (Beijing: Culture and Art Publishing House, 1999), 215. The translation is that of Wing-tsit Chan. See Chan's *Sourcebook in Chinese Philosophy* (Princeton, N.J.: Princeton University Press, 1963), 547–548.

10. Chen Lai, "The Discussion of Mind and Nature in Zhu Xi's Philosophy," in *Chinese Philosophy in an Era of Globalization*, ed. Robin R. Wang, trans. Robert W. Foster (Albany: State University of New York Press, 2004), 92.

11. I am oversimplifying here. See Kwong-loi Shun, "Zhu Xi's Moral Psychology," in *Dao Companion to Neo-Confucian Philosophy*, ed. John Makeham (Dordrecht, Neth.: Springer, 2010), 185–186, 488.

12. Daniel K. Gardner and Confucius, *Zhu Xi's Reading of the Analects: Canon, Commentary, and the Classical Tradition* (New York: Columbia University Press, 2003), 79–82.

13. Zhu Xi, *Chu Hsi's Family Rituals: A Twelfth-Century Chinese Manual for the Performance of Cappings, Weddings, Funerals, and Ancestral Rites*, trans. Patricia Ebrey (Princeton, N.J.: Princeton University Press, 1991), 234.

14. Norman Kutcher, *Mourning in Late Imperial China: Filial Piety and the State* (New York: Cambridge University Press, 1999), 31.

15. Francesca Bray, "Decorum and Desire: An Architectonics of Domestic Space in Late Imperial China," in *Li jiao yu qing yu: qian jin dai Zhongguo wen hua zhong de hou/ xian dai xing*, ed. Ping-chen Hsiung and Miaofen Lü, eds., (Taibei, Taiwan: Zhongyang Yanjiuyuan Jindaishi Yanjiusuo, 1999), 31.

16. For a more detailed description, see Endymion Wilkinson, *Chinese History: A Manual* (Cambridge, Mass.: Harvard University Asia Center for the Harvard-Yenching Institute, 2000), 597–598.

17. Jonathan Chaves, trans., *The Columbia Book of Later Chinese Poetry: Yüan, Ming, and Ch'ing Dynasties (1279–1911)* (New York: Columbia University Press, 1986), 253.

18. David Hawkes, Preface, in Eifring, *Minds and Mentalities*, xii.

19. Joseph R. Levenson, *Confucian China and Its Modern Fate: A Trilogy* (Berkeley: University of California Press, 1968), 44.

20. Zhuangzi, *Chuang-tzŭ: The Seven Inner Chapters and Other Writings from the Book Chuang-tzŭ*, trans. A. C. Graham (London: Allen and Unwin, 1981), 123–124.

21. Hung-tai Wang, "A Life of Love and Art," in *Li jiao yu qing yu: qian jin dai Zhongguo wen hua zhong de hou/xian dai xing*, ed. Ping-chen Hsiung and Miaofen Lü (Taibei, Taiwan: Zhongyang Yanjiuyuan Jindaishi Yanjiusuo, 1999).

22. Bray, "Decorum and Desire," 43–47.

23. See, generally, Kutcher, *Mourning in Late Imperial China*, 30–31.

24. David T. Roy, "Songs of the Self: Self-expression through Song Lyrics in *Jin Ping Mei*," in Eifring, *Minds and Mentalities*, 19.

25. Ibid., 27.

26. The list of what was considered the standard emotions varied somewhat in premodern China. According to Confucians, the emotions were: joy (*xi*), anger (*nu*), grief (*ai*), fear (*ju*), love (*ai*), hate (*wu*), and desire (*yu*). Brian King, "The Conceptual Structure of Emotional Experience in Chinese" (PhD diss. University of Ohio, 1989), 24.

27. Ibid., 2.

28. Halvor Eifring, "Chinese Faces: The Sociopsychology of Facial Features as Described in 'The Story of the Stone," in Eifring, *Minds and Mentalities*, 94.

29. Zufferey, "Quelques réflexions," 501–521, 507.

30. Ibid., 508.

31. Christoph Harbsmeier, "Weeping and Wailing in Ancient China," in Eifring, *Minds and Mentalities*, 317–422.

32. Harbsmeier's argument can help us make sense of the public wailing observed in North Korea following the death of Kim Jong il.

33. Andrew Plaks, "Self-enclosure and Self-absorption in the Classic Chinese Novel," in Eifring, *Minds and Mentalities*, 33–34.

34. Dorothy Ko, "Thinking about Copulating: An Early-Qing Confucian Thinker's Problem with Emotion and Words," in *Remapping China: Fissures in Historical Terrain*, ed. Gail Hershatter et al. (Stanford, Calif.: Stanford University Press, 1996), 62–65.

CHAPTER 4

EMOTIONS HISTORY
IN EASTERN EUROPE

MARK D. STEINBERG

It would be unwise, even harmful, to approach a regional history of emotions looking for essential patterns of national or ethnic character. To be sure, many people have claimed defining emotional traits for their own culture. In the early 1900s, for example, it was common for Russians to speak of a "Russian soul" naturally inclined toward "brooding and melancholy."[1] More deleterious have been claims about other cultures: Serbs are belligerent, Romanians are intensely emotional, "Gypsies" are impassioned but irresponsible, Germans desire order, Jews are avaricious. National and ethnic cultural stereotypes have histories and are worth studying as revealing constructions and for their effects on people's lives. But as a method of analysis, arguments about culturally essential emotional personalities are as problematic as arguments about emotions being hardwired into human neurophysiology and thus universal across place and time. Of course, bodily affect does exist—strong feelings such as fear or anger have corporeal elements that precede their cultural narration and interpretation—though what matters more for studying the complexities of human society and history is how feelings develop in differing contexts. A regional approach opens a valuable space for examining what contexts mean in practice, but only if approached critically, with an awareness of the dangers of cultural essentialism as well as of the (also often dangerous) historical power of such imagery. Following newer approaches to regional geography, it is most useful to view regions not as stable or homogeneous places but as spaces constituted by social relationships and thus marked by difference, conflict, and change interacting with common and stable features.[2]

Emotions, we know, are a slippery and treacherous terrain and also indispensable as we seek deeper and fuller answers to the most difficult questions historians pose: not least, the search for causation and the hermeneutic search for past meanings. As such, we must view emotions as social practice, as inseparable from the ways individuals in social settings and in social relationships perceive, evaluate, judge, and act in their world. This is an understanding of emotions as formed at the intersections of bodily affect; tangible circumstance (poverty, violence, etc.); social difference (including the experiences of gender, class, ethnicity, religion, and differentials of power); culture (especially language); communication (including both the desire to be understood by others and the likelihood of misunderstanding); and change over time.[3]

"Eastern Europe" is a particularly unstable, imprecise, and shifting category. Indeed, some scholars have used the term to illustrate how geographic regions are always social and historical constructs, always situated and relational: in this case, the product of a western-European "orientalizing" gaze (Europe's backward "east") or the particular historical legacy of communism (or Russian domination, as many saw it).[4] Even if we limit ourselves to the nineteenth and early twentieth centuries, the lands roughly from the Elbe to the Urals (some would exclude Russia, perhaps as too "eastern" to be "European," though I will not) and from the Baltic to the Adriatic have been divided among empires (Hohenzollern, Habsburg, Romanov, Ottoman) in changing relations of alliance and conflict, reconfigured and realigned as the communist "eastern bloc," and, most recently, divided again into nations both allied and at (sometimes violent) odds. And even the definition of "nation" has been unstable and contested. This is a region rich in its diversity of ethnicities, languages, and religions. Even the common academic designation for study of this region, Slavic studies, has long included, alongside people speaking Slavic languages, the great many ethnicities and nationalities in close historical relations with Slavs—varyingly, relations of domination, subjugation, and alliance—including Lithuanians, Latvians, Estonians, Finns, Hungarians, Romanians, Georgians, Armenians, Azeris, Jews, Roma, Tatars, Kazakhs, Uzbeks, Kyrgyz, Turkmen, Tajiks, and others. Since the end of communist rule, as connections between these groups have grown more strained, it has been repeatedly asked whether this is a "region" at all. But if we hold to the definition of *region* as a space constituted by social relationships rather than by commonalties of culture, eastern Europe is very much such a relational space, with its distinctive legacies of enormous diversity and often sudden change, and especially of forceful modern attempts to unify and stabilize relationships by absorbing difference into empires and multinational states or attempting to eradicate difference.

The "emotional turn" in the study of eastern Europe has been strong in recent years, stimulated by new work in various fields and by the challenges of interpreting the disruptions and enthusiasms the region experienced after the fall of communism. Historians, literary scholars, and anthropologists have led the way in systematically asking new questions about the workings of passions, feelings, moods, dispositions, and affects in the construction of human experience, thinking, perception, judgment, and action, past and present. Numerous conferences, workshops, and talks—including in the region—have been organized around the study of emotions, and a growing body of research has begun to appear in print.[5] The variety of methodological influences evident here reflects the luxuriant growth of emotion studies generally. Theories of subjectivity, discourse, performativity, memory, gender, and power—and comparative research on these questions—have been evident in various combinations. But for all this variety, most scholars now share the view of emotions as relational and situated social practice. Thus, the focus of new work has been on mapping and analyzing the particular mutual relationships between emotions and the social, ranging from the experiences of everyday life to extraordinary political actions in the public sphere. These new studies have deepened our understanding of these histories and challenged interpretations that are limited to "rational" calculations and motives.

It has been suggested that emotions are most intense when self or society (particularly self *in* society) are troubled, especially when individual agency is obstructed.[6] This is demonstrated all too well by the modern history of eastern Europe. It is not surprising that research on emotion history in the region has tended to focus on emotions attached to the most difficult public conditions and experiences, such as violence and material suffering, and emotions like anger, hatred, fear, and despair. But no less powerful in the modern history of the region have been histories of passionate vision, hope, and exhilaration, including the embrace of the redemptive (even utopian) promise of happiness in times of revolution—whether nationalist, socialist, communist, or, at the fall of communism, market liberal. Research on emotions in the history of eastern Europe is too large and varied to capture in a single chapter. I will focus, therefore, on four broad areas—all in the modern era, indeed in which modernity is itself often the key problem,[7] and all of which involve politics broadly defined, particularly the "cultural politics of emotion," which concerns how people apprehend their world and actively pursue some desired good.[8] Although these areas are often entwined, I will group and name these separately as *emotional identities* (especially nationalisms), *moral emotions* (especially around the self in society), the *emotional politics of happiness* (especially the pursuit of modernity and freedom), and the persistent power of *emotional dissent* (the refusal to believe the most authoritative discourses of what is proper and normal or how to achieve happiness).

A word on translation is needed, especially given my insistence on situated practices and meanings. At the very least, we must recognize what is lost when we translate emotion words—even the word *emotion*—from other languages into English, given the rich complexity of contextual meanings imbedded in different languages. There is no easy way to navigate, as we must, between the Scylla of assuming transcultural equivalence between words (and, as expressions of emotion, assuming universality of feeling as well as meaning) and the Charybdis of seeing only cultural difference. Explicit attention to local meanings and uses are a minimum necessity.[9] More than this, we must recognize that the *evidence* of emotion is already a translation—between, for example, bodily affect and culturally shaped emotions, between given emotion words and historically particular meanings and uses, between their past and our present. Translation, it has been argued, must be a practice that not only seeks to convey the most authentic rendering of meanings (and feelings) between two languages but one that questions assumptions about authenticity and recognizes that all communication involves translation, even for oneself.[10] Loss in translation is certainly part of this story. But critical attention to the ubiquity of translation can turn loss into interpretive possibility, at least into useful questioning of our assumptions. Without explicitly saying so, the best recent work on emotion history tries to see and think about these ubiquitous acts of translation.

EMOTIONAL IDENTITIES: BELONGING AND OTHERNESS

Collective identification, Ronald Suny has argued in his work on nationalism and empire, is largely an "affective tie" involving feelings of love and pride that bind, as well as dissociating feelings of fear, resentment, and hatred of "others."[11] Scholars of the region, like Suny, have begun to explore nation, ethnicity, and religion (often mutually reinforcing) as *emotional* communities, often defined in contradistinction to alien outsiders. Of course, care is needed not to succumb to the easy fallacy of reducing national and similar identities to unchanging, primordial feeling, as so many popular accounts of ethnic violence in the region have continued to do, speaking of "age-old hatreds" and emotional memories and identities existing since "time immemorial." The ways people identify with ethnicity, religion, and nation and how they define and exclude others, most scholars recognize, are historically constructed conceptions of attachment and rejection, located in language and memory and in social and political conditions, none of which are fixed or stable. This approach to collective identities and enmities can be allied to quite varied cases—from anti-Jewish violence to class consciousness and hatred, for example. But most attention has been focused on nationalism. In eastern Europe in the modern era, this has mainly involved feelings of affective unity and alienation in context of the disintegration of regional empires (as distinct from overseas colonial empires) and multinational states, notably the Russian, Habsburg, and Ottoman empires, the Soviet Union, and Yugoslavia.

The "Armenian genocide" of 1915, for example, is a historically significant event, but also a contested interpreting term, which still rouses strong feelings of affective identification, fierce hatred, resentment, and unresolved mourning. As Suny has noted, this genocide (the first to be so called) occurred in a particular and significant context: as the new Young Turk leaders of the disintegrating Ottoman Empire reconceptualized their state away from the Ottomanist ideal of a multinational society toward a national vision of Turkey. From one point of view, the Young Turks were acting rationally and strategically to remove the danger of a rebellious population group, among whom nationalist identity was also growing. This could be translated into brutal massacres only through the prism of an emotional construction of the Armenian enemy that distorted perceptions of reality and thus heightened fears of an existential threat. Feelings of enmity toward and resentment of the Armenian "other" were aggravated by a crisis in which old structures, relationship, and certainties were eroding. This context is essential. But emotions are not simple reflections of conditions. In this case, emotions themselves (especially the emotional construction of the enemy) became part of the social conditions shaping action. The case reminds us of a general point for emotions history and its contribution to our methods: attention to how affective dispositions shape evaluations of reality, public action, and political decisions can illuminate, as Suny argued, how "seemingly irrational or ultimately destructive choices" can be thought by actors to be both rational and positively effective.[12]

Interpretations of ethnic violence amid the disintegration of the multinational state of Yugoslavia—including "ethnic cleansing" and "genocide," terms now used often in both legal and popular interpretations of these events—have frequently relied on arguments about emotion and affective identities. Too often, especially in journalistic interpretations but also among policymakers, the linkage between emotions and genocide has been essentialist, reductionist, and ahistorical. Nurtured by western stereotypes about "the Balkans" as a primitive and fractured land, whose various ethnicities have for centuries harbored unchanging enmity toward one another, violence during the Yugoslav wars of the 1990s has often been interpreted as a release of ancient hatreds that had been kept in bay by the now failed state. As an implied theory of emotion, these arguments reflect the old "hydraulic" model in which feelings "are like liquids within each person, heaving and frothing, eager to be let out," but controlled by various forms of emotional management and control, including by the rational self, the discipline of "civilization," and the controlling state.[13] Recent work on the history of violence in the postsocialist Balkans—mostly by anthropologists and sociologists—agree about the importance of emotions in nationalism and ethnic violence, but insist on the unstable complexities of each local instance: the influence of particular and changing social and political contexts (with rapid economic change and disruption, poverty, property relations, and political regime particularly salient); different cultural interpretations of past and present; and a good deal of inner conflict and ambivalence.[14]

History has been central to this violence. The emotional uses of stories and images of the past to inspire passionate loyalty to one's group and hatred of a significant "other" has been very common. There have been numerous cases of politicians, writers, and public intellectuals translating the past into emotional memories with strong national and political purpose. The Serbian president Slobodan Milošević's use in 1989 of the already legendary Battle of Kosovo of 1389, when Ottoman Turks decimated a Serb army, to stir up feelings of persecution and resentment among Serbs but also heroic solidarity is perhaps the most notorious instance of a ubiquitous practice. Throughout the region we see portrayals of the nation-state as a kin group with natural bonds of blood and place; contempt, fear, and hatred of outsiders who threaten these kinlike solidarities with impurity; and the trope of histories of national suffering, including violent defeat or conquest, imposed borders that cut through "natural" ethnic and national geographies, the traumas of World War II, and other examples of perceived historical ill treatment at the hands of others.

Emotional memories of collective victimization, but also of endurance and survival proving national worth, have been used by many groups and individuals throughout the region. What recent scholarship reminds us, though, in contrast to widespread popular accounts, is that these are not fixed or uniform memories—indeed, as *historical memories* they are constructed and reconstructed, including in their emotional content, as they are used socially and politically. The Battle of Kosovo, for example, was not a stable emotional memory unchanged for six hundred years, but an evolving and varied story, which had included an apocalyptic religious vision of the struggle between

Christianity and Islam and political arguments about the need for mutual affection and devotion between a ruler and his vassals.[15] Emotional memories
of history, at the level of individuals and dissenting groups, can also *resist* po-
liticized discourses of exclusive national belonging and ethnic purity, allowing
alternative emotional judgments and drawing on diverse experiences and values
from the past. An example, much discussed, are nostalgic memories in Croatia
and Bosnia of cooperation and mutual respect among Serb, Croat, and Muslim
neighbors, who lived and worked side by side, even intermarried. The suffering
nation to be liberated from threatening impurities through violent exclusion
of the other was not the only emotional memory in play.[16]

MORAL EMOTIONS: SOCIETY AND THE PERSON

That so much of the modern history of eastern Europe has involved great suffering for individuals and groups, often interpreted as injustice, and radical movements to end suffering and injustice, has placed questions of moral judgment
and moral vision at the center of this history. However, moral conceptions of
what is "right," "fair," "virtuous," and "just," and how people respond to perceived violations of these norms, almost always involve emotions, including
feelings of pleasure, hurt, shame, anger, and love. When such affective evidence
is marginalized, as it has been until quite recently, we limit our understanding
of how people are able to define suffering as moral wrong and how they experience and interpret both misery and salvation. Very often, especially in eastern
Europe, moral appraisal and moral emotions are also closely linked to ideas
and feelings about the human person, especially the fate of the self in social life.

Members of the Russian radical intelligentsia of the nineteenth century, for
example, built their ideology on the inseparability of reason and feeling and the
relation of both to the self. As Vissarion Belinsky put it, anticipating twentieth-
century theories about the interdependence of emotion and cognition, "For
me, to think and feel, to understand and suffer are one and the same thing."[17]
The generation of intelligentsia "fathers," notably Alexander Herzen, Mikhail
Bakunin, and Belinsky, formed their philosophical and ideological edifices not
only with adapted theories from the likes of Schelling, Fichte, and Hegel, and
with European ideas about historical progress, the natural dignity and rights of
man, just social and economic relationships, and the need for civil and political
freedom but also with strong emotions: especially a theory of selfhood naturally
imbued with love for the other and love of self but also pain and disgust in the
face of violations of personhood. The politics of the Russian intelligentsia were
as intensely aesthetic as they were ethical and intellectual: love of spiritual and

physical beauty and nausea at the sight of social and political ugliness (all too common, they noticed, not only in tsarist Russia but also in the "bourgeois" West). No less, the intelligentsia as a social group was defined by bonds of intimacy and love in which conventional boundaries of private and public were completely blurred, as were the boundaries of philosophy and emotion. The radical "sons" of the 1860s, notably Nikolai Chernyshevsky, Nikolai Dobroliubov, and Dmitry Pisarev, though insisting that they were scientific rationalists, having ostensibly rejected the romantic idealism of the "fathers," built their ideologies out of faith in sensation, reliance on instinctual desires of the self, belief in the pursuit of pleasure and avoidance of pain as the natural purpose of life, love for humanity, and disgust in the face of poverty and the suffering self. For Russian political radicals—and this would remain true into the twentieth century, with a major exception being Vladimir Lenin's attempt to purge moral emotion from political thought—justice was a moral judgment and morality a product of ideas and "feeling." The nineteenth-century "new man" was a person marked by an intensity of emotion entwined with moral conviction and thus the readiness to fight and sacrifice oneself for the truth.[18]

The Soviet "new man," too, even the Stalinist version, was recognizable by his moral feelings. As Glennys Young has shown in her analysis of the Great Purges, Stalin's notorious (and fatal for many) division of party leaders into "us" versus "them" was based strongly on alleged moral-emotional qualities. The new communist person was expected to do the public emotional work required to develop a new communist self. This was a cultural politics of emotion that required enthusiastic devotion to the party and its cause, absence of negative feelings (gloominess and pessimism were to be purged from the soul of a true communist), and lack of sentimental attachments, but also hiding, even trying to obliterate, the realm of private feelings.[19] Similarly, during the de-Stalinizing "thaw," as Polly Jones has shown, emotional memories of the terror were expected always to possess moral clarity and emotional confidence in defining good and evil.[20]

The intertwining of emotion, moral judgment, and constructions of self were ubiquitous in the history of Russian socialism. This was not a stable or fixed emotional politics, but intensely argued over. Consider, for example, Marxist working-class poets and writers in Russia in the decades on the two sides of 1917. Russian worker authors, echoing older intellectual traditions but also interpretations of their own immediate social lives, insisted that human experience, judgment, and actions are composed of emotion as well as rational perception, of feelings that derive from both body and spirit, of moral sensibilities as well as ethical convictions—elements they combined in notions such as "life feeling" (*zhizneoshchushchenie*). At the center of this philosophy of emotion, especially as a political and moral philosophy, was the familiar principle of the human person, of *lichnost'*—a keyword also for the nineteenth-century intelligentsia. This idea, however, especially in its emotional development, reached in two contradictory directions: on the one hand, toward moral outrage at violations of natural human dignity and rights, leading to an optimistic vision of a radically different society in which every individual is honored and nurtured (democracy, freedom, and socialism were the most common terms for this hopeful moral vision); on the other hand, a troubled focus on the wounded and suffering self, inspiring not heroic defiance or faith in redemption but disenchantment, hopelessness, melancholy, powerless rage, and alienated withdrawal. Thus, workers' poems employed a rich moral vocabulary to describe the emotional harm inflicting on the person by modern society: "insult," "humiliation," violated "dignity," denied "happiness," and "hell," said to produce in the worker's spirit intense "suffering," "misery," "grief," "pain," "nausea," and "tears." As an emotional politics, this vocabulary of moral suffering could produce narratives of "boldness," "hope," "heroism," "courage," "faith," and "struggle." But even many Marxist workers found it difficult to reconcile this allegedly correct "proletarian" mood with the obvious realities of the world around. As Soviet critics complained during the 1920s, too many working-class writers continued to view the world through "alien motifs" of "anguish," "confusion," "pessimism," and "melancholy"—feelings that a true proletarian "ought not to know."[21]

These entwined histories of moral and emotional evaluation draw our attention repeatedly to the efforts of authorities (and authoritative communities) to control, manage, and manipulate emotions—another large and potentially useful comparative theme in the history and theory of emotions. Soviet communist efforts to purge negative emotions and stimulate positive ones had many analogues in the history of the region, notably during wartime and when states mobilized populations for both modernization and combat. To guide and regulate how political subjects understand and express emotions is a key practice of power, both to maintain stability and, when needed, to direct people in collective action. These practices can be compared across boundaries, but they are always marked by the particularities of place, time, and situation. At the same time, these workings of power rarely act without challenge, deviance, and dissent—also rooted in moral judgments and evaluative emotions. As the example of worker poets in Russia reminds us, even the most cohesive "emotional regime"—or, in different formulations and models, "emotional culture" or "emotional community"—contains dissenting values, judgments, and feelings that question authoritative normativities and turn away from the forceful insistence on conformity.[22] Such acts of difference are as much a part of the modern history of this region as authoritarian regimes and intolerant group identities.

THE EMOTIONAL POLITICS OF HAPPINESS: MODERNITY AND FREEDOM

The modern history of eastern Europe has been marked by movements of extravagant political optimism, even utopian faith in the promise of happiness. Happiness, of course, is closely tied to notions of self and morality: the happy life, it is often believed, is when one's whole being can enjoy life that is "good," including by doing good, however varyingly goodness may be defined in relation to objects, practices, and feelings.[23] Indeed, different answers to the question of how to define happiness as a social and moral state have played a large role in the development of movements where the desire for happiness is a key drive, whether these are for national autonomy, social revolution, modernization, or the eradication of enemies to these goals. Of course, movements for happiness have victims—and not only "enemies" of the cause. As Sara Ahmed has emphasized in her critical study of the "promise of happiness," we need to attend to the arguments of "feminist, black, and queer scholars" who have shown "how happiness is used to justify oppression."[24] As a social and moral standard—often a hegemonic normativity—happiness can be deeply painful to those whose lives preclude access. In eastern Europe, this has included not only women, many ethnic minorities, and homosexuals (and we should note that the experiences of gays, lesbians, and transsexuals in the history of eastern Europe still remains largely in shadow and silence) but also individuals and groups who refused to embrace the powerful ideologies promising happiness, much less the faith that it had arrived. Stalin's famous slogan of 1936 that "life has become more joyous, comrades" had its analogues—and its skeptics—in many histories in the region (and beyond). That this slogan was soon followed by a bloody terror was not a contradiction but characteristic of the potential exclusion, oppression, and violence against "others" in movements for happiness.

The promise of becoming more "European," which was to say more civilized and modern, was widely embraced in eastern-European history as a bright path out of darkness and suffering toward light and happiness. We see this especially in the history of cities and how contemporaries imagined them. Modernizing cities like Budapest, Cracow, Vilnius, St. Petersburg, Odessa, Baku, and Tashkent[25] were seen as precisely where the keys to happiness could be found. A newspaper columnist in St. Petersburg observed (though skeptically) in 1913

83

that so many provincials were attracted to the big city as if it were a "bright temple" where a person could escape the dark and oppressive corners of "age-old silence."[26] Newspapers throughout the region in the late nineteenth and early twentieth centuries wrote of modern life as allowing a new modern self-hood to develop, of the city as a place of freedom and opportunity, a place to find happiness and even love. And this was reflected in city moods: city folk felt "bright faith" in progress and a "mood that is bold and filled with the joy of life."[27] Enthusiasts of modernization insisted that "modern man" feels joy and love for the material embodiments of this happy "civilization": electricity, flight, telephones, phonographs, the cinema, gigantic bridges, tunnels through mountains, tall buildings, and new technologies.[28] The goal of all this modernity, it was often argued, was nothing less than "happiness."[29] Appropriately, the most popular novel in early-twentieth-century Russia was *The Keys to Happiness* (published between 1910 and 1913 and made into a movie in 1913), which dwelled at melodramatic length on a modern woman's "thirst for happiness" and the difficult search for its path.[30] Modern commerce marketed (and markets again, after communism, with renewed faith and gusto) to the desire for happiness and the belief that it could be found in the material objects of the capitalist marketplace. Fashion and shopping were explicitly treated as sites of pleasure. Urban entertainment, even for the poor, was defined by a mood of "fun and laughter" and the devoted "pursuit of happiness."[31] Advertisements for patent medicines (many imported from the West) made a particular point of promising users—whom they understood often failed to achieve this state of mind—"joy in life" (*zhizneradostnost'*) and happier "moods."[32]

Marxists made much the same argument about modernity's promise of happiness, though reworked with a dialectical insistence on revolution, which would reveal the false promises of capitalism and overcome the social obstacles to modernity's potential to making the lives of more than an elite happy. Thus, Marxist cultural critics were sure that proletarians, even while suffering the oppressions of capitalism, feel "love" for modern streets, crowds, factories, and machines and an exhilaration of hope in this environment, because "in the whirl and noise of spinning wheels is born a new life."[33] Lenin was especially insistent that the ideal communist personality, suitable for making revolution and then for building socialism, was driven not only by rational knowledge of the telos of historical movement but also by positive emotions. He praised revolutionaries who displayed boldness and optimism and voiced contempt for people who succumbed to pessimism, despair, or demoralization—terms he spoke of with disgust.[34] Lenin's most famous plea for emotional boldness as the necessary revolutionary mood came in October 1917, when he condemned party leaders who hesitated to support his insistence that the time had come to take power as guilty of "shameful" vacillation, intolerable "hopelessness," and a "pessimism" rooted in unrevolutionary fear and "sadness."[35]

The revolutionary year 1917 was imbued with emotions and talk of emotion. For many Russians, the revolution was above all about "freedom," a ubiquitous slogan marked strongly by affect: the promise of happiness and pleasure but also the sense of living in a miraculous time. In the early months of the revolution, especially, public discourse was dominated by a hyperbolic emotional rendering of freedom as a "Great Joy," a "sacred" time of "Resurrection," a source of "infinite feelings," the expectation of "Happiness" (capital letters, and often exclamation points, seemed essential to make clear that there was nothing modest or commonplace about these feelings).[36] As so often, these political emotions were tied to moralities, especially concerning the treatment of the individual person. Letters to the press, petitions to those in authority, and resolutions at meetings, especially by workers, soldiers, and peasants, insistently framed the revolution in terms that blended moral right with emotional passion: joy, happiness, love, light, honor, truth, and salvation, but also, when faced with enemies of change, shame and betrayal. Most important, the revolution was envisioned as a moral drama in which the "insults" and "humiliations" of the past would be replaced by a society in which the human person was honored and loved: a new world of "justice" and thus "happiness." To elevate both meaning and moods, metaphoric language was especially predominant—figurative language, it has been argued, is often involved in how we construct emotions[37]—notably the melodramatic opposition of, on the one side, bloodsuckers, vermin, and vampires, producing slavery and the abyss, and, on the other side, brave fighters and saviors with pure hearts whose struggles produced the sun of freedom, salvation, and heaven.[38]

Perhaps the most extreme case of political "optimism of feeling" about modern change—and the one with the most victims—was Stalinism, which eventually embraced the whole of eastern Europe. The years of Stalin's "Great Turn" (as the drive for industrial, social, and cultural transformation was officially known) favored a cult of happy moods, even stronger than during the revolutionary years. The most radical years, during the First Five-Year Plan of 1928–1932, were marked not only by iron-fisted control, compulsion, and repression but also by enormous mobilization of "enthusiasm"—a keyword of the time, echoed in speeches, news reports, films, and memoirs—for socialist construction and the fight against hated class "enemies." Stalinism cultivated a language of radical optimism, especially in the face of obstacles and opponents—as Stalin was fond of saying, "there are no fortresses Bolsheviks cannot storm." Even failures, such as surrounded the initial assaults of mass collectivization, were attributed to an admirable, but harmful, excess of enthusiasm ("dizziness with success," in Stalin's famous phrase). Talk of happiness, in both the struggle itself and as the end goal, was ubiquitous. By 1935, slogans like "Long Live Our Happy Socialist Motherland" were everywhere, as were displays of happy, smiling workers. Victims of the "Great Purge" of the late 1930s were accused of lacking sufficient faith in this march of happiness, even of committing what Glennys Young has called "emotion crimes," especially dishonesty about one's true feelings and "hatred" for the revolution and its leaders.[39]

EMOTIONAL REFUSAL AND DISSENT

The liberating promises of the modern capitalist city, or of national independence, or of revolutionary socialism clearly did not stand unchallenged, even from within. Authoritative discourses defining these as emancipatory and felicitous paths met with skepticism and resistance, also often constructed of moral and emotional elements. If "unhappiness" can be "a form of political action"[40]—a moral and political practice of feeling the lies, exclusions, and hurt—the modern history of eastern Europe has been rich in such refusal to be happy in the face of wrong. Affect, morality, and the self often entwined to form these oppositional, or at least disenchanted or alienated, cultural politics. Many examples could be considered (and a few have been noted already): ethnic and religious minorities, who had good reason to feel marginalized in both national empires and national communist states; communist-era "dissident" intellectuals, but also earlier liberal and socialist intelligentsias, who felt politics to be meaningful only when inspired by moral values (especially the natural dignity of the human person) and humanistic emotions (love for others, self-sacrifice, moral passion, etc.), and thus found current conditions offensive morally and emotionally; artists and writers whose use of sentiment and emotion deviated from the state's desire to mobilize citizens—for example, a lyrical and melancholy inwardness rather than collectivist enthusiasm—even if they were only allowed to create works "for the desk drawer," as it was said in the Soviet Union; women who felt the insult of being treated as different and subordinate in politics and society or valued only for "feminine" contributions like motherhood; gays and lesbians whose feelings of self, desire, and love refused to conform to societal norms, often in the face of ostracism and violence; and others. I will illustrate the point with two general cases, framing the two ends of the twentieth century, reaching across the region, and marking a modern history defined by the unrealized promise of modernity and capitalism to deliver happiness: fin-de-siècle urban public culture and fin-de-millenium "postsocialism."

That the rapid development of urban modernity in a capitalist mode was not simply a history of social and economic change but also a history of emotions can be seen in recent historical writing about central- and east-European cities in the fin de siècle. In the capital of the Russian empire, for example, the experience of the pathologies of urban modernity were intensified by rapid development and by the context of a highly authoritarian political order, but also by an intellectual and cultural sphere that nurtured ideas and feelings about alternatives. It mattered that St. Petersburg, from the moment of its founding by Peter the Great "to cut a window through to Europe," stood emphatically for the development of "western civilization," particularly the idea of constructing civilization in a conquered and primitive space—a theme that the communist modernization of the Soviet Union would later echo. This was clearly not a uniquely Russian idea. Indeed, the ways Petersburg was represented and interpreted echoed a longer history of interpreting cities, especially the modern city. In particular, Russians elaborated on the view of the city as defined by contradiction, including in its emotional experience: as the expression of both human achievement and human failure, both delight and dread, what Charles Baudelaire famously called the typically modern urban experience of "rapture," "joy," and "intoxication," but also "darkness," "despair," and "mourning."[41]

Russian urban writers (from modernist poets to tabloid journalists) appreciated the intoxicating pleasures of bustling streets, bright lights and windows, new technologies, and opportunities for entertainment, but they mostly dwelled on the dread. Yes, city dwellers could be happy, energetic, and filled with dreams, but they were most likely to be lonely, tired, sick, depressed, and sorrowful. The partial distinctiveness of this experience can be seen, for example, in comparison to the American "strangers in the city" who focused more on the possibilities for love, as described by Pam Epstein in this volume (chapter 6) (Russians often observed that Americans were not as gloomy as Russians about the modern experience). Perhaps, as some contemporaries thought, this darker response was because of the still fresh shock of the new in Russia, especially in the political context of persistent authoritarianism. But the shock was not simply a result of backwardness: on the eastern margins of European modernization, Russians were well positioned to perceive the dark sides of urban capitalist modernity as a whole, encouraged by a rich intellectual history—their own and adapted from the West—of skepticism about the human costs of progress. Of course, rapid change can heighten both perception and feeling. Whatever the reasons, we see in urban Russia an intensely emotional judgment of modernity as marked by moral transgression and disorder, illusoriness and deception, harm to the self, sickness, and death, producing moods of disorientation and incomprehension if not outright disgust and fear.[42]

In the early 1900s, the experience of life in the Russian capital—constant change and instability, the endless "struggle for existence," the dangers of sharing the public spaces of the city with strangers (and being a stranger), the many stories of moral "fall" and "degradation," and other hallmarks of modernity— was reflected in what the mass media (newspapers, magazines, popular fiction, cinema) diagnosed as a troubled "social mood": strong "depression," feelings that the "time has shattered the foundations" for hope, the disillusioned realization that "reality does not bring happiness," and other feelings (so widespread as to amount to an "epidemic," they thought) of "pessimism," "despair," and "hopeless emptiness."[43] A rather telling word often used to describe and interpret this mood—and to highlight the workings of emotion as interpretation and interpretation forming through emotions—was *razocharovanie*, or disillusionment, disenchantment, and disappointment. Again, this was not a uniquely Russian experience: it has been argued that "sentiments of disenchantment" were a defining affect of classic modern capitalism.[44] But each environment has its own forms and elaborations. In prerevolutionary Russia, such feelings were exceptionally intense and unusually "democratic" in their reach across classes. Journalists of quite different ideologies agreed that the "public mood" was marked by a "prevailing tone of disenchantment."[45] Partly this was thought to be *political* disillusionment and disaffection, the collapse of hopes for change in the wake of the revolution of 1905. But mostly it referred to a systemic problem: the recognition of "the senselessness and purposelessness" of modern life.[46] A well-known public-health physician diagnosed widespread "disillusionment, revulsion, and despondency," produced by the modern atmosphere of "emptiness" and "artificiality."[47] Such disenchantment, a religious critic wrote, had become for "the modern person" the chief way of "emotionally perceiving the world" (*mirooshchushchenie*).[48] Most of these writers explained these moods as a response to the "cultural conditions of modernity."[49] Writers debated which conditions were most to blame, but they did not disagree about the emotional effects and its social and historical roots. "Modern reality," a magazine essayist wrote melodramatically, but not unusually, in 1909, "has filled the human soul with indescribable sorrow."[50]

Ironically, the collapse of communism in eastern Europe inspired the sort of hopes that socialism itself once offered as a remedy for disenchantment. Especially in the first years after 1989 (or 1991 in the Soviet Union), we see exhilaration at finally being "free," the faith that capitalism would bring European modernization and democracy to the still "backward" east, in other words, that the undelivered promise of happiness would now be realized. Words like freedom and democracy were spoken with euphoric anticipation. This hope was attached to a quite material view of happiness: that the great prosperity enjoyed in the West (exaggerated to mythic proportions) would quickly be theirs. But these feelings were also tied to moral evaluations: that state social-ism had harmed the human person and that freedom (including economic) was a superior moral condition. The emancipation of suppressed ethnic and national minorities, but also nationalism among once dominant nations like the Russians, added to these postcommunist enthusiasms the emotions of free belonging. But disillusionment—though taking different forms in differ-ent settings—again became widespread, especially among the poor, the old, and the disadvantaged, particularly in countries with weaker economies. Un-employment, increasing social inequality, corruption, and crime, made worse as experience by deliberate shredding of the social safety net and framed as a supposedly salutary "shock therapy," caused many to feel disorientation, loss of familiar meanings, damaged selves and identities, and even trauma. The sense of "loss" and "ruin" was overwhelming; hence the rise of both violent reaction against the new establishments and quieter but sometimes painful nostalgia for the socialist era.[51]

This recent history of hope and disenchantment—though both strong faith and strong disappointment have weakened since the turbulent 1990s—has been much described in the press and extensively examined by scholars. My emphasis here, however, is not so much on these depressed feelings of disen-chantment and hopelessness or their similarity to earlier emotional arguments but on the ways unhappiness functioned as political dissent, as refusal to ac-cept the new mythic "promise of happiness" of postsocialist leaders (and their western economic and political advisors). Again, this response was often tied to expressions of moral outrage, especially concerning new violations of human dignity evidently produced by the rise of "democratic freedom"—which discon-tented Russians dubbed *dermokratiia*, or shitocracy—especially in the form of unregulated capitalism in both the workplace and the consumer marketplace. This moral dissent could take private forms ranging from kitchen-table talk of discontent, which continued an important socialist-era space for shared dismay and disaffection as well as anger and bitter laughter,[52] to suicide, though these were sometimes enacted demonstratively in front of others. Very often, this dissension was quite public, especially in the many depictions in cinema and literature of the suffering and longing of ordinary people after communism. Sometimes, feelings of loss, moral injury, and resentment produced open anger and defiance: demonstrations, strikes, and violence, inspired by emotional and moral claims and fueled by collective emotions. Most recently, disgust (a particularly important political emotion in recent history) at the seemingly corrupt and cynical rule of new elites has helped bring many thousands into the streets of postsocialist cities.

Studies of postsocialist labor protest, for example, have noted the importance of narratives of suffering, often grounded in established moral models of rights and entitlements—ironically, often nurtured by the old socialist critique of capitalism. In many situations, we know historically, contextually constructed models of moral right and justice—such as the inviolability of the person, the value of labor, the purpose of society as the common welfare—produce outrage at the violation of these norms, indeed a sense of moral entitlement to anger at this violation.[53] In postcommunist eastern Europe, scholars have noticed the deliberate "performance" of social suffering in social and political protest, where litanies of "suffering" form communities and serve as "emotional capital" (and moral capital) enabling injustice to be defined and protest legitimated.[54] A study of violent strikes by miners in Romania in the late 1990s, for instance, reveals how workers translated feelings of loss and suffering into legitimate political anger and action, though also how authorities did everything they could to delegitimate these same emotions (with increasing effectiveness) by interpreting them as irrational and regressive. Under socialism, in Romania as elsewhere, Marxist histories taught that working-class anger in capitalist conditions was a primitive first stage of class feeling on the way to real class consciousness—thus legitimate but requiring directing control. Miners interviewed in the 1990s about their motivations indirectly echoed and appropriated these arguments as "entitlement" to resentment, disgust, outrage, and action in the face of impoverishment, political corruption, and a growing culture of greed.[55] As here, litanies of unhappiness—of loss, decline, injury, and fear, especially when sustained by available moral standards—can be political acts with great public consequence.

It is significant that capitalism, communism, and postcommunist capitalism in eastern Europe have been experienced in comparable ways: as promises of happiness (sometimes, or for some, realized) along with a great deal of loss, decline, corruption, inequality, and decline of community, producing feelings of disenchantment, melancholy, sorrow, and despair. The meanings of these words and feelings are shaped strongly by time and place, however. Successive experiences with, for example, the promise of "happiness" and the feeling of "disenchantment" have unfolded in new contexts, though have also drawn on stories of past experience. Very important, postsocialists possess a knowledge that socialism is not the answer. That once promising exit seems closed. What might seem to be a continuation of moral and emotional protest is less effective this time, for it is necessarily less directional and thus less hopeful. Histories of civic unhappiness remind us that emotional language is not an expression of universal affect but part of a contextual story. Anger, mourning, melancholy, and fear are protean emotions—restless, adaptable, hybrid, resilient[56]—that tell tales about comparable but always particular experiences.

Laughter has been a persistent part of how people have responded to the predicaments of their lives, complicating these histories further. Laughter can be interpreted as part of a cultural politics of emotion expressing disenchantment and dissent, but also as a means of coping, even healing. The final years of tsarist Russia, to take a less familiar example than the communist era, were accompanied by a great deal of public laughter. A journalist in 1912, echoing many other commentators, remarked that the whole nation seemed to be "shaking with gay, uncontrollable laughter, such that one "might think that we have finally reached the kingdom of bright joy."[57] Laughter meant many different things, journalists recognized. What it almost never meant in that context, they concluded, was real happiness. This was not "life-affirming laughter"; it was repeatedly observed with regret. Sometimes, as in slum humor, it was the "cheerful horror" of the desperate. Sometimes it was a tormented hysteria, or "Mephistophelean laughter," or the laughter of "self-flagellation." Sometimes it was the "humor of the doomed" defined psychologically by feelings of disgust and "nausea" over the "ugliness" of the world. Perhaps, it was suggested, "modern guffawing Russia" was only a self-deluding mask over "suffering" and "sadness." Perhaps, more positively, it was a means to "chase away the spiders of humanity's lies and crassness." Most often, it was felt, this was "pessimistic" laughter, which sees evil but doubts that it can be chased away.[58] Most politically, laughter was viewed as ironic, a laughter that announces the dissonance between expectations and realities. This might even lighten the weight of disappointment with the world. But all too often, contemporary commentators worried, it degraded into apathy and detachment. Journalists observed that the "ironic smile . . . worn at all times and in every situation" had become the main emotional mechanism for coping with the world. And many found nothing positive in this, only the emotional weapon of the weak and pessimistic: a corrosive and alienating "ha-ha" that made modern life endurable but could change nothing.[59] Perhaps, as Karl Marx suggested, "gaiety" is a characteristic sign of the end of a historical epoch, a means by which people are able to reconcile themselves to the tragic loss of their past.[60] Or as a Russian journalist put it, when "the melancholy city-dweller laughs," he can "forget and let others forget" without having to deny the truth about the world that this melancholy expresses.[61] This may have been a weak political gesture, but it was one. And perhaps a less harmful one, in the long run, than the bold certainty of people like Lenin (and, more violently, Stalin) that they held the keys to happiness.

Communism, it has been often said, especially in its later more moribund stages, was an ideal environment for humor. The problem is that the emotions humor expressed was diverse and subtle, as was the political significance of laughter. Contemporaries could find many different emotional and political meanings in a joke like, "What is the difference between capitalism and communism? Capitalism is the 'exploitation of man by man' and communism is the other way around." Mikhail Bakhtin, a Soviet philosopher of language famous for his work on Rabelais and carnival, argued that laughter can call into question the sanctity of the established language and the system it sustains, shattering for a moment the absolutism of authority and authoritarian lies, including the promises of happiness.[62] But such laughter, even when mockingly subversive, tends not to give voice to the sort of outrage and anger that might inspire action, but rather, it enables one to accept suffering and wrong through irony, sarcasm, and mockery. Still, the disenchanting remains, producing at least the space in which flashes of a defiant emotional politics can arise.

Of course, laughter can be the opposite of political dissent, transgression, and promised change, as we see in recent work on laughter under socialism, which has described an emotional politics that deployed laughter as a weapon of power and even violence. The Soviet leadership continually sought and promoted a vision of a well-managed socialist laughter (most evident in satirical journals like *Krokodil* and in stage comedians) that would sustain the socialist system. As the Commissar of Enlightenment, Anatoly Lunacharsky, argued in 1931, "laughter is a weapon—and a very serious weapon at that—of a social self-discipline of a particular social class." The collective laugh, for Lunacharsky, was a "laughter of fellowship" that both united "us" and distanced us from "them."[63] Lunacharsky did not envision this, but in Stalin's time, such disciplining and distancing social laughter could take on violent forms, as during the purges when it was used to demolish the language victims used to protest their treatment (especially when they tried to defend themselves through the principles of socialism and the traditions of the party) and to emotionally crush judged enemies like Nikolai Bukharin as well as embolden the victors as they sent so many to their graves.[64]

Catastrophe, it has been argued, is the dark face of the modern experience, with violence, loss, and suffering no less defining of modern history than positive progress. The dreamworlds of capitalism and communism have both been histories marked by disastrous harm.[65] East Europeans tend to think they have had more than their fair share of modern catastrophe and thus are especially justified in feeling a disenchanted melancholy if not outright trauma. Of course, these can be unruly and self-destructive emotions. Just as dreams of happiness can produce cruelty and violence, so can the emotional refusal to believe produce what Sianne Ngai has called "ugly feelings," which are often the result of obstructions to freedom and agency.[66] Ugly feelings such as anger, outrage, disgust, hatred, mourning, and despair can have a certain defiant force when arising as responses to the moral and social ugliness of the world. But like laughter when it turns ugly, these can have hellish consequences for oneself and others. Melancholy, historians have observed, can be a type of defiant heroism in a modern world of loss.[67] But melancholy and its sister feelings have often, notably for eastern Europeans, been an abyss of dark feelings that have undermined political hope and action.[68]

· · ·

Just as a "region" is not a fixed and homogenous cultural place but a space defined by relationships, where boundaries and connections and meanings are continually reconfigured, so should a regional history of emotions be grounded in relations: between people and their environments and between people and the lives and emotions of others, in all their particularity, complexity, and instability. The risks of a regional approach are all too familiar. The examples I have described could be read—and often have been read by policymakers, journalists, and some scholars—as reflecting persistent affective dispositions among national or ethnic groups. Although few insist any longer on unchanging national characters, still common are arguments about the inescapable legacies of the past: cultural traditions, histories of belief, experiences of political domination, and cycles of ethnic violence, for example, shaping lasting emotional cultures—if not for the whole of Slavic civilization (as in the "clash of civilizations" model), then for particular national, ethnic, and religious groups. The strength and potential of exploring emotional geographies is in the centrality of contexts and relations. *Context* is a small and dry word for all that it must carry as the heart of both historical and geographic study, though its etymological meanings of connection and relation point to what is essential. In thinking about contexts and relations, and their instabilities, we confront the challenge for doing any history of experience and subjectivity: how to weave together (the meaning of the Latin original *contexĕre*) bodily sensation, material and social structures and relationships (including those of power), discourse, communication, memories, and change; and how to create an interpreting narrative that describes patterns without becoming more tightly woven and symmetrical than real life allows. Also, the particularities of context must be kept in dialogue with comparisons reaching beyond particular instances. Eastern Europe's distinctive historical experience of imperial domination of minorities, ethnic and national conflict, brutally modernizing states, and persistent social deprivation for the majority were variations, not exceptions, in human experience. These conditions, and the emotions interpreting and shaping them, can and should be compared—as instances, as sources of new questions, as evidence of important differences—to other cases of domination and violence, other hatreds of social and ethnic others, other expressions of disgust and anger at subordination, other examples of mourning and melancholy in the face of the promises of "happiness" or "progress," and other dreams of political salvation.

NOTES

I am grateful to Jan Plamper, Judith Pintar, Jane Hedges, participants in the Illinois "Kruzhok," the volume editors, and the anonymous reviewers for their valuable comments.

1. Skitalets ["The Wanderer," the pen name for Osip Blotermants], "Bodrye liudi," *Gazeta-kopeika*, April 10, 1911, 4; L. A. Vilikhov, "Idealizm i material'naia kul'tura," *Gorodskoe delo* 1912, no. 11–12 (June 1–15): 742–743.

2. This relational approach to space has been a theme in the influential work of the geographer Edward Soja.

3. See especially Peter N. Stearns and Carol Z. Stearns, "Emotionology: Clarifying the History of Emotions and Emotional Standards," *American Historical Review* 90:4 (October 1985): 813–836; Catherine S. Lutz and Lila Abu-Lughod, eds., *Language and the Politics of Emotion* (Cambridge: Cambridge University Press, 1990); William Reddy, *The Navigation of Feeling: A Framework for the History of Emotions* (Cambridge: Cambridge University Press, 2001); Sara Ahmed, *The Cultural Politics of Emotion* (New York: Routledge, 2004); Barbara Rosenwein, *Emotional Communities in the Early Middle Ages* (Ithaca, N.Y.: Cornell University Press, 2006); Daniel Gross, *The Secret History of Emotion: From Aristotle's "Rhetoric" to Modern Brain Science* (Chicago: University of Chicago Press, 2007). For a recent overview of theoretical issues relevant to the historical study of emotions, see Susan Matt, "Current Emotion Research in History: Or, Doing History from the Inside Out," *Emotion Review* 3:1 (January 2011): 117–124.

4. See Maria Todorova, *Imagining the Balkans*, updated edition (Oxford: Oxford University Press, 2009); Larry Wolff, *Inventing Eastern Europe: The Map of Civilization on the Mind of the Enlightenment* (Stanford, Calif.: Stanford University Press, 1996).

5. Key publications include Sheila Fitzpatrick, "Happiness and Toska: An Essay in the History of Emotions in Pre-War Soviet Russia," *Australian Journal of Politics and History* 50:3 (September 2004): 357–358; Ronald Grigor Suny, "Why We Hate You: The Passions of National Identity and Ethnic Violence" (February 1, 2004), Berkeley Program in

Soviet and Post-Soviet Studies, http://repositories.cdlib.org/iseees/bps/2004_01-suny (accessed March 25, 2013); Maruška Svašek, ed., *Postsocialism: Politics and Emotions in Central and Eastern Europe* (New York: Berghahn, 2005); Glennys Young, "Emotions, Contentious Politics, and Empire: Some Thoughts about the Soviet Case," *Ab Imperio* 2 (2007): 113–151; John Randolph, *The House in the Garden: The Bakunin Family and the Romance of Russian Idealism* (Ithaca, N.Y.: Cornell University Press, 2007); Mark Steinberg, "Melancholy and Modernity: Emotions and Social Life in Russia between the Revolutions," *Journal of Social History* 41:4 (Summer 2008): 813–841; Valeria Sobol, *Febris Erotica: Lovesickness in the Russian Literary Imagination* (Seattle: Washington University Press, 2009); Jan Plamper, ed., "Emotional Turn? Feelings in Russian History and Culture," special section of *Slavic Review* 68:2 (Summer 2009); Jan Plamper, Schamma Schahadat, and Marc Elie, eds., *Rossiiskaia imperiia chuvstv: Podkhody k kul'turnoi istorii emotsii* (Moscow: NLO, 2010); Mark D. Steinberg and Valeria Sobol, eds., *Interpreting Emotions in Russia and Eastern Europe* (DeKalb: Northern Illinois University Press, 2011).

6. Sianne Ngai, *Ugly Feelings* (Cambridge, Mass.: Harvard University Press, 2005), 3. She defines emotions, in this light, as "interpretations of predicaments."

7. On the emotional history of modernity and the related history of modern emotions, see Peter Stearns, "Modern Patterns in Emotions History," chapter 1 of this volume.

8. See Ahmed, *Cultural Politics of Emotion*, and Lutz and Abu-Lughod, eds., *Language and the Politics of Emotion*, though these authors treat culture, politics, and emotion in rather different ways.

9. Anna Wierzbicka, *Emotions across Languages and Cultures: Diversity and Universals* (Cambridge: Cambridge University Press, 1999); Zoltán Kövecses, *Metaphor and Emotion: Language, Culture, and Body in Human Feeling* (Cambridge: Cambridge University Press, 2003).

10. Amid large and growing literature, see Lawrence Venuti, ed., *The Translation Studies Reader* (New York: Routledge, 2004); Paul Ricoeur, *On Translation* (London: Routledge, 2006).

11. Ronald Suny, "Thinking about Feelings: Affective Dispositions and Emotional Ties in Imperial Russia and the Russian Empire," in Steinberg and Sobol, *Interpreting Emotions*, 116–123. See also chapter 8, "Emotion and Political Change," by Nicole Eustace in this volume.

12. Suny, "Thinking about Feelings," 123.

13. Barbara Rosenwein, "Worrying about Emotions in History," *American Historical Review* 107:3 (June 2002): 834. For an earlier critique of the hydraulic metaphor, see Robert C. Solomon, *The Passions: Emotions and the Meaning of Life* (New York: Anchor Press/Doubleday, 1976).

14. See discussion and sources cited in Maruška Svašek, "Introduction: Postsocialism and the Politics of Emotions," in Svašek, *Postsocialism*; and Judith Pintar, "Emplaced and Displaced: Theorizing the Emotions of Space in the Former Yugoslavia," in Steinberg and Sobol, *Interpreting Emotions*, 181–188.

15. Pintar, "Emplaced and Displaced," esp. 182–182.

16. Ger Duijzings, *Religion and the Politics of Identity in Kosovo* (New York: Columbia University Press, 2000); Katherine Verdery, *What Was Socialism and What Comes Next?* (Princeton, N.J.: Princeton University Press, 1996); Verdery, *The Political Lives of Dead Bodies: Reburial and Postsocialist Change* (New York: Columbia University Press, 1999); Maria Todorova, *Bones of Contention: The Living Archive of Vasil Levski and the Making of Bulgaria's National Hero* (Budapest: Central European University Press, 2009); Carolin Leutloff-Grandits, "Claiming Ownership in Postwar Croatia: the Emotional Dynamics of Possession and Repossession in Knin," in Svašek, *Postsocialism*, 115–137 (also chapters by Svašek and Zlatko Skrbiš in the same volume); Pintar, "Emplaced and Displaced."

17. Letter from V. G. Belinskii to V. P. Botkin, March 1, 1841, in *Polnoe sobranie sochinenii* 12 (Moscow, 1956), http://az.lib.ru/b/belinskij_w_g/text_3900.shtml (accessed March 25, 2013). For later research and theory, see the psychology journal *Cognition & Emotion* (1987–present).

18. Among many scholarly studies, see especially Lydia Ginzburg, *On Psychological Prose* (Princeton, N.J.: Princeton University Press, 1991; first Russian edition, 1971); Isaiah Berlin, *Russian Thinkers* (New York: Viking, 1978); Randolph, *House in the Garden*; Sobol, *Febris Erotica*; Victoria Frede, "Radicals and Feelings: The 1860s," in Steinberg and Sobol, *Interpreting Emotions*, 62–81. For a later extension of this mentality, see Barbara Walker, *Maximilian Voloshin and the Russian Literary Circle: Culture and Survival in Revolutionary Times* (Bloomington: Indiana University Press, 2004).

19. Glennys Young, "Bolsheviks and Emotional Hermeneutics: The Great Purges, Bukharin, and the February–March Plenum of 1937," in Steinberg and Sobol, *Interpreting Emotions*, 128–151; Igal Halfin, *Terror in My Soul: Communist Autobiographies on Trial* (Cambridge, Mass.: Harvard University Press, 2003).

20. Polly Jones, "Breaking the Silence: Iurii Bondarev's *Quietness* between the 'Sincerity' and 'Civic Emotion' of the Thaw," in Steinberg and Sobol, *Interpreting Emotions*, 152–176.

21. See especially the criticisms levied against worker poets by Pavel Lebedev-Polianskii, head of the Proletcult and later of the Soviet censorship office, in his "Motivy rabochei poezii," *Proletarskaia kul'tura*, no. 3 (August 1918): 7; and essays in *Proletarskaia kul'tura*, no. 5 (November 1918): 42; nos. 9–10 (June–July 1919): 65–66; S. Rodov, "Motivy tvorchestva M. Gerasimova," *Kuznitsa*, no. 1 (May 1920): 23–24; A. Voronskii, "O gruppe pisatelei 'Kuznitsa,'" *Iskusstvo i zhizn': sbornik statei* (Moscow, 1924), 136. See discussion in my *Proletarian Imagination: Self, Modernity, and the Sacred in Russia, 1910–1925* (Ithaca, N.Y.: Cornell University Press, 2002).

22. See Stearns and Stearns, "Emotionology"; Reddy, *Navigation of Feeling*; Rosenwein, *Emotional Communities*.

23. For a recent and insightful critical discussion, Sara Ahmed, *The Promise of Happiness* (Durham, N.C.: Duke University Press, 2010). See also essay on happiness by Darrin McMahon in this volume (chapter 5).

24. Ahmed, *Promise of Happiness*, 2.

25. Among recent studies that have focused on the cultural and emotional meanings of modern urban life, see especially Peter Hanak, *The Garden and the Workshop: Essays on*

the *Cultural History of Vienna and Budapest* (Princeton, N.J.: Princeton University Press, 1998); Roshanna Sylvester, *Tales of Old Odessa: Crime and Civility in a City of Thieves* (DeKalb: Northern Illinois University Press, 2005); Nathaniel D. Wood, *Becoming Metropolitan: Urban Selfhood and the Making of Modern Cracow* (DeKalb: Northern Illinois University Press, 2010); Mark D. Steinberg, *Petersburg Fin de Siècle* (New Haven, Conn.: Yale University Press, 2011).

26. Ol'ga Gridina, "Gorod-obmanshchik," *Gazeta-kopeika*, December 24, 1913, 3.

27. Quotes from the Petersburg magazine *Ogonek* 1913, no. 1 (January 6): n.p.

28. Al. Fedorov, "K solntsu!" *Peterburgskii kinematograf*, February 12, 1911, 2; *Peterburgskii kinematograf*, January 5, 1911, 2.

29. For instance, Skitalets, "Dvizhenie," *Gazeta-kopeika*, July 20, 1911, 3.

30. See Laura Engelstein, *The Keys to Happiness: Sex and the Search for Modernity in Fin-de-Siècle Russia* (Ithaca, N.Y.: Cornell University Press, 1992), 404–414.

31. For example, "S novym schast'em," *Peterburgskii listok*, January 1, 1914, 2. See also Louise McReynolds, *Russia at Play: Leisure Activities at the End of the Tsarist Era* (Ithaca, N.Y.: Cornell University Press, 2003).

32. See Susan K. Morrissey, "The Economy of Nerves: Health, Commercial Culture, and the Self in Late Imperial Russia," *Slavic Review* 69:3 (Fall 2010): 645–675.

33. Pavel Lebedev-Polianskii, "Motivy rabochei poezii," *Proletarskaia kul'tura*, no. 3 (August 1918): 5.

34. For example, V. I. Lenin, "Ivan Vasil'evich Babushkin (nekrolog)," *Rabochaia gazeta*, December 18/31, 1910, in Lenin, *Sochineniia*, 4th edition (Moscow: Gosudarstvennoe Izdatel'stvo, 1954–1962), 16:333–334.

35. V. I. Lenin, "Pi'mo k tovarishcham," published in *Rabochii Put,'* October 19, 20, 21, 1917, in Lenin, *Sochineniia* 26:166–184.

36. Mark Steinberg, *Voices of Revolution, 1917* (New Haven, Conn.: Yale University Press, 2001), 8, 79–84, 110, 128, 146.

37. For example, Kovecses, *Metaphor and Emotion*.

38. Steinberg, *Voices of Revolution*.

39. Young, "Bolsheviks and Emotional Hermeneutics." See also Katerina Clark, *The Soviet Novel: History as Ritual* (Bloomington: Indiana University Press, 1981); Stephen Kotkin, *Magnetic Mountain: Stalinism as a Civilization* (Berkeley: University of California Press, 1997); Karen Petrone, *Life Has Become More Joyous, Comrades: Celebrations in the Time of Stalin* (Bloomington: Indiana University Press, 2000); Choi Chatterjee, *Celebrating Women: Gender, Festival Culture, and Bolshevik Ideology, 1910–1939* (Pittsburgh, Pa.: University of Pittsburgh Press, 2002); David Hoffmann, *Stalinist Values: The Cultural Norms of Soviet Modernity, 1917–1941* (Ithaca, N.Y.: Cornell University Press, 2003); Jochen Hellbeck, *Revolution on My Mind: Writing a Diary under Stalin* (Cambridge, Mass.: Harvard University Press, 2009).

40. Ahmed, *Promise of Happiness*, 207.

41. See Charles Baudelaire, *Les Fleurs du mal* (1857), *Le Spleen de Paris* (1862), and *Le Peintre de la vie moderne* (1863). See also Burton Pike, *The Image of the City in Mod-*

ern Literature (Princeton, N.J.: Princeton University Press, 1981); Marshall Berman, *All That Is Solid Melts into Air: The Experience of Modernity* (New York: Viking, 1982); Judith Walkowitz, *City of Dreadful Delight: Narratives of Sexual Danger in Late-Victorian London* (Chicago: University of Chicago Press, 1992); Vanessa Schwartz, *Spectacular Realities: Early Mass Culture in Fin-de-Siècle Paris* (Berkeley: University of California Press, 1998); Robert Alter, *Imagined Cities: Urban Experience and the Language of the Novel* (New Haven, Conn.: Yale University Press, 2005).

42. Steinberg, *Petersburg Fin de Siècle*; V. N. Toporov, *Peterburgskii tekst russkoi literatury: izbrannye trudy* (St. Petersburg: Iskusstvo–SPB, 2003).

43. N. V., "Itogi minuvshago goda," *Vesna* 1908, no. 1 (January 6): 1; "Novogodnye mysli," *Tserkovnyi vestnik* 1908, no. 2 (January 10): 43; R. Blank, "1909–yi god," *Zaprosy zhizni* 1909, no. 11 (December 29): 1; "S novym godom," *Tserkovnyi vestnik* 1908, no. 1 (January 3): 1; *Ogonek* 1913, no. 1 (January 6), n.p. See discussion in Steinberg, *Petersburg Fin de Siècle*, chapter 7.

44. From Paolo Virno's 1996 essay "The Ambivalence of Disenchantment," quoted and discussed in Ngai, *Ugly Feelings*, 4.

45. For example, Protopopov, "Sud'ba russkikh gorodov," *Gorodskoe delo* 1911, no. 24 (December 15): 1715.

46. N. Rubakin, "Dlia chego ia zhivu na svete," *Novyi zhurnal dlia vsekh* 1912, no. 6 (June): 67.

47. D. Zhbankov, "Polovaia prestupnost,'" *Sovremennyi mir* 1909, no. 7 (July): 90–91; "Sovremennye samoubiistva," *Sovremennyi mir* 1910, no. 3 (March): 29, 47–50.

48. "Sovremennost' i dumy," *Tserkovnyi vestnik* 1913, no. 31 (August 1): 945–946, 948.

49. Georgii Chulkov, "Demony i sovremennost'" (mysli o frantsuzskoi zhivopisi)," *Apolon* 1914, no. 1–2 (January–February): 66, 70–71.

50. Ashkinazi, "Ot individualizma k bogostroitel'stvu," *Novyi zhurnal dlia vsekh* 1909, no. 6 (April): 105.

51. These are themes in the great many studies based on ethnographic research in the region since 1989.

52. See Nancy Ries, *Russian Talk: Culture and Conversation during Perestroika* (Ithaca, N.Y.: Cornell University Press, 1997).

53. For an early development of this argument, see Barrington Moore, *Injustice: The Social Bases of Obedience and Revolt* (New York: M. E. Sharpe, 1978).

54. For example, Dimitrina Mihaylova, "Social Suffering and Political Protest: Mapping Emotions and Power among Pomaks in Postsocialist Bulgaria," in Svašek, *Postsocialism*, 53–71.

55. Jack Freidman, "A Genealogy of Working Class Anger: History, Emotions, and Political Economy in Romania's Jiu Valley," in Steinberg and Sobol, *Interpreting Emotions*, 200–223.

56. See Robert Jay Lifton, *The Protean Self: Human Resilience in an Age of Fragmentation* (Chicago: University of Chicago Press, 1993).

57. L. Logvinovich, "Smekh i pechal,'" *Zhizn' dlia vsekh* 1912, no. 1 (January): 107.

58. S. Liubosh, "Petersburgskii zametki," *Sovremennoe slovo*, June 2, 1910, 2; K. Chukovskii, "Mark Tven," *Rech,'* April 10, 1910, 3; K. Chukovskii, "Iumor obrechennykh," *Rech,'* April 17, 1910, 2; L. Logvinovich, "Smekh i pechal,'" *Zhizn' dlia vsekh* 1912, no. 1 (January): 107–114.

59. K. Chukovskii, "O khikhikaiushchikh," *Rech,'* December 20, 1908, 3.

60. See Walter Benjamin, *The Arcades Project* (Cambridge, Mass.: Harvard University Press, 1999), 467 (convolute N5a,3), quoting and interpreting Karl Marx, "Zur Kritik der Hegelschen *Rechtsphilosophie*" (1844).

61. L. Logvinovich, "Smekh i pechal,'" *Zhizn' dlia vsekh* 1912, no. 1 (January): 107–114.

62. See Katerina Clark and Michael Holquist, *Mikhail Bakhtin* (Cambridge, Mass.: Harvard University Press, 1984), 289, 299–300; Gary Saul Morson and Caryl Emerson, *Mikhail Bakhtin: Creation of a Prosaics* (Stanford, Calif.: Stanford University Press, 1990), chapter 10.

63. See the thematic cluster on "Soviet Jocularity" in *Slavic Review* 70:2 (Summer 2011), especially the Introduction by Serguei Oushakine, 247–255 (he quotes Lunacharsky's article "On Laughter" on page 252). See also Igal Halfin, *Intimate Enemies: Demonizing the Bolshevik Opposition, 1918–1928* (Pittsburgh, Pa.: University of Pittsburgh Press, 2007).

64. Young, "Bolsheviks and Emotional Hermeneutics," 139.

65. See a version of this argument, influenced by Walter Benjamin, in Susan Buck-Morss, *Dreamworld and Catastrophe: The Passing of Mass Utopia in East and West* (Cambridge: MIT Press, 2000).

66. Ngai, *Ugly Feelings.*

67. See discussions of redemptive and political melancholy (and concerning other negative feelings) in Jonathan Flatley, *Affective Mapping: Melancholia and the Politics of Modernism* (Cambridge, Mass.: Harvard University Press, 2008), esp. chapter 1; and Ngai, *Ugly Feelings.*

68. One can see this also in late Soviet and post-Soviet "chernukha," the "dark" movies and literature that dwelled on depression, amorality, violence, and social sources of individual suffering. More recently, the director of Russia's most respected independent polling agency concluded that there is "a dark and depressive mood in society, . . . a growth of anxiety, a feeling of stagnation and degradation." Quoted by Seth Mydans, "Putin's Eye for Power Leads Some in Russia to Ponder Life Abroad," *New York Times*, October 1, 2011.

PART III

PROBING
SPECIFIC
EMOTIONS

CHAPTER 5

FINDING JOY
IN THE HISTORY
OF EMOTIONS

DARRIN M. McMAHON

Are historians of emotions a negative lot? Do they give greater weight to angst and animosity, sadness and fear than they do to the positive human emotions? Indeed, might the field of the history of emotions as a whole suffer from something of a "negative bias," a tendency to accord greater prominence to the role played by negative emotions in constituting the human past? Consider the titles of a recent, semester-long speakers' series at the Max Planck Institute for the Study of the History of Emotions in Berlin:[1] "Sorrow carved in stone: Expressions of grief and suffering in Ottoman Muslim epitaph"; "'A Legacy of Fear': The 1857 Uprising and the colonial imagination"; "German Angst—The West German peace movement of the 1980s and the memory of the Second World War"; and "Threat and Emotions. Anarchist bombings in nineteenth-century Paris." To be sure, the same series included several neutral titles—a paper on methodology in the study of religious emotion, another on the emotional lives of "born again" Muslims among Pakistani youth, and a third on philosophy and therapy in the seventeenth century. There was even a contribution on love, for the most a positive emotion, even if this particular paper considered it in the rather bleak context of "times of total war." But though the great majority of these research projects were undoubtedly serious, interesting, and well-conceived, what is conspicuous for its absence, to judge by the titles, is any discussion of happiness or joy.

Needless to say, the title list of a semester's research colloquium at a single institution in a single country is hardly an adequate basis for generalization. To answer the questions posed at the outset of this article with any measure of scientific certainty would require extensive bibliographic research in a variety of different languages and a great many national literatures. That is certainly a venture worth undertaking, but it is far beyond the scope of the present inquiry. So in the absence of this kind of hard data, I would like to treat my anecdotal account simply as the basis for presenting a soft conjecture—a plausible hypothesis, perhaps, though far from a statement of fact—that the history of emotions *does* suffer from a negative bias. And having broached the claim, I would like to consider a number of the reasons why it might actually be true, before then considering some of the consequences and entertaining some possible remedies. How, I want to inquire, might it be possible to put a little more joy in the history of emotions?

NEGATIVE BIAS IN THE SOCIAL SCIENCES
AND THE HUMANITIES

If the discipline of the history of emotions *were* to suffer from a negative bias, then that would not be terribly surprising. Human beings, after all, are themselves prone to what psychologists describe as a "negativity bias" or a "positive-negative asymmetry effect."[2] In general, that is, information with a negative valence impacts us more strongly than does positive information, and we seem to be constructed in such a way as to spend more time worrying about threats and mulling over injuries than we do fantasizing about or reliving the sources of pleasure or joy. Painful events stay with us longer in memory and are recalled more often, while negative emotions like fear, anger, guilt, anxiety, shame and regret seem to have played such a crucial evolutionary role in ensuring our survival that they are simply more powerful than their positive counterparts. In the pithy formulation of the psychologist Roy Baumeister, one of the leading researchers in this domain, "Bad is stronger than Good."[3]

There is also more of the "bad" to choose from. Classifications of the emotions, of course, always leave room for disagreement and debate, and it is undoubtedly true that for every negative emotion, one can identify a positive counterpart. Though we may all feel shame, as Aristotle observed in one of the earliest attempts to list and classify the emotions, we all feel shamelessness too. And yet it is also the case that negative emotions are more differentiated than positive emotions. As one philosopher with an interest in psychology observes, "There are far more ways to describe negative emotional experiences than there are for positive ones."[4] In English, for example, even though there are more words with positive than negative connotations, the opposite is true of words used to describe emotion. Thus, whether it is actually the case that "there are more ways in which a situation can be unpleasant than pleasant," it is clear that we have greater linguistic resources at our disposal to describe it as such—more ways, in effect, to bitch and moan.[5] It follows that if historians of emotions are drawn inordinately to the negative end of the spectrum, they may simply be affirming their humanity.

And there are other factors at play besides human biology. When one thinks of the pioneering work in the field of the history of emotions, good cheer is not likely to be the first thing that comes to mind. Indeed, when the great French historian Lucien Febvre first put forth, in the pages of the *Annales*, his seminal 1941 call to devote research to the affective dimensions of human history, he did so in understandably dark tones. Writing in the shadow of the Nazis, he wanted to understand the source of political passions. One might protest, he noted, that "the history of hatred, the history of fear, the history of cruelty, [and] the history of love" constituted a kind of "idle chatter." "But that idle chatter," he responded, "will tomorrow have turned the universe into a fetid pit of corpses."[6] To study hatred, fear, cruelty, and love (which in Febvre's handling always had the capacity to turn dangerous), was to make a plea, as Barbara Rosenwein observes, for writing histories of the "dark side."[7] When, some decades later, Peter and Carol Stearns issued a no-less seminal plea to continue the pioneering work of Febvre and others in self-consciously formalizing the study of "emotionology," they were separated from the catastrophe of the Second World War by the summer of love.[8] The 1960s and 1970s were hardly decades to spurn the positive emotions. And yet the novel forms of historical inquiry that were developed most forcefully in this period, particularly in social history, which the Stearns saw as the history of emotion's natural terrain, were often motivated by righteous indignation at the injustices and exclusions of the past. In drawing attention to the plight of ordinary people, the marginalized, and oppressed, many historians not surprisingly chose to focus on the structures of power or "emotional regimes" that limited, curtailed, and exploited them.[9] It is perhaps not so surprising, then, that social historians working on the history of emotions should also focus in this way. It is surely striking that a great number of the field's landmark studies—from Jean Delumeau's classic work on fear, to the Stearnses' work on anger, to a spate of important studies dealing with sadness, grief, humiliation, and disgust—have focused heavily on negative emotion. Insofar as seminal studies map the way for others, these works would seem to have opened up pathways for studying civilization and its discontents.

The allusion to Freud hints at another factor likely at play in shaping negative bias in the field of the history of emotions: the negative bias, for much of its history, in the field of psychology itself. Modeled on the discipline of medicine, which long has focused overwhelmingly on pathology, psychology, too, since its nineteenth-century inception, aimed to identify and remedy the causes of disease. Understanding in order to treat the sources of negative emotion—depression, anger, anxiety, resentment—was its stock in trade, with many practitioners abjuring altogether the attempt to cultivate positive emotion. Freud's aims were more restricted still. Given, as he believed, that sustained human happiness was simply not possible, the goal of what he came to call psychoanalysis should be to remove gratuitous or self-imposed suffering (neurosis) with the aim, as he put it in his *Studies on Hysteria*, coauthored with Josef Breuer, of restoring "common" or "ordinary" unhappiness (*gemeines Unglück*).[10] Some even went so far as to move to have happiness classified officially in the *Diagnostic and Statistical Manual* as a psychiatric disorder![11] Admittedly, that was an extreme view, but it reflected a much wider suspicion of happiness among members of the profession.

That general, and at one time, pervasive attitude has come under intense scrutiny and challenge since at least the 1990s, when Martin Seligman and a host of like-minded colleagues launched an explicit effort to cultivate *positive* psychology, a psychology that would focus not on human pathology but on human strengths. Positive psychology's rapid rise to prominence and rather startling international success is well-known to professionals and the public alike and has even generated something of a backlash. But its effort to draw attention to negative bias in the discipline of psychology has had the ancillary effect of aiding and abetting attempts to do the same in other disciplines. Thus, economics, which long wore its description as the "dismal science" as a badge of pride, now boasts an exciting and robust effort to focus on the economic underpinnings of human happiness, with positive psychologists and economists of happiness working in close collaboration.[12] In sociology and the social sciences, too, fields that in their focus on the underpinnings of class conflict and exploitation, social injustice and poverty, were long skeptical of the allegedly Pollyannaish study of happiness, a focus on the positive is now common. Ruuth Veenhoven, the director of the World Happiness Database in the Netherlands and one of the leading researchers today working on comparative well-being, recalls how his dissertation advisor, upon hearing of his young student's shocking interest in positive affect, told him in the 1960s to never mention happiness again if he hoped to get a job as a sociologist![13] That world has changed.

But what about the humanities? Here, too, I think it is fair to point to a long-standing and reflexive, if often unexamined, bias in favor of the same "dark side" that originally drew Lucien Febvre. One might invoke a number of provisional and deep-seeded causes: the belief, nourished in Western culture, at least, by centuries of Christian reflection, that pain is deep and ennobling, and that pleasure, where not sinful, is often shallow and trite; the related notion, furthered by the Romantics and maintained in Bohemian circles ever since, that suffering is profound, and that, call it what you will—melancholy, spleen, *Weltschmerz*, alienation, *ennui*—is the inevitable lot of artists, intellectuals, and all who dare to confront the world with open eyes; the conception that the proper role of humanists is to exercise a critical function, calling attention to human faults and societal shortcomings, not "cheerleading" for what might be done well; and finally, a tendency to associate happiness and positive affect with the complaisance and hedonism of consumer societies. Happy are those who have a Coke and a smile, not who read Kafka or Sartre or contemplate the Shoah or the depths of the poetry of Sylvia Plath. This list of "causes" is not meant to be categorical or complete. Some might be expanded, others added, others emended or cut. But collectively they do point to a thought worth entertaining by self-reflexive scholars: namely that the "emotional community," to borrow Rosenwein's term, of humanists themselves, has a propensity to be fault-finding, querulous, and rather pessimistic at times, and in our current climate even more so.[14] "There is no document of civilization which is not at the same time a document of barbarism," Walter Benjamin once famously declared, setting the mood as it were for a great many historians, philosophers, and students of modern languages and cultural studies.[15] The members of the fictitious English department of Manhattan College in Rachel Kadish's 2006 novel, *Tolstoy Lied*, might well have agreed. Whether or not they had read Benjamin, they were affected by a serious case of the blues. The narrative of Kadish's novel revolves around a young assistant professor Tracy Farber, who is pursuing happiness and tenure in New York. The two goals are not compatible, she learns, complaining that it is almost impossible "to find a good nontragic American novel on Academia's approved reading list."[16] Her own interest in happiness in the American literary tradition is thus a nonstarter. "Talking about happiness is career suicide," she concludes.[17]

To be sure, *Tolstoy Lied* (the title is meant as an assault on the first line of Tolstoy's *Anna Karenina*, "Happy families are all alike") is a work of fiction, and a satire at that. But the characters are recognizable, and the situation—until recently, at least—rang true. Fortunately, things have begun to change. English professors and students of comparative literature have recently begun to exhibit an altogether healthy, and far from uncritical, interest in happiness, and that interest is evident elsewhere in the humanities.[18] Classicists are now devoting interesting work to rediscovering what was for the Greeks and Romans, as for many others, a foundational concern.[19] And philosophers, too, like students of religious studies, have begun to reconnect with their long-forgotten point of departure, posing the question, "How to live the good life?" in dialogue with positive psychologists and contemporary happiness studies.[20] Finally, historians, not least, have seen fit to investigate a variety of documents of civilization that are arguably less than fully barbaric, following pursuits of happiness and pleasure where they might lead.[21]

With some notable exceptions, however, the majority of this new historical work has been carried out mostly by philosophers, intellectual historians, and other scholars not drawing self-consciously on the methodology and the source bases of the history of emotions.[22] That is a shame, because the kind of careful, nuanced studies produced by historians in this field—studies that are concerned to push investigation beyond the domain of high culture and into the affective realms of the lives of ordinary people—are perfectly placed to complicate, enrich, and expand the interest in positive emotion that is now animating other regions of the humanities and social sciences. What better place to study the history of positive emotion than from the discipline of the history of emotions? Might it be time for the field to take a positive turn? And if so, what might such a turn look like in practice? Although no single individual can provide a prescriptive answer to such questions, of course—let alone an "outsider" (albeit an interested one) from the field of intellectual history like myself—perhaps it would not be amiss to offer a few preliminary reflections on what would seem to be one promising area for further research: the study of joy.

THINKING ABOUT THE HISTORY OF JOY

But why joy and not, say, happiness, the history of which has already drawn a good deal of attention in recent years? The two are related, of course, and in turn they gesture toward a spectrum of positive emotions ranging from mild delight and good cheer to ecstasy, rapture, and bliss, all of which might be studied by historians of emotion with real benefit. But the study of the history of happiness is complicated by the fact that for much of its development, happiness was not considered to be exclusively or even primarily an emotion at all.[23] Indeed, until roughly the late seventeenth century, happiness in the Western tradition was thought of primarily as an evaluation (an *objective* evaluation) of an entire life, and so was considered less a function of feeling than an ethical ideal, the product of living well. When Aristotle said that happiness (*eudaimonia*) is a life lived according to virtue; when Roman Stoics concluded that a truly virtuous man may be happy even on the rack; or when Christians emphasized that true happiness could come only in death, they underscored the extent to which happiness was conceived as an ethical, not an affective, state. That conception was challenged, it is true, beginning in the seventeenth century, and by the eighteenth century it was increasingly common to think of happiness in terms of pleasurable feelings, sensations, and states in ways that might readily be equated with joy. And yet even still, the older ethical evaluations retained a stubborn force. One might *feel* happy, but to *be* happy continued to require (and perhaps does still) a certain equanimity and balance extended over the long run. To this day, we ask, for example, if individuals are happy in their relationships or in their careers, or if they have lived happy lives in ways that connote something more than a simple summation—an addition and subtraction—of the positive and negative emotion contained therein.

Joy, by contrast, though it too long possessed an ethical register, has rarely been mistaken for anything but an emotion, an emotion and flood of feeling more concentrated and intense than happiness, and hence generally of shorter duration. It is an emotion, moreover, that en-joys a central place in the earliest development of human feelings. As the philosopher Martha Nussbaum has observed:

> From the first there are agencies in the environment [of an infant] that minister to its needs, supplying what it cannot supply for itself. These agencies therefore take on an intense importance in the infant's inchoate and as yet undemarcated awareness of the world. Its relationship to them focuses, from the first, on its passionate wish to secure what the world of nature does not supply by itself—comfort, nourishment, protection.[24]

For the newborn infant, Nussbaum continues, "a felt need for the removal of painful or invasive stimuli, and for the restoration of a blissful or undisturbed condition" is an overriding concern, yet one over which it possesses little agency or control. The infant's world is one "in which the best things arrive as if by lightning, in sudden penetrations of light and joy."[25] The literary historian and critic Adam Potkay has developed Nussbaum's insight in his own wonderfully insightful study of joy in Western culture, describing these lightning flashes as themselves a "regressive recuperation of the blissful totality of pre-birth experience."[26] Joy, in this reckoning, is from infancy onward always "to a certain degree, an aftertaste of a pre-linguistic totality," an account that helps to explain why joy is frequently described as indescribable.[27] It also helps to explain a crucial (if complicated) distinction of usage—the difference between joy and ecstasy and rapture. If ecstasy connotes, in keeping with the Greek root *ekstasis*, a "standing outside of oneself," and so a certain degree of abandonment and self-loss, joy more often implies self-recovery and return, completion, and the longing for recurrence. Be that as it may, Nussbaum and Potkay's accounts of joy as a primal and even prenatal emotion, the original object-directed passion, helps explain both its universality and its endless variability. Joy, according to the psychologist Paul Ekman and his many colleagues and disciples, is one of the archetypal emotions recognizable across cultures in facial expressions from infancy until death.[28] But like other emotions it is also always uniquely adapted to the narratives and experiences of selves—selves that are, in turn, indelibly shaped by culture and context. The expression of joy, in other words, may be universal, but like every emotion, it is also culturally specific and culturally distinct. Channeled, structured, shaped and imparted, joy is taught and joy is learned as part of the emotionology of all societies. As Aristotle observed, in an insight with potentially wide application, much of education is, and in his view should be, concerned with imparting a sense of "when to rejoice aright."[29] Just as friends find joy in the same things, communities and societies share and impart notions of when to "rejoice as one should."[30]

Aristotle's insight that "no man is just who does not take joy in acting justly" aimed at self-consciously encouraging a particular affinity between joy and virtue, which takes us some way from Nussbaum's lighting strikes of emotion.[31] The affinity had strong resonance in the ancient world, particularly among the Stoics, who continually reaffirmed the connection, distinguishing between ethical joy, rightly conceived, and allegedly irrational pleasures, such as sex and inebriation, to which they gave another name. Thus does Cicero, in a gloss on the Stoic tradition, differentiate, with other Latin writers, between *gaudium* (joy), which is used "when the soul has this satisfaction rationally and in a tranquil and equable way," and *laetitia*, which applies when "the soul is in a transport of meaningless extravagance," an "exuberant or excessive delight."[32] The distinction endured in the principal Romance languages where *laetitia* becomes *allégresse* (French), *alegría* (Spanish), *allegrezza* (Italian), and "joy" derives, as in English (via the French *joie*), from *gaudium*. Just as importantly, the distinction endured in a long tradition of "ethical joy" that, building on ancient precedents, reemerged in the eighteenth century in a compelling form in the writings of Anthony Ashley Cooper, the third earl of Shaftesbury. Shaftesbury's reading was broad, and he drew on many influences, including the new science of the seventeenth century. But his conception of joy was partially indebted to the

Stoic tradition, and along with his theory of happiness, it exerted a major influence on the century's moralists. Joy in his reckoning was one of nature's tools for promoting well-being in the species, and it followed that we were naturally inclined to take joy in good things. This included performing virtuous acts or in seeing them performed by others. To behold the "exercise of benignity and goodness" brought "natural Joy" to the mind, which reflected upon the "beautiful, proportioned, and becoming action" of virtue—whether one's own, or that of others.[33] Indeed, central to Shaftesbury's understanding—and a key element of his extensive impact in the eighteenth century as an impetus to the development of theories of moral sentiments—was his belief that through sympathy we may vicariously experience the joys and sorrows of others. The contention would have an important impact not only on influential philosophers in the eighteenth century such as Francis Hutcheson and David Hume, but also on novelists such as Henry Fielding and Samuel Richardson, whose popular writings moved readers with empathetic description of the virtues, joys, and sorrows of their protagonists. When eighteenth-century readers wept, they shed bitter tears for the trials of Clarissa but also tears of joy for the likes of Pamela. As the poet Mark Akenside observed in his "The Pleasure of the Imagination" (1744), beautiful moral spectacles—supreme acts of virtue—"invite the soul to never-fading joy."

Akenside's Shaftesburian (and Platonic) linking of virtue, beauty, and joy in the context of a discussion of the soul reminds us of the central place of conceptions of joy in the Christian tradition, as well. Ancient understandings of ethical joy undoubtedly exerted an important influence, at least through the eighteenth century. But the Christian tradition was ultimately the stronger (and broader) force, acting alongside it. As Potkay rightly observes, "Were it not for the frequency and urgency of 'joy' (*chara*) and 'rejoice' (*chairō*) in the gospels and throughout the epistles, the general story of joy in the West would be markedly different and probably less central than it is."[34] The main words for joy in the New Testament—*chara* (joy) and *chairō* (to rejoice)—occur 133 times, giving credence to the claim by one theologian that "the Gospel as such is a message centered on joy."[35] And the word itself—closely akin to the Greek *charis* for "grace"—emphasizes to a much greater degree than the Latin tradition of ethical *gaudium* the way in which joy can come upon us, as Nussbaum emphasizes, in a flash, bestowed, as it were, miraculously from outside. Like grace or a mother's nourishment, joy is freely given, it is a gift, the source of flourishing and life.

And just as it is present at birth, it is present, in the Christian tradition, at *the* birth, the birth of Jesus, whose annunciation the angel of the Lord describes in

Luke 2:10 as "good news that will cause great joy for all the people."[36] Jesus, who is "full of joy" (John 3:29) promises eternal joy: "I will see you again and you will rejoice and no one will take away your joy" (John 16:22). Joy in the future, but also joy in the present in the expectation of the fulfillment of his promise. "Rejoice and be glad"—now—"because great is your reward in heaven" (Matt. 5:12). Jesus, the man of sorrows, is at the same time a fountain of joy, who can transform the one into, and in the presence of, the other.

Jesus's transformative capacity worked another wonder, as well. And that was to recast the value associated with a whole range of what were deemed lesser joys, the joys of this earth, the joys of the flesh. For of course, neither the ancient understanding of ethical joy nor the new joys of Christian eschatology and fellowship could completely deny or do away with the many joys of this world, the sundry joys that have drawn human beings since infancy, each according to her/his taste, the joys that we moderns now catalogue with our endless variety of titles—the joys of cooking, the joys of living, the joys of sex. The Jewish tradition, that great font and foil of the Christian, had provided one way of dealing with this dilemma. God, as the giver of all joy, had sanctified joy, making many of its earthly varieties holy and just. As the scholars Erich Beyreuther and Günther Finkenrath observe, "In the Old Testament there is no apology for joy in the good things of life, such as health (Sir. 30:16), wise children (Prov. 23:25), eating and drinking (1 Ki. 3:1; cf. Ps. 104:14 f), peace in the land."[37] Joy may be had happily, healthily, in the fruits of the table and the fruits of one's loins. And though it is also true that such joys are transitory, as the author of Proverbs cautions—for "even in laughter the heart may ache, and joy may end in grief" (Prov. 14:13)—they are not to be disdained or dismissed in and of themselves.

The Christian attitude—or rather one tendency of the Christian tradition— was more skeptical, and on the whole, less accommodating to the joys of this earth. Worldly joy was deemed just that—worldly—potentially fleshly, carnal, and so a gateway to sin, an open door that could easily lead to gluttony, lasciviousness, greed, and sloth. One should beware fleeting pleasures and fleeting joys for they turned the heart astray. Yet if such a joyless orientation toward the things of this world is an undeniable tendency in the Christian tradition—the stuff indeed of frequent caricature and cliché—it is only one side, and arguably the less important, of the Janus-face. For the command to be joyful—the injunction to rejoice and be glad in all things—was also a spur to confront the world with a very different demeanor. And though there were ample precedents for assuming this kind of regard in the Catholic tradition—"it is not right for the servant of God to show sadness and a dismal face," Saint Francis observed, he should strive "ever to be joyful"—it was ultimately Protestants who wrestled to the greatest extent with the ambiguities of the command to rejoice.[38] Luther, for example, takes very seriously Christ's injunction. As he repeatedly affirms, "all sadness is from Satan" (*Tristitia omnis a Sathana*): it is a clear sign of the absence of God's grace and the absence of the redemptive power of the word.[39] Joy, by contrast, was a measure and sign of their presence, and so it followed that "we can mark our lack of faith by our joy; for our joy must necessarily be as great as our faith."[40] The true Christian *ought* to be "joyful in all things," Luther insisted, and a perfect Christian would continually rejoice, even in the sorrows of the passion.[41] As Calvin, who also insisted on the importance of joy, observed: "If praise and thanksgiving to the Lord can only proceed from a cheerful and joyful heart—and there is nothing which ought to repress these emotions in us—it is clear how necessary it is to temper the bitterness of the cross with spiritual joy."[42] The great poet John Donne, an Anglican convert from Catholicism, put it best when he enjoined in a sermon, "rejoice always . . . in your prosperity [and] . . . in your adversity too."[43] Joy was a religious duty. In this vision, the return to God and the return to the self were one and the same.

As both Adam Potkay and I have suggested in separate, if related, arguments, this Protestant moralization of mood had the curious consequence of both sanctioning joy and happiness as presumptive signs of God's grace *and* of increasing anxiety about their attainment.[44] If good Christians *should* feel joy and *ought* to experience happiness in this life, it followed ineluctably that failure to do so was to be doubly damned. Sadness was not only sad, it was a sign of sin, a sign that one might prefer to hide from one's neighbor and from oneself while busy in pursuit. Be joyful, in short, or be condemned.

Reformed Christianity's moralization of mood and its treatment of positive affect as both religious obligation and spiritual validation had analogues, as well, in strains of Catholicism and Judaism, especially the Hasidic tradition, which placed a great emphasis on the cultivation of joy. Collectively they played an important role in shaping later, more secular, attitudes toward positive affect, whether happiness, joy, gladness, or good cheer, which in the eighteenth century were endorsed by a variety of enlightened voices, religious and otherwise, as indicators of the *natural* default setting of human beings, the way we are supposed to be when we are being well. Indeed, the notion that one ought to be joyful and that to be so is well and good—an outward sign of inward flourishing—remained a consistent feature of discussions of joy throughout the eighteenth century and beyond. Even when its more obvious connections to religion were downplayed or overlooked entirely—such as in the revived classical discourse of ethical joy in the eighteenth century, or the Romantics' efforts to recover a pristine infant joy, or in Nietzsche's explicitly anti-Christian "joyful science" of the late nineteenth century—joy remained an ideal state, and the joyful human being the image of the integrated, harmonious, and flourishing self. "Joy is a delight of the mind, from the consideration of the present or assured approaching possession of a good," John Locke was already observing in the late seventeenth century in a predominately secular idiom.[45] And though he was well aware that the good(s) that one possessed might differ markedly from mind to mind, joy, he deemed, was generally good in itself. To feel it was to be right in the world—with ourselves and with others. It is not a notion to be lightly dismissed. As the neurologist Antonio Damasio has argued recently, in departing from the reflections of another seventeenth-century philosopher and early theorist of the Enlightenment—in this case, the materialist and atheist Baruch Spinoza—"The current scientific knowledge regarding joy supports the notion that it should be actively sought because it does contribute to flourishing."[46] Damasio goes even farther, observing, on the strength of Spinoza, that "I see primary sorrow and joy as having played, and still playing, a principal role in the construction of justice."[47]

One need not share that sentiment entirely to acknowledge the important role joy has clearly played in Western history (to say nothing of the many other traditions in which its presence and absence is no less central). This short, and admittedly selective, consideration of the intellectual history of joy has sought only to suggest that importance in an impressionistic fashion, highlighting some of the ways that men and women in the West's broad emotional regime have been schooled in joy, educated as Aristotle observed, to "rejoice as one should." But it goes without saying that men and women were taught in many other ways, too—both within the West and without—and the emotional communities of which they formed parts received their lessons in different fashions, while giving lessons of their own, lessons that were in turn disobeyed or reimagined, repeated, reinvented, or altogether dismissed. Attending to some of the nuances of that reception and dissemination, it is clear, is a task that historians of emotion are well-placed to continue—deepening, complicating, and enriching as they do. For of course a consideration of the intellectual history of joy, like the intellectual history of happiness, is only the beginning of a much broader consideration of joy's place in the past, a history that by and large remains to be written. What of the fraught and, in modern times, closely connected relationships between joy and happiness? How have human beings given different expressions to the frequent coexistence of sadness and joy—at weddings, births, and graduations, or in love? In what ways have human beings imagined joy on the horizon—in utopian communities, and concrete visions of progress and the future? And how have they experienced it collectively in different places and in different times? From religious festivals to birthdays to rock concerts and sporting events, the possibilities would seem vast.[48] Finally, in what ways did the affective "Sattelzeit" of the long eighteenth century—an age that granted unprecedented importance to the desirability and attainability of positive emotion, from happiness to gladness to good feeling to joy—impact the emotional lives of ordinary men and women, for better or for worse? Are there analogous moments in other cultures? Where and when does joy assume a primary place?

These are only a few of the questions that historians of emotion might formulate more sharply themselves, doing so, moreover, by focusing in on specific, and particularly revealing, instances, episodes, and events. Consider—to take only one ready example—the famous night of August 4th, 1789, when deputies of the three estates to the French National Assembly came together in unprecedented concord to abolish the vast complex of feudal dues, restrictions, and privileges that had long defined royal France. This was the night, as one historian describes it, that the "old Regime ended," and virtually all contemporary accounts agree on its extraordinary, even magical mood.[49] "We wept with joy and emotion," one witness remembered typically. "Deputies, without distinction, treated one another with fraternal friendship."[50] The "famous Night of 4 August," William Reddy observes, "has all the trappings of a sentimentalist gesture."[51] And given that joy was the evening's primary passion, it behooves us to examine more closely how it was articulated, expressed, and recalled. For joy in fact was a central emotion of the Revolution as a whole, with its continual will to enact celebrations and sponsor festivals and to give birth to a new, regenerated humanity. As the night of August 4th illustrates, joy was often contagious, serving not only to register responses to revolutionary action but to initiate it via a joyous appeal to human brotherhood and moral uplift. Swept up in the flood of joy of the night of August 4th, deputies initiated motion after motion that sought to give expression to the Revolution's loftiest ideals and hopes. The connection to virtue is conspicuous in this case—joy is at once cause and consequence of acts of moral grandeur—in a way that registers nicely the eighteenth century's own sentimental education.

But one might consider another, later example of collective joy—the reception of news throughout Europe of the declaration of war in 1914—to illustrate how this same infectious feeling can well up from very different sources. The infamous image of the smiling face of Hitler, celebrating the declaration in a crowd before the Feldherrnhalle on the Odeonsplatz in Munich, on August 2nd, 1914, is a particularly graphic illustration of the point. But the same scene was repeated across Europe, as exultant crowds responded to the news of war with spontaneous jubilation. August 1789, we might say, in a Nietzschean idiom, was "Apollonian," whereas August 1914 was "Dionysian." And although, as Nietzsche himself took pains to emphasize, the two tendencies are surely present in many times and places, there is nonetheless something distinctive to the autumnal summer of 1914 about the Dionysian joy taken in impending violence and destruction. Whether his words were present in the backpacks of soldiers on the Western Front, Nietzsche's repeated insistence that "joy and pain are not opposites," and that joy, domination, and power are a piece was part of the collective sensibility of the time.[52]

Exploring that sensibility in context, and registering its specific emotional inflections in contrast to that of previous and subsequent ages, is a task that awaits historians of emotion. It is to be hoped that they will undertake it, extending as they do so the sweep of their interests to include the range of positive emotions that have done so much to give meaning and value to human lives in the past. For if it is true, as Jan Plamper suggests, that the historical profession has undergone an "emotional turn" in recent years, then perhaps one way to continue the trajectory in the years ahead is by continuing in a positive direction, finding a little joy along the way.[53]

NOTES

1. The titles are taken from the Colloquium for the Winter Semester 2011–2012 at the Center for the History of Emotions at the Max Planck Institute for Human Development in Berlin: http://www.mpibberlin.mpg.de/sites/default/files/media/pdf/28/koll_programmws1112_neu_1.pdf (accessed April 22, 2013).

2. Paul Rozin and Edward B. Royzman, "Negativity Bias, Negativity Dominance, and Contagion," *Personality and Social Psychology Review* 5 (2001): 296–320; G. Peeters and J. Czapinski, "Positive-Negative Asymmetry in Evaluations: The Distinction between Affective and Informational Negativity Effects," in *European Review of Social Psychology*, ed. W. Stroebe and M. Hewstone (New York: Wiley, 1990), 33–60.

3. Roy F. Baumeister, Ellen Bratslavsky, Catrin Finkenauer, and Kathleen D. Vohls, "Bad Is Stronger than Good," *Review of General Psychology* 5 (2001): 323–370.

4. Aaron Ben Zéev, "Are Negative Emotions More Important than Positive Emotions?" *Psychology Today* (July 18, 2010): http://www.psychologytoday.com/blog/in-the-name-love/201007/are-negative-emotions-more-important-positive-emotions (accessed March 26, 2013).

5. Ibid.

6. Lucien Febvre, "La sensibilité et l'histoire: Comment reconstituer la vie affective d'autrefois?" *Annales d'histoire sociale* 3 (January–June 1941): 5–20.

7. See Barbara Rosenwein's discussion of Febvre in "Worrying about Emotions in History," in *American Historical Review* 107 (June 2002): 2–4.

8. Peter N. and Carol Z. Stearns, "Emotionology: Clarifying the History of Emotions and Emotional Standards," *American Historical Review* 90 (1985): 13–36.

9. William Reddy, *The Navigation of Feeling: A Framework of the History of Emotions* (Cambridge: Cambridge University Press, 2001), Ch. 4.

10. Sigmund Freud and Josef Breuer, *Studies on Hysteria*, trans. and ed. James Strachey (New York: Basic Books, 2000), 305.

11. Richard P. Bentall, "A Proposal to Classify Happiness as a Medical Disorder," *Journal of Medical Ethics* 18 (June 1992): 94–98.

12. A nice introduction to the extensive literature on economics and happiness, comprising many of the leading practitioners in the field, is provided in Amitava Krishna Dutt and Benjamin Radcliff, *Happiness, Economics, and Politics: Towards a Multi-Disciplinary Approach* (Northampton, Mass.: Edward Elgar, 2009).

13. Veenhoven's anecdote was shared with the author in a personal conversation. See also Derek Bok, *The Politics of Happiness: What Government Can Learn from the New Research on Well-Being* (Princeton, N.J.: Princeton University Press, 2010).

14. Barbara H. Rosenwein, *Emotional Communities in the Early Middle Ages* (Ithaca, N.Y., Cornell University Press, 2007); David Watson, *The Question of Morale: Managing Happiness and Unhappiness in University Life* (New York: Open University Press, 2009).

15. Walter Benjamin, "Theses on the Philosophy of History," *Illuminations*, ed., Hannah Arendt; trans. Harry Zohn (New York: Schoken Books, 1968), 256.

16. Rachel Kadish, *Tolstoy Lied: A Love Story* (New York: Mariner Reprint Edition, 2007), 4.

17. Ibid., 5.

18. See, for example, Adam Potkay, *The Story of Joy: From the Bible to Late Romanticism* (Cambridge: Cambridge University Press, 2007); and also Vivasvan Soni, *Mourning Happiness: Narrative and the Politics of Modernity* (Ithaca, N.Y.: Cornell University Press, 2010); and numerous articles in the special issue of *Nineteenth-Century Contexts* 33, no. 2 (2011), "The Pursuit of Happiness."

19. Julia Annas, *Morality of Happiness* (New York: Oxford University Press, 1993); or see the Oslo Happiness Project, devoted to investigating ancient conceptions of the good life: http://www.hf.uio.no/ifikk/english/research/projects/happiness/ (accessed March 26, 2013).

20. The list is long and growing longer. See Sissela Bok, *Exploring Happiness: From Aristotle to Brain Science* (New Haven, Conn.: Yale University Press, 2010); Daniel Haybron, *The Pursuit of Unhappiness: The Elusive Psychology of Well-Being* (Oxford: Oxford University Press, 2008); Philip J. Ivanhoe, "Happiness in Early Chinese Thought," in *Oxford Handbook of Happiness*, ed. Ilona Boniwell and Susan David (Oxford: Oxford University Press, 2012); Brent A. Strawn, ed., *The Bible and Pursuit of Happiness* (New York: Oxford University Press, 2012); Hava Tirish-Samuelson, *Happiness in Premodern Judaism: Virtue, Knowledge and Well-Being* (Cincinnati, Ohio: Hebrew Union College Press, 2003); and Nicholas P. White, *A Brief History of Happiness* (Oxford: Blackwell, 2006).

21. Jennifer Michael Hecht, *The Happiness Myth: Why What We Think Is Right Is Wrong*

(San Francisco: Harper, 2007); Darrin M. McMahon, *Happiness: A History* (New York: Atlantic Monthly Press, 2006).

22. Those notable exceptions include, Peter N. Stearns, "Defining Happy Childhoods: Assessing a Recent Change," *Journal of the History of Childhood and Youth* 3, no. 2 (Spring 2010): 165–186; and Christina Kotchemidova, "From Good Cheer to 'Drive-by Smiling,'" *Journal of Social History* 39, no. 1 (August, 2005): 5–37. Rosenwein also discusses joy intermittently in *Emotional Communities*.

23. McMahon, *Happiness: A History*; Soni, *Mourning Happiness*. On the (sometimes subtle) distinctions between joy and happiness, see Potkay, *Story of Joy*, 20–29.

24. Martha C. Nussbaum, *Upheavals of Thought: The Intelligence of Emotions* (Cambridge: Cambridge University Press, 2001), 182.

25. Ibid., 183–184.

26. Potkay, *Story of Joy*, 15. In the discussion of joy that follows, I draw extensively on Potkay's rich study.

27. Ibid., 17.

28. David Matsumoto and Paul Ekman, "Facial Expression Analysis," *Scholarpedia* 3, no. 5 (2008): 4237.

29. Aristotle, *Politics*, 8.5.17: http://www.perseus.tufts.edu/hopper/text;jsessionid=734 F2BB0C317AC7A2866ECEB1EED2B96?doc=Perseus%3atext%3a1999.01.0057 (accessed April 23, 2013).

30. See the discussion of Aristotle in Potkay, *Story of Joy*, 167, and 268, n. 18. The following section on joy's history draws heavily, and gratefully, on Potkay's fine study.

31. Aristotle, *Nichomachean Ethics*, 1099a: http://www.perseus.tufts.edu/hopper/ text;jsessionid=734F2BB0C317AC7A2866ECEB1EED2B96?doc=Perseus%3atext %3a1999.01.0053 (accessed April 23, 2013).

32. Cicero cited in Potkay, *Story of Joy*, 6.

33. Anthony Ashley Cooper, 3rd Earl of Shaftesbury, "An Inquiry Concerning Virtue and Merit," in *Characteristicks of Men, Manners, Opinions, Times*, Foreword Douglas Den Uyl, 3 vols. (Indianapolis, Ind.: Liberty Fund, 2001), 2: 60, 61.

34. Potkay, *Story of Joy*, 30.

35. Peter Beyerhaus, "Joy," in *Baker's Dictionary of Christian Ethics*, ed. Carl F. H. Henry (Grand Rapids, Mich.: Baker Books, 1973), 356.

36. All citations from Scripture are from the New International Version.

37. Cited in Potkay, *Story of Joy*, 34.

38. Saint Francis cited in McMahon, *Happiness*, 121.

39. Luther cited in McMahon, *Happiness*, 173.

40. Luther cited in Potkay, *Story of Joy*, 78.

41. Luther cited in McMahon, *Happiness*, 165.

42. Calvin cited in McMahon, *Happiness*, 173.

43. Donne cited in Potkay, *Story of Joy*, 86.

44. See McMahon, *Happiness*, esp. 164–175; and Potkay, *Story of Joy*, 94.

45. John Locke, An *Essay Concerning Human Understanding*, ed. Peter H. Nidditch (Oxford: Clarendon, 1975), 231.

46. Antonio Damasio, *Looking for Spinoza: Joy, Sorrow, and the Feeling Brain* (Orlando, Fla.: Harcourt, 2003), 285.

47. Ibid., 321.

48. Barbara Ehrenreich's *Dancing in the Streets: A History of Collective Joy* (New York: Metropolitan, 2007), though not a work of original scholarship, offers some suggestions in this regard.

49. Michael P. Fitzsimmons, *The Night the Old Regime Ended* (University Park: Pennsylvania State University Press, 2003).

50. Cited in Timothy Tackett, *Becoming a Revolutionary: The Deputies of the French National Assembly and the Emergence of a Revolutionary Culture (1789–1790)* (Princeton, N.J.: Princeton University Press, 1996), 175.

51. Reddy, *Navigation of Feeling*, 182.

52. See Walter Kaufmann, *Nietzsche: Philosopher, Psychologist, Antichrist*, 4th edition (Princeton, N.J.: Princeton University Press, 1974), 272–273.

53. Jan Plamper, "The History of Emotions: An Interview with William Reddy, Barbara Rosenwein, and Peter Stearns," *History and Theory* 49 (May 2010): 237.

CHAPTER 6

ADVERTISING FOR LOVE

MATRIMONIAL ADVERTISEMENTS AND PUBLIC COURTSHIP

PAMELA EPSTEIN

In June 1864, a man signing himself "Bertram" printed a remarkable matrimonial advertisement. At forty-three lines long and three hundred and seventy-two words (but only three sentences), it took up nearly a quarter of a column in the *New York Times*. Describing himself as a "young gentleman in all respects favorably situated in life," with all the qualities a privileged man should have: "prepossessing appearance and manners . . . no ordinary capabilities and attainments, independent in thought and action, enlarged, liberal and charitable in views," he nevertheless lamented that he was "still wanting the essential element of happiness," a wife. The reason for this lack, he explained, was "the narrow bigotry and conventionalities of society, which, by imposing barriers to the free intercourse of the sexes, and thus limiting our choices, condemn multitudes of even the most favored to lives of celibacy and misery."

Bertram was convinced, however, that the world somewhere contained his "'bright particular star'—the light of whose blessed presence and sweet influence his social confines, extensive as contracted souls would consider them, have shut him out from," so he turned to "this method as the only one open to him." Dismissing any "worldly advantages," he requested only respectability, "agreeable person, expressive face and engaging manners," and anyone who did not "unite *brains* and *heart* (the latter especially)" need not reply. The only women who should answer were those "with resources of soul and wealth of affection greater than their opportunities . . . [who could] rise above the prejudice of mode and tyranny of custom." In conclusion, he hoped to "[escape] the relentless social constriction which crushes our best aspirations within the folds of its 'circles' and thus dooms us to become the helpless victims of mere matrimonial chance or accident."[1]

This ad may have been unique in length, but it was not alone in its sentiment. Bertram spoke for many men when he lamented the "narrow bigotries and conventionalities" of social etiquette that forbid the "free intercourse of the sexes" and which constrained marriage choices to one's "circles." Who Bertram really was is a matter of conjecture—his name was a pseudonym likely borrowed from Shakespeare's *All's Well That Ends Well*—but his ad was representative of many matrimonials. Men and women who printed these ads echoed his complaint. Not all of them shared his eloquence, but they expressed the same frustration with the difficulty of meeting a spouse due to restrictive social etiquette as well as isolation in big cities. Whether or not they expressed it as plainly as did Bertram, however, advertisers chose to overcome these obstacles by turning to an unconventional form of public, urban courtship, one that they acknowledged as irregular, but necessary nonetheless.

Matrimonials date back to at least the late seventeenth century; according to one historian, the first appeared in a British periodical in 1692.[2] The *London Times* was the first mainstream newspaper to publish one in 1786.[3] In the United States, articles began to appear referring to matrimonials as early as 1811.[4] However, they did not become a regular feature in newspapers until the second half of the nineteenth century as classified ads in general became more common. The *New York Herald*, the paper with the most famous matrimonial column, began publishing them on a semiregular basis in about 1855, where they became a near-daily presence by 1860, and other papers nationwide began printing them with varying degrees of frequency at about the same time. Although these ads were in papers across the country, they were most common in urban areas, especially in big cities.

Matrimonial advertisements provided a space, for urban dwellers in particular, in which to experiment with a new kind of personal interaction. Matrimonials revealed individuals who were on the move—both geographically and socially—circulating themselves in public in an attempt to find intimacy. In order to do so, they deliberately circumvented middle-class rules of etiquette, and their actions were disturbing to many observers. Where lonely, single people saw advertising as an opportunity to make connections in an anonymous urban world, critics saw people bringing the private institution of marriage up for sale in the public marketplace. Yet matrimonials demonstrate the opposite is true. Where before love was something that people hoped to find within a marriage, the radical decision by many to advertise for spouses shows that expectations had changed; men and women wished to marry for love before all else. At the same time, however, they were accepting a new definition of love, one in which it became a commodity that could be found in a newspaper classified.

Much has been written about the rocky growing pains of the middle class in the nineteenth century as a result of rapid urban growth and capitalism, and matrimonial ads give a new and unique insight into the way these transformations affected people's intimate lives and their approach to experiencing love. Matrimonial advertisers provide an excellent window into how these upheavals in society were negotiated; they were ordinary men and women who wanted nothing more than to conform to a middle-class lifestyle but felt forced to find traditional relationships in an unconventional fashion. Even "extraordinary" men like Bertram wanted the same thing: to find a loving partner. The strikingly similar language that many advertisers used shows how alike they were: highly literate, well-educated, and instilled with middle-class ideals about romance, marriage, and intimacy. In the midst of change, Americans stayed committed to the traditional ideals of love. Yet at the same time, they redefined the place of love—from a private, sacred emotion shared only between partners, love was now placed squarely in the public eye and the market.

Matrimonials began to appear more frequently at the same time as an ideological shift was taking place in middle-class notions of marriage. The unprecedented emphasis on love had begun to develop in the previous century—Nicole Eustace's essay, later in this volume, deals with this change and its extension into politics; a number of historians have charted the earlier impact on romantic ideals. But it was in the nineteenth century that this shift began to translate more widely into standard definitions of the basis for marriage. From a tacit recognition that financial stability was a necessary precondition for a successful marriage, Victorians began to elevate love over any other consideration— indeed, they believed that love was the *only* justifiable reason for marrying. This shift took place as a result of the increased influence of the market on all aspects of life. Although love is a personal experience, it is socially constructed, and with "the transformation from an agrarian to a capitalist economy, love was also transformed."[5] The more commerce dominated everyday interaction, the more people valued marriage as something separate and distinct from the outside world. Stephanie Coontz writes that "Victorians were the first people in history to try and make marriage the pivotal experience in peoples' lives.... Victorian marriage harbored all the hopes for romantic love, intimacy, personal fulfillment and mutual happiness."[6] Previous expectations that people would "[learn] to love someone from within the marriage relation" implied that other considerations—specifically financial ones—were more important than romance in making marriage choices.[7]

Therefore matrimonials were problematic, because although they reflected these Victorian ideals of marriage, the public courtships were still solicited and arranged in a commercial fashion. Indeed, matrimonials made marriage openly commercial. Advertisers offered their own appearance, social standing, and education as qualities with concrete value at a time that Victorians believed that love was an "uncontrollable and baffling force," which was sudden and abstract.[8] The ads were troubling because the authors were taking romantic relationships meant to be sacred and mysterious and giving them quantifiable value.

There are no records of the people who submitted these ads. Except in a small handful of cases that made their way into the news, the ads are completely anonymous. Like Bertram, the people involved often used pseudonyms, first names, or initials, and directed letters to the newspaper or post offices; they are utterly untraceable. In many ways, this makes them questionable sources at best. The cases where advertisers can be identified are often examples of fraud: men and women who published ads, or responded to them, in order to steal money from the other party. The dishonesty could be less dangerous; sometimes people simply lied about their age, physical appearance, or financial status. There were also several cases of intrepid reporters who wrote matrimonial ads to amuse their readers with the replies. Therefore none of them can be taken at face value.

This does not mean, however, that we can draw no conclusions about the authors. Bertram was especially loquacious, but he was not the only person who wrote a lengthy ad, and the longer an ad, the more it would have cost. In fact, in 1862, the only year for which advertising rates for the *New York Herald* are available, a matrimonial was double the cost of any other ad, meaning that the authors must have had some disposable income.[9] More important, many of the advertisers were not just literate; they were highly educated. They quoted and adapted famous writers, such as one man who borrowed from Dante's *La Vita Nuova* when he wrote, "Romance will never see its end, nor a noble heart half its treasure. So says the poet." Advertisers referenced works of literature, historical figures, indulged in witty wordplay, and even composed their own poetry. One man wrote that he wished to meet a woman "whose piano is not her only forte, who will make the winter of his discontent glorious summer." Another, who signed himself "A Bashful Man," wrote a twelve-line ad all in rhyme, closing: "I ask not, I offer not silver and gold; a wife I'll not purchase, nor will

I be sold. But I have a hand to labor, and I have a heart to love. Lady, wouldst thou win my favor, a true helpmeet thou must prove."[10] Women tended to be less eloquent in their ads—likely because lengthy ads cost more money—but they too wrote in a style that indicated a genteel background. Critics assumed that even the most romantic ads were at best from social outcasts whom no one wanted to marry and at worst from clever imposters, but even if this was true, they were highly educated, well-written, and intelligent imposters and outcasts.

Why these highly educated people found it necessary to advertise for their spouses is not always clear; however, matrimonials did represent a populace in motion, both socially and geographically. Many of the advertisers were part of a growing middle class, people who had migrated from smaller towns and rural areas as agricultural opportunities shrank and white-collar positions in businesses in cities increased. There were considerable opportunities for promotion for men within business bureaucracies as managerial positions were growing more quickly than clerical jobs."[11] Because growth was always possible, the middle class was always on the move, and its members were always trying to move up the social ladder. As a result, transition became a permanent condition.[12]

Men and women who had migrated to the cities found themselves bereft from family and community ties, and "set adrift in a maelstrom of people."[13] And they consciously saw themselves as outsiders. The migrants referred to themselves as being "strangers in the city"; this phrase appeared without alteration for decades. For example, in 1860 one man wrote: "A gentleman, a stranger in the city, desires to make the acquaintance of a domestic young lady, with a view to matrimony."[14] In 1894, another man echoed him, writing: "Gentleman (34) . . . stranger in the city, wishes to make the acquaintance of a widow under 40; object, matrimony."[15] Despite being over thirty years apart, these two advertisers expressed the same problem in identical language.

Advertisers moved to big cities from all over the country, sometimes from rural areas, sometimes from smaller towns. "A young man, having recently arrived in the city, with but few lady acquaintances," published an ad to find a wife. One man wrote he had only "lately returned from abroad." Another, claiming to be originally from New Orleans, explained that he was "detained North on business, and [had] no lady acquaintances." More poignantly, one ad read: "Is there an intelligent, kindly disposed young lady, or widow . . . 15 to 50, anywhere, matrimonially inclined, who appreciates temperance, loyalty, and truth, who craves the exceptional devotion of [an] exceptional young man? Am stranger everywhere, traveling the world alone." In addition, with cities changing so rapidly, it was possible to leave and come back to a different place. As one man "recently returned home" after living abroad for several years discovered, he was "himself almost a stranger in his native city."[16]

Women, like men, often explained that their decision to print a matrimonial was because they were strangers in the city. For example, a "lady from the East with few acquaintances in the city" published an ad in the *Chicago Tribune* in the hopes of finding a husband, while a "lady from the West, a stranger in the city," did the same in New York. Nearly twenty years later, a lady in New York "just from San Francisco" advertised to marry a man in business.[17]

In addition to being isolated due to geographic mobility, men and women were also segregated due to the changing nature of work, which could affect people native to cities as well as new residents. The increasing demands on men's time in business made it more difficult for them to have extensive social lives. As many historians have observed, it was in the nineteenth century that work and home life became separate; as more and more men moved to cities and entered the corporate world, the less their time was spent in society. In an era that idealized the "self-made man," economic success defined a man's worth. Max Weber writes in *The Protestant Ethic and Spirit of Capitalism* that the work ethic became about "the earning of more and more money, combined with the strict avoidance of all spontaneous enjoyment of life," so that a man would be "dominated by the making of money, by acquisition as the ultimate purpose of his life."[18] This kind of work ethic would have further cut off migrant men, but even those with larger social networks could become disconnected from society if they were "chained" and "bound" to their desks all day long. Thus, the "individual's very independence and mobility often brought, not heightened dignity and achievement, but, on the contrary, a sense of anonymity and isolation."[19]

Therefore, it was common to see ads in which a man might write, for example, that his "attention has been occupied with business to the neglect of his social ties"; another explained that "business demands his constant attention." Similarly, one man wrote over twenty years later that his "business require[d] all his time" and so he felt compelled to use an advertisement "in the hopes of being able to make the acquaintance of a respectable lady."[20] As the writer of one etiquette book commented, "Instances have . . . occurred where gentlemen, driven with business, and having but little time to mingle in female society, or no opportunity . . . desirous of forming the acquaintance of ladies, have honestly advertised for correspondence."[21] Echoing this, a busy merchant explained that he was "out of society" and a lawyer wrote that he had "but limited time to mingle in general society."[22]

Both men and women complained frequently of their lack of social ties. Men claimed their reason for placing an ad was being "deprived . . . for the past few years of the pleasure of society," who "through the removal of friends and family from the City, [were] left without female company" or were "by circumstances deprived of the enjoyments of parents and home." Women echoed them. A young widow wrote that her "acquaintance in the city is very limited," and another young lady explained that she was "placed in a position which almost precludes the possibility of any acquaintance with the opposite sex."[23]

Thus, loneliness was a pervasive theme in many of these ads. A young gentleman wrote that he was "wearied of hotels and boarding houses." A "lonely" widower echoed him, writing that he was "weary of solitary rooms." An eighteen-year-old girl agreed, saying she was "wearied of a life of single blessedness," and a "widowed lady" said that she was "tired of living alone."[24] The few existing letters in response to matrimonial ads reflect the same sentiment. One woman wrote to a researcher who had posed as a matrimonial advertiser: "I am horribly lonely, having no society of gents outside of business relations." Another explained, "I am very lonesome at times . . . but [have] not yet seen any [men] that I could trust." A woman responding to an ad from a curious reporter echoed her, writing: "[a]nswering a personal is, I realize, rather a risky way of becoming acquainted. However, I plead loneliness as my excuse."[25] Also in response to a curious reporter, one girl in Chicago explained, "[m]y friends would ridicule me if they knew that I had answered a personal. But I dread the thought of being alone in the world."[26]

One of the greatest barriers middle-class people faced were the strict rules guiding interactions between men and women. Members of the opposite sex could not meet without a formal introduction, and for recent transplants from small towns, or for people who lived and worked almost exclusively with members of their own sex, introductions were difficult to come by. The rules that Bertram and his fellow advertisers complained about were very strict: introductions could not be given without prior consent of a lady, and could not be suggested unless it was certain that the acquaintance would be mutually beneficial. So although city-dwellers actually had more potential marriage partners to choose from, explains Ellen Rothman, "they were more likely . . . to be choosing from among strangers. . . . The city became both a more open and more hazardous place to find a mate than the small town . . . far more complex, heterogeneous, and dynamic, it was also more divided by class, geography, and gender."[27]

Arthur MacDonald, a psychologist with the U.S. Bureau of Education, published an entire book of letters he received from women in response to ads asking either for a correspondent or for a wife. From them, he concluded that "unfortunately, courtship and love under . . . favorable conditions are too infrequent . . . owing to social artificiality, there seems to be little arrangement by which the proper people can meet and become well acquainted in a natural way."[28] He described his correspondents as "a class of young refined women who need and really desire a home [but they] are too refined to marry a man who is vulgar or coarse, and so have remained single. This illustrates a want of social arrangements where people of mutual adaptation may meet. . . . Such matters are left too much to accident or incident."[29] As one journalist asked, "[h]ow many young men in large towns are anxious to be married, but have never obtained admission into a circle of acquaintance from which a wife could be chosen?"[30] No one offered a solution, but as a young woman observed in 1864, "many a man out of even a very large circle of lady friends will acknowledge there is not one of them he would marry. This is perhaps the reason why so many matrimonial advertisements find their way into our newspapers."[31]

Matrimonials show how the search for love had become constrained by social niceties. Like Bertram, men expressed frustration with their inability to move in larger circles. For example, one man wrote that he had decided to print an ad because "the prevailing conventional rules of society in a great degree prevent social intercourse, and acquaintance between the sexes especially in matrimonial matters." Another admitted that he found "the ordinary formalities too irksome and too little understood" by himself to find a wife in a more proper fashion.[32]

Men justified their decision to write a matrimonial by dismissing the necessity of etiquette; one explained that he turned to a matrimonial advertisement because he did not wish to be a "slave to ceremony." Another wrote that because he had "sought in vain for a kindred spirit within the circle of his acquaintance he [concluded] to turn to the virtue of advertising to reach the rest of womankind." And one advertiser claimed that he "spurn[ed] the 'social lie' which thinks and says the Press is no fit medium of introduction. 'If their hearts be right it matters little how they met.'"[33]

Advertising for a spouse became a pragmatic solution to a difficult quandary. Most people in cities were surrounded by a growing consumer culture; commerce would have been a daily part of their lives. So when it came time to solve the problem of finding a spouse, with no socially acceptable alternative, they turned to what was familiar: the market. Finding a husband or wife in the same place one might find a job, a servant, or a place to live, while appearing vulgar to many observers, would have made sense in the context in which many urbanites lived; after all, most migrants to the city had come specifically to take part in the market economy.

At the same time, ads gave a unique chance for self-expression. While the stereotype of Victorian repression has been largely disproved, in public life, men were expected to act with restraint. Middle-class businessmen relied on their behavior and demeanor to help them further their ambitions; displaying emotion was a sign that a man lacked self-control. Matrimonial ads, however, gave men a chance to express themselves freely. Often anonymous, the ads did not risk public exposure, and advertisements were often full of romantic language—much like Bertram's. However, even the less eloquent could be expressive, such as one man who wrote that he wished "to be adopted by some young lady who can appreciate a kind, honorable [gentleman with a] loving disposition and generous instincts."[34] Another man, who admitted he was publishing an ad "for the romance of the affair," hoped he could meet a woman capable of "a loving disposition" and added that he had no interest in money—"as only a warm, unfettered heart is asked for one as good in return."[35] Matrimonials gave a rare opportunity to speak openly in an era that prized serious, unemotional behavior.

However, some onlookers saw nothing but evil in the ads. Believing that the advertisers were at best social rejects and at worst villains, critics abhorred matrimonials. They argued that people who printed these ads had one goal in mind: to marry someone rich and steal all of his or her money. And because many matrimonial advertisers, men as well as women, included wealth as a prerequisite for their desired spouse, critics assumed that such people were mere money grabbers. But by the mid–nineteenth century, Americans were celebrating a material culture based on a mass production economy that encouraged consumption; in other words, everyone wanted more money. People wanted to marry either their equals or someone in an even better position; members of the middle class—indeed, of any class—were always looking to move up the social ladder, not down. While idealists and moral arbiters believed that love mattered above all else, Americans lived in a society where consumer goods were the key to success (and thus implicitly to happiness), and this influenced men and women's decisions when it came to choosing a marriage partner.

And matrimonials did often specify that only wealthy people should respond, especially those from women. In two typical examples, one man wrote that he "desire[d] to meet a lady possessing some means," while a young lady requested "to correspond with a gentleman of means."[36] Men's reasons for stipulating that their ideal spouse be wealthy varied. Some frankly stated that they needed the extra income, such as the man who wrote that he "desire[d] to find a lady as a partner in business . . . with a view to matrimony. One with some means . . . preferred."[37] But most men who requested that only wealthy women reply gave no explanation; they merely claimed that they were rich themselves and that they expected their wives to be so as well.

However, there is some evidence that these men were not always motivated by greed. For example, one man explained that he wanted to meet a woman with some means "as a bar to all mercenary motives." Another man, whose ad rivaled Bertram's in its length and romantic language, wrote that his wife needed to have "a fortune in her own right capable of at least supporting her in independence during life, if she should not marry, as the advertiser is determined not to marry, knowingly, any young lady who marries simply for a home and to be supported." These advertisers may have been swindlers whose goal was to entrap wealthy women and steal their money, but it is true that there were many women advertising for husbands out of financial distress, or who requested letters from "wealthy gentlemen (none other need reply)."[38] It is reasonable to suppose that men wanted to be sure that their wives were marrying them for love instead of for support.

In any event, most men who advertised shared Bertram's opinion that money was not an issue or, as one man put it, money was "no object, although I should not object to it." On the contrary, many advertisers indicated that they were seeking a wife at that time because they finally were comfortable enough to support one; one man explained that "having amassed a moderate competency," he was "desirous of opening a correspondence with a prepossessing young lady with a view to matrimony." Similarly, another man wrote that "having recently amassed a fortune and safely invested the same, [he] wishe[d] to meet with a young lady or widow . . . with a view to matrimony." Many a man was proud that, as one wrote, his "means [were] ample for the comfort of married life, and therefore he is not actuated by mercenary considerations."[39]

Women's ads were more likely to address the need for financial stability, a tendency that horrified critics; even more than men, women were expected to be emotional creatures who were only interested in romance. Unfortunately, it was very rare that a woman had enough of an income to ignore her future spouse's financial situation. The matrimonial advertisements from women make it clear that love, while desirable, often—though not always—took a backseat to support. "A widow lady of respectability and agreeable manners desires to meet with a gentleman of good standing and means to support a wife," read one typical example. Another widow wrote that she wanted to correspond "with an elderly gentleman of means, with a view to matrimony . . . [who was] able to support a wife comfortably. To such I would offer a loving heart."[40]

Some observers accepted the fact that women had to marry wisely as a necessary reality; Arthur MacDonald, for example, wrote that if "both man and woman are without means, it is a question whether she should marry him at all; for the truest love cannot always pay debts."[41] Another writer, attempting to debunk the myth that "unfortunate girls are exposed for sale by their cruel, heartless, and avaricious mothers," argued that the issue was more complex. "A certain number of women marry solely for love," he explained, but a "certain, and perhaps larger, number marry for reasons in which love and the desire to have a home of their own are mixed up." Blaming money-grabbing mothers, he concluded, was not fair; after all, "poverty and virtue" are not better than "riches and virtue," and who would not want the best for their children?[42]

As one lady who exchanged several letters with Arthur MacDonald explained, "I look through this unconventional medium, where there are good as well as bad, for a life companion—a suitable husband. . . . I seek love and affection, but I and you have lived long enough to know money is convenient . . . so I do not want a man with no resources." However, she added, "I do want a big, warm heart, one who needs just me to round out his life and make it complete; one to whom I could 'be all the world,' make his every hour happy, and who would value the wealth of affection I have to dispose."[43] Nevertheless, whatever they might want for themselves emotionally, women had to marry someone who was capable of providing lifelong security.

And men who advertised for wives seemed to understand and accept that most women married with financial considerations in mind. Like women, they put themselves on the market, with financial status listed alongside all their other desirable qualities. Most men stated their own worth upfront, whatever it was, sometimes going so far as to name their exact salary or the value of their property. Men without as much to offer would admit this fact with some level of apology or self-deprecation; one man described himself as a "gentleman, with some disadvantages, to wit: - Over 40 and of slender means." Another, with even more good humor, wrote: "A young man, receiving the princely salary of $5 per week, and has only had his wages lowered once in four years, wishes to find some young lady foolish enough to marry him; beauty and money will not be sneered at."[44] Men who printed matrimonials, in other words, were far more pragmatic than the critics who attacked them; they wanted a loving spouse, but they recognized that no matter how affectionate, kind-hearted, and devoted they were, women had to find a husband who could support as well as love them.

In her analysis of nineteenth-century love letters, Karen Lystra argues that men "phrased their identification of love and money in terms of their ambition to provide for women's comfort and happiness, often insisting that their economic concerns were motivated by the heart."[45] Men understood that their ability to make money determined their ability to be good husbands. For example, one man wrote that he "has a self maintenance, and possesses in brief, every qualification to render an amiable, true-hearted, lovely woman happy in wedded life." Some advertisers explicitly connected their financial status with their manliness; in one notable example, in 1862 a man who described himself as "nearly bankrupt, for crediting the South" prior to the Civil War, felt obliged to mention that despite his poverty, he was still "every inch a man."[46]

Whether honest or fraudulent, however, it is clear that advertisers at least felt that marriages formed through the market could be successful, and requesting that potential spouses have money would not be repellent. Nor did advertisers themselves appear to see any contradiction. One man, who published his ad several times, wrote that he had "a good presence, and a kind, loving heart," and wished "to correspond, sincerely, with an amiable and prepossessing lady of wealth." Another man wrote, "A bachelor would like to marry—The lady must be like himself—wealthy, cheerful, of undoubted social position, and possess qualities of head and heart calculated to make home happy." One ad exemplified the conflation of love and financial security perfectly. The man who published it "desire[d] a lady with some capital to form business and matrimonial partnership. Being interested in a lucrative old established business, he wants to buy it out. Rare chance to acquire happiness and fortune honestly."[47]

And while the method used may have been the market, the goal of many advertisers was anything but commercial. Whether or not money was mentioned, the primary motivation for most men was the desire for a loving wife. Advertisements varied in their length, specificity, and tendency toward romance, but the men wrote that they wanted to meet someone who was "affectionate," "kind-hearted," "loving," or some other variation on the same theme. Bertram is only one example of advertisers who expressed their longing in passionate terms. "The world is so full of poetry, beauty, and glory, and I have no one to share it with me," lamented one man. Another, quoting Henry Wadsworth Longfellow, wrote: "'No one is so accursed by fate, / No one so utterly desolate, / But some heart, though unknown, / Responds unto his own.' A gentleman awaits a response from a lady of culture and refinement." Another quoted freely from two different authors to express his desire for "someone to love in this wide world of sorrow" who could bring about "Two souls with but a single thought / Two hearts to beat as one." Even ads that were shorter often highlighted the desire for love; one such read: "A bachelor of means, position, and influence seeks sweet wife with loving, kind heart." More simply yet, another man merely wrote: "With a view to matrimony, the advertiser wishes the acquaintance of a fair-haired, blue-eyed, kind-hearted girl."[48]

To a lesser degree, there were women whose ads were purely romantic. Though women never rivaled men like Bertram in length or eloquence—perhaps because money was always an issue even for women who were not in dire straits—there were some who focused on love. One girl described herself as a "young and romantic miss" who hoped "she could meet with one who could excel all her most fond and brilliant imagination; one whom she could trust, honor, and obey." Another young lady "of sweet sixteen" requested to meet "one whom she may learn to love."[49]

Letters from women were more openly idealistic. "I believe in matrimony and mutual happiness, as far as the true love and affection are there, and as sure as there is heaven to gain and a hell to shun, the real true thing in life worth living for is love," wrote one woman who carried on a long correspondence with Arthur MacDonald. Not all the women who wrote him were so articulate, but they expressed the same feelings. For example, one wrote: "If I had a real good man I would do all in my power for him to make him happy."[50] In response to a reporter posing as a "Western gentleman," one young lady concluded her letter by saying, "You may doubt the reply as not being genuine, but I assure you it is from an honest, petite, lovable *little girl*."[51] All of these letters and advertisements indicate that, despite critics' concerns, both men and women were very much desirous of loving marriages. In a sense, they were in, but not of, the market.

Nevertheless, for horrified critics, just the idea of finding a spouse through a public courtship in the market could be dangerous to American society as a whole. Marriage was the most important contract in American society. "It was the simultaneously private and public contract that defined the obligations between husband and wife, bound their union to the political order, and shaped construction of gender," explains historian Norma Basch; "it was the irrevocable contract that made all other contracts possible."[52] The institution was so central that the Supreme Court itself determined in 1888 that it was the "foundation of family and society, without which there would be neither civilization nor progress."[53]

Seen in this context, it is not hard to understand why matrimonial advertisements were threatening. Marriage was the defining moment of people's lives, especially women; indeed, through "marriage and maternity, [a woman] completes her own being," wrote one author.[54] By the mid–nineteenth century, this institution had to be founded on the basis of love, with no other reason being acceptable to the middle class. Therefore, people finding marriage partners in a businesslike fashion would have destabilized the foundations of society itself. As Nancy Cott argues, "[i]f marriage produced the polity, then wrong-fully joined marriages could be fatal. The presence of such marriages and their perpetrators might infect the whole body politic."[55]

Yet the critics' concern that people using matrimonials were never marrying for love was unfounded. While there were ads that were strictly business, most people advertised in the hopes of finding a loving spouse, whether or not they included financial qualifications. To be sure, many of those ads could have been dishonest—using romantic language to draw in lonely, lovesick marks. But, despite what contemporaries assumed, there is evidence that many of the ads were sincere. Even some skeptical critics admitted this must be the case. "For many men and women the 'personal' columns of a newspaper have a strong attraction and in some cases have even brought about a desirable change in human fortune," admitted one journalist, concluding "that a great many strong friendships, and even marriages are brought about by the answering of news-paper 'personals.'"[56] Another observer wrote that it "would probably surprise many if they knew that not a few of both those who advertise, and those who respond to such advertisements, occupy very respectable positions in society, with no fear of poverty before their eyes; and . . . many marriages annually take place from an acquaintanceship formed in this manner."[57]

And there were verifiable instances of successful marriages through ad-vertisements. Arthur MacDonald reported one widow who met her husband through an advertisement. "When I was a young lady I answered a 'personal,'" she wrote when MacDonald chastised her about the danger of using matrimo-nials. "A widower called. . . . We became well acquainted, and finally he went to see my parents. . . . A happier marriage there never was." She had answered MacDonald's advertisement out of curiosity, and explained her decision to try again by saying, "I know that these 'personals' are not inserted with good intentions, but some are. I thought possibly I might find a suitable husband in this way. . . . A man will go and find a wife, and this is the only method I have."[58] Marriage announcements in various papers around the country also attested to the success of matrimonials; one reported that the couple was "as happy as two sunbeams."[59] Another recorded the "romantic marriage" of a couple who had met through the "'Personal' column of a New-York paper."[60] Though not very common, announcements such as these indicate that at least some advertisers were sincere.

Critics of these advertisements saw them as symptomatic of a new era of commercialization and commodification and feared that the results would be dangerous—not only to individuals but to society as a whole. As the ads multiplied, they only provided proof that the market was intruding into private life in an unprecedented manner. What critics failed to recognize was that economics had always played a role in private lives, especially marriage. Matrimonial ads, far from an outcome of the growing market economy, were merely part of a tradition that had existed for generations. The only difference was that they were open and public. But while on the surface they suggested that little had changed, and that marriage for financial reasons still dominated despite changing ideals, upon closer inspection, they make it clear that love was an equally important factor. The means of gaining a spouse may have been influenced by the market, but the end goal was exactly what idealists desired. Like anything else, matrimonials were used by different sorts of people for a variety of different reasons. However, most advertisers at least claimed they wanted to conform to the middle-class ideal; they desired the same thing: a happy, loving, and financially secure marriage.

If matrimonials had a heyday, it was over by the 1890s. By that time, entrepreneurial businesspeople had latched onto the ads as a moneymaking venture: creating "matrimonial bureaus" to match lonely men and women together. Often full of fraudulent promises to help people find wealthy spouses, ads from these clubs would have likely discouraged sincere individuals from publishing their own matrimonials.

Nevertheless, at their best, matrimonials offered a chance for people who were isolated by social and geographical mobility to circumvent etiquette in order to find love despite their circumstances. For the men and women using them, matrimonials provided a way to use the public market to create private, intimate relationships.

These ads never disappeared entirely. Matrimonials appeared in newspapers throughout the twentieth century, and computer dating had its origins as early as the 1960s with services such as Data Mate and Phase 2. Both these programs required clients to fill out lengthy questionnaires demanding precise, detailed answers, which were then fed into a computer, in a time when computers were the size of a small room. Through mathematical analysis, the computer would match clients together, at least sometimes successfully.[61] (Computer dating never had a positive image, however; decades after these services were established, the 1992 film *Sneakers* mocked the trend as the purview of the socially inept and undesirable.)

City papers such as New York City's *Village Voice* and *Observer*, and the *Chicago Defender*, among others, ran personals columns starting in the 1970s and 1980s. In 2001 the *New York Times* reinstated its personals column after a gap of approximately 135 years. Nevertheless, it was not until the advent of online dating that advertising for a partner once again became widely acceptable.

Online dating has once again redefined the quest for love. According to a recent study commissioned by Match.com, one in six couples who were married between 2007 and 2010 met online, and "more than twice as many marriages occurred between people who met on an online dating site than met in bars, at clubs and other social events combined."[62] Meanwhile, eHarmony claims that from "January 1, 2008 through June 30, 2009 an average of 542 people were married every day in the United States" who met through its service.[63]

These data demonstrate just how much dating through personals is now part of mainstream life, and given the outrage personals once elicited, it is worth discussing what led to this transformation. First, although women still earn less as a whole than men, they are no longer financially dependent on husbands or fathers as they once were. Therefore, while financial stability and even gain still plays a role in many marriages, it is not as crucial a factor, and money does not appear prominently as an important quality a potential spouse must possess (except in websites such as MillionaireMatch.com). One of the most oft-repeated criticisms of matrimonials was that people used them to marry for money; if money only rarely plays a role in personals today—at least openly—such a concern is no longer at issue.

In addition, in a post-Victorian era, women's virtue is neither as fragile as it once was nor as in need of protection from male predators. Although there are risks associated with using personals, they are no more dangerous than dating through any other method for either men or women. Ultimately, alongside the increase of gay marriage, some conservative concern over premarital sex, skyrocketing divorce rates, and various other "threats" to the "sanctity of marriage," the use of personals seems comparatively harmless.

Discomfort with personals still lingers, although the stigma is shrinking daily. In 2003, the *New York Times* announced that "Online Dating Sheds Its Stigma as Losers.com," but seven years later in 2010, the *Chicago Tribune* was only just making the same discovery, stating that "[o]nline dating grows [and] sheds its stigma."[64] Couples who have met online are still occasionally embarrassed to admit it; single people who sign up for accounts often feel the need to justify their decision. Whatever the *Times* reporter wrote in 2003, online dating still has a slight taint of "Losers.com." What makes this significant is the degree to which people offer the exact same reasons why using personals is shameful today as they did over a hundred years ago. One critic wrote in 1896 that the only people who used matrimonials were "old bachelors, decayed rakes, and other discarded single gentlemen."[65] Echoing him, a writer in the *Washington Post* argued in 2010 that the same view persists: online dating is still seen by some as "the realm of the desperate."[66]

This uneasiness with online dating is not a holdover from when personals were reviled by mainstream critics—very few people are aware that personals existed before the late twentieth century. So it is significant that the stigma associated with personals now is much the same as it was over a hundred years ago; the negative connotations associated with online dating developed independently and yet reproduce many of the earlier criticisms. The problem with personals, therefore, is that they are at odds with a fundamental sense that finding romance in a public place—putting oneself on display for others to accept or reject—is wrong. Public courtship is the last resort: if a person could meet a partner anywhere else, he or she would not be browsing or publishing personals. In addition, there is also a lingering sense that marriage is still a sacred institution that should be unsullied by crass commercialism, and most online dating services promote marriage, or at least long-term, committed relationships, as the end goal.

Nevertheless, with social networking sites like Facebook and MySpace, as well as a plethora of online dating sites that each offer their own special methods of finding Mr. or Ms. Right (or at least Mr. or Ms. Right Now), there is no doubt that personals, despite their rocky origins and occasional snafus, will sooner or later make the stigma of finding intimacy in a public market disappear. It is hard to condemn a trend that has been consistently and demonstrably successful. As one of the cofounders of the dating site OkCupid has pointed out, "[O]nce you have a friend who's in a relationship that started online, you're at a crossroads. . . . Either your friend is weird and you're friends with weirdos, or it's not weird."[67]

So, the anxious critics of the nineteenth century proved to be wrong; matrimonial advertisements did not lead to the dissolution of society. The people who used and continue to use the ads are not the dregs of society. On the contrary, as the research funded by Match and eHarmony makes clear, personals have helped bring people together. In their willingness to search for love in unconventional ways, "Bertram" and others like him were far ahead of their time. By advertising for spouses in newspapers, these men and women asserted the stance that love—a private, sacred emotion—could be found in the most unexpected location of all: the marketplace.

The history of matrimonial advertisements in the nineteenth century, and the intriguing connections with recent developments, shows the power of the kind of emotional standards for marriage that began to emerge in the eighteenth century and that gained wider credence from the 1850s onward. Even criticisms of public advertisement show the power of assumptions that marriage and love should intertwine. The combination of emotional expectations and the greater impersonality of modern, urban life launched the effort to use new media and develop new organizational supports for the emotional quest on which marriage might be built. The process is ongoing.

NOTES

1. *New York Times* (hereafter *NYT*), June 4, 1864: 3.

2. H. G. Cocks, *Classified: The Secret History of the Personal Column* (London: Random House, 2009), vii.

3. Stephen Winkworth, *Room Two More Guns: The Intriguing History of the Personal Column of the Times* (London: George Allen and Unwin, 1986), 23.

4. "Matrimonial Advertisement, in Reply to Modestus," *Freemasons Magazine and General Miscellany* 2, no. 2 (November 1811): 130.

5. Francesca M. Cancian, "Love and the Rise of Capitalism," in *Gender in Intimate Relationships, A Microstructural Approach*, ed. Barbara Risman and Pepper Schwartz, (Belmont, Calif.: Wadsworth, 1989), 12.

6. Stephanie Coontz, *Marriage, A History: From Obedience to Intimacy; or, How Love Conquered Marriage* (New York: Viking, 2005), 177–178.

7. Elizabeth White Nelson, *Market Sentiments: Middle-Class Market Culture in Nineteenth-Century America* (Washington, D.C.: Smithsonian Books, 2004), 172.

8. Karen Lystra, *Searching the Heart: Women, Men, and Romantic Love in Nineteenth-Century America* (New York: Oxford University Press, 1989), 29.

9. Chas. B. Norton, *Catalogue of a Large and Valuable Collection of Books Relating Chiefly to America* (New York: John A. Gray, Printer, Stereotyper, and Binder, 1862), back page. Presumably this fee remained the same throughout the 1860s and perhaps throughout the nineteenth century, but the *Herald* did not print the fees in the paper and no other record seems to remain with this information.

10. *New York Herald* (hereafter *NYH*), January 15, 1863: 7. The Dante quote is "Love and the noble heart are but one thing / Even as the wise man tells us in his rhyme"; *NYH*, February 14, 1862: 6; *NYH*, February 11, 1860: 11.

11. Stuart Blumin, *The Emergence of the Middle Class: Social Experience in the American City, 1760–1900* (New York: Cambridge University Press, 1989), 292.

12. Karen Halttunen, *Confidence Men and Painted Women: A Study of Middle-Class Culture in America, 1830–1870* (New Haven, Conn.: Yale University Press, 1986), 30.

13. Gunther Barth, *City People: The Rise of Modern City Culture in Nineteenth-Century America* (New York: Oxford University Press, 1980), 3.

14. *NYH*, January 19, 1860: 11.

15. *NYH*, July 8, 1894: 1.

16. *NYH*, October 20, 1859: 9; *NYH*, February 19, 1860: 3; *NYH*, July 2, 1865: 6; *NYH*, August 19, 1879: 4; *Washington Post*, November 9, 1902: 26; *NYH*, June 10, 1863: 6.

17. *Chicago Tribune*, September 16, 1888: 8; *NYH*, April 11, 1865: 2; *NYH*, September 9, 1883: 2.

18. Max Weber, quoted in Michael Kimmel, *Manhood in America: A Cultural History* (New York: Free Press, 1996), 104.

19. John Kasson, *Rudeness and Civility: Manners in Nineteenth-Century Urban America* (New York: Farrar, Straus, and Giroux, 1991), 82.

20. *NYT*, April 18, 1862: 1; *NYH*, March 26, 1860: 7; *NYH*, March 6, 1885: 7.

21. Thomas E. Hill, *Hill's Manual Social and Business Forms: Guide to Correct Writing* (Chicago: Hill Standard Book Co., 1884), 115.

22. *NYH*, August 3, 1860: 8; *NYH*, June 4, 1882: 3.

23. *NYH*, April 8, 1858: 9; *NYH*, August 6, 1860: 6; *NYH*, October 19, 1862: 3; *NYH*, March 24, 1865: 7; *NYH*, November 27, 1861: 6.

24. *NYH*, April 18, 1867: 2; *NYH*, April 11, 1863: 8; *NYH*, March 15, 1860: 9; *NYH*, August 31, 1873: 13.

25. "Romance in a 'Personal,'" *Kansas City Star*, October 22, 1899: 24.

26. "Matrimonial Advertisements," *Chicago Tribune*, December 28, 1884: 12.

27. Ellen Rothman, *Hands and Hearts: A History of Courtship in America* (New York: Basic Books, 1984), 192.

28. Arthur MacDonald, *Abnormal Woman: A Sociologic and Scientific Study of Young Women: Including Letters of American and European Girls in Answer to Personal Advertisements, with a Bibliography* (Washington, D.C.: Self-published), 171.

29. Ibid., 44

30. "Marrying Made Easy," *Spirit of the Times* 30, no. 44 (December 8, 1860): 526.

31. Jenny Miller, *American Monthly Knickerbocker* (January 1864): 83.

32. *NYH*, May 5, 1860: 9; *NYT*, February 11, 1860: 3.

33. *NYH*, April 8, 1858: 9; *NYT*, May 18, 1864: 7; *NYT*, April 15, 1861: 7.

34. *NYH*, February 21, 1863: 7.

35. *NYT*, July 17, 1866: 1.

36. *NYH*, June 28, 1874: 14; *Chicago Daily Tribune*, June 26, 1880: 26.

37. *NYH*, February 5, 1863: 6; *NYH*, February 10, 1863: 3.

38. *NYH*, December 5, 1880: 4; *NYH*, January 3, 1863: 2; *NYH*, March 15, 1860: 9.

39. *NYH*, April 5, 1861: 3; *NYH*, March 19, 1863: 3; *NYH*, April 9, 1863: 5; *Chicago Tribune*, April 18, 1861: 1.

40. *NYH*, August 26, 1860: 7; *NYH*, January 13, 1863: 6; *NYH*, April 11, 1865: 1.

41. Arthur MacDonald, *Girls Who Answer "Personals": A Sociologic and Scientific Study of Young Women, Including Letters of American and European Girls in Answer to Personal Advertisements, with a Bibliography*, 2d ed. (Washington, D.C.: Self-published), 5.

42. "The Marriage Market," *Living Age*, May 29, 1897: 624.

43. MacDonald, *Abnormal Woman*, 94.

44. *NYH*, March 3, 1878: 19; *NYH*, January 5, 1862: 7.

45. Lystra, *Searching the Heart*, 133.

46. *NYH*, March 12, 1860: 3; *NYH*, December 7, 1862: 8.

47. *NYT*, March 5, 1866: 2; *NYH*, April 6, 1858: 1; *NYH*, December 29, 1860: 11.

48. *NYT*, March 9, 1866: 1; *Atlanta Constitution*, October 22, 1899: 10; *NYH*, February

11, 1863: 7. The first quote is from a song entitled "Someone to Love" (1860), the second is from the play *Der Sohn der Wildnes* (1843) by the Austrian playwright Frederick Halm; *Atlanta Constitution*, July 3, 1898: 11; *NYT*, March 21, 1866: 1.

49. *NYT*, March 24, 1866: 2; *NYH*, February 11, 1863: 7.

50. MacDonald, *Abnormal Woman*, 22, 90, 91.

51. "Matrimonial Advertisements," *Chicago Tribune*, 12.

52. Norma Basch, *Framing American Divorce: From the Revolutionary Generation to the Victorians* (Berkeley: University of California Press, 1999), 3.

53. Michael Grossberg, *Governing the Hearth: Law and the Family in Nineteenth-Century America* (Chapel Hill: University of North Carolina Press, 1985), 18.

54. "Matrimonial Man-Traps," *Georgia Weekly Telegraph Journal & Messenger*, September 16, 1881: F.

55. Nancy Cott, *Public Vows: A History of Marriage and the Nation* (Cambridge, Mass.: Harvard University Press, 2000), 155.

56. "The Wife Market: Ambiguous Phraseology of Matrimonial Advertisements—Seeking a Life Partner in the Newspapers," *St Louis Globe-Democrat*, November 14, 1885: Col E, 7.

57. "A Bad Way to Get Married," *Knickerbocker* 60, no. 4 (October 1862): 351–353.

58. MacDonald, *Abnormal Woman*, 96.

59. "She Came for Him," *Atlanta Constitution*, May 31, 1891: 7.

60. "Not Young, but So Romantic," *New York Times*, December 12, 1893: 3.

61. Iris Shur, "The Shur Thing: Computer Dating, '60s Style," *Naples Daily News*, March 22, 2010, http://www.naplesnews.com/news/2010/mar/22/shur-thing-computer-dating-60s-style (accessed April 9, 2010); Iris Shur, "Re: Data Mate," email message to the author, April 13, 2010.

62. Match.com and Chadwick Martin Bailey 2009–2010 Studies, "Recent Trends: Online Dating," http://cp.match.com/cppp/media/CMB_Study.pdf (accessed September 10, 2010).

63. Match.com and Chadwick Martin Bailey; eHarmony.com and Harris Interactive, "Study: 542 People Married Every Day in U.S., on Average, through eHarmony," http://www.eharmony.com/press/release/31 (accessed September 10, 2010).

64. Amy Harmon, "Online Dating Sheds Its Stigma as Losers.com," *New York Times*, June 29, 2003, http://www.nytimes.com/2003/06/29/us/online-dating-sheds-its-stigma-as-loserscom.html?pagewanted=1 (accessed September 10, 2010); Wailon Wong, "Online Dating Grows, Sheds Stigma," *Chicago Tribune*, July 22, 2010, http://articles.chicagotribune.com/2010-07-22/business/sc-biz-0723-online-dating—20100722_1_dating-online-meeting (accessed September 10, 2010).

65. "Matrimonial Advertisements," *Milwaukee Sentinel*, December 12, 1896: 4.

66. Ellen McCarthy, "Meredith Fineman, Blogging Past the Stigma of Online Dating," *Washington Post*, August 9, 2010, http://www.washingtonpost.com/wp-dyn/content/article/2010/08/05/AR2010080507364.html (accessed September 10, 2010).

67. Wong, "Online Dating Grows," 2.

PART IV

EMOTIONS
IN SOCIETY

CHAPTER 7

RELIGION AND EMOTIONS

JOHN CORRIGAN

The practice of emotions history in the field of religious studies has developed apace with the flowering of scholarly interest in everyday practice, embodiment, locality, and the constructed self over the past several decades. Most previous religious history from the earlier twentieth century,[1] whether focused on western monotheisms or on Asian or indigenous religions, was inclined to illustrate its narratives about feeling with ideas collected from theological discourses, or, at the very least, with language sampled from Christian glossaries of belief and worship.[2] For much religious history, confessional perspectives supplied the basis for interpretation—including the preoccupation with meaning itself—and the freight of medieval and early modern scholastic arguments provided grounding for the evaluation of feeling in historical analyses of religious life. The authority of Augustine, Gregory of Nyssa, and Aquinas, filtered through Bernard, Hadewijch, Luther, a broad array of Continental Pietists, and Scottish realists still exercised a profound influence on Christian writers in the post-Enlightenment West. This came through, for example, in the writings of the German pastor Friedrich Schleiermacher (d. 1834), who identified a unique emotion, "the feeling of absolute dependence," that he presented as universally associated with religious experiences.[3] That proposal remained central to much subsequent theorizing in the nineteenth and early twentieth centuries, finding expression most famously in German theologian and comparativist Rudolf Otto's (d. 1937) *Das Heilige*, where the holy remained mysterious, feeling was transcendent, and history was replete with instances—such as the experiences of Martin Luther—that evidenced the reality of the unanalyzable and ineffable "numinous."[4]

There was good reason to look to Augustine and Aquinas and to their predecessors among ancient Greek and Roman writers. The history of emotion in the West and the history of religion in the West have been intertwined for millennia. Religion was de facto queen of the sciences long before it was officially designated "Divinity" and set upon its medieval academic throne. Following the Christian recasting of the Greek *paideia*, philosophy, rhetoric, ethics, natural science—the full *encyclopedia*—fell into orbit around religion, and the conventions of religious reasoning were applied to the production of knowledge overall, including the defining of emotion.[5] This was most noticeable in the area of ethics. That legacy remains strong, although many who draw upon Christian writers in theorizing ethics do so with a less explicit investment in transcendence than Otto or Schleiermacher. But as intellectual history of a certain sort, the nearness of emotion to religion in the historical study of ethical thought models the ongoing influence of Christian language and the assumptions of emotional universality that are inscribed on that language.[6] This is visible even in scholarly writings that address the history of non-Western ethical thought.[7] The ongoing resistance to claims for the constructedness of emotion in historical religious settings is less doctrinaire than it was in the mid to late twentieth century, but there is a strong impulse to take religious statements of emotion at face value. The result is some ongoing cultural tension between the scholarly querying of emotion and Christian-inflected thinking about religion.

In the following overview, I return occasionally to the issue of constructedness while remarking on several kinds of inquiry, including those having to do with 1) popular and official religion; 2) embodiment and objectification; 3) words, knowledge, and feelings; 4) religious meaning; and 5) prospects. I note that in the discussion below, I have not attempted to so thoroughly schematize research in the area of religion and emotion as to overlook how research in one area overlaps with that in another. Outside of the difference in voice between theologically tinctured writing (which is not receptive to constructivist interpretations) and a more standard historical approach, there is no simple way to categorize the current state of the field. Studies intersect in many ways, and it is good that we see, at this relatively early stage of a new phase of research on religion and emotion, where those intersections are and how they affect the overall project.

OFFICIAL AND POPULAR RELIGION

Late-twentieth-century historical scholarship about religion began to change as part of the surge of academic interest in the study of emotion. In historical studies, attention to emotion emerged largely as a subset of historians' turn to social history, the practice of everyday life, and reconsiderations of previous schemings of events as manifestations of "public" and "private" spheres and "official" behaviors and beliefs vis-à-vis popular culture. All this applied strongly to religious history, which was being redirected by compelling studies of early modern religion that challenged the previous focus on religious orthodoxy and official authority with detailed cases of the ubiquity, vitality, and power of popular religion. Historical analysis of the religious lives of Europeans was reoriented by degrees to a consideration of religious activity that took place outside the parameters set by orthodox determinations of sacred calendar, holy place, and vested authority. It especially challenged the tendency of previous religious historians to conceive of feeling as a mostly private matter—what Luther felt in his prayer closet as he wrestled with thoughts about salvation—while taking public worship, doctrine, and authority as the principal components of the religious world. Just as Emile Durkheim in the early twentieth century had discovered in the seemingly private worlds of suicide and religious experience a profoundly social phenomenon, so also did historians find emotional performances to be central to religious life in both official and unofficial settings. They accordingly inquired into the performance of emotion in religious practice as it was evidenced in harvest festivals, at dinner tables, and on pilgrimages as much as in religious ceremony, public worship, or otherwise before the altar.[8] The "thick description" promoted by anthropologist Clifford Geertz as a means of articulating the process of construction of social performances, and the application of that approach to historical investigation—visible in the writing of Robert Darnton, among others—contributed to the redirecting of researchers' attention to a focus on locality. That development in turn opened possibilities for taking the immediate social and material contexts of religious activities as keys to understanding emotional expression.[9]

The turn to the study of emotion among academics who study religion—a turn fostered by developments in the social sciences—was abetted by the maturation of religious studies as a field shedding theological baggage that directly or indirectly had shaped its agenda for decades. The late-twentieth-century concentration of religion scholars in state universities served as a platform for rethinking theory, research agendas, styles of argument, and curriculum. The default position of scholars with regard to the role of emotion in religion—that it was an irreducible datum that could be marshaled in a pinch to explain behavior and belief—began to give way to more precise formulations of both emotion and religion. As scholars became less anxious about "reducing" religion to social or biological factors, traditional debates about reductionism increasingly were dismissed as shopworn and unproductive, with the result that space was cleared for bolder investigations of emotion as an analyzable aspect of religious life.

The historical study of religion and emotion accordingly was advanced, initially, through close scrutiny of local religious events, such as in William A. Christian Jr.'s analysis of religious weeping at several sites in early modern Iberia. Drawing insight from ethnographies by Alfred Radcliffe-Brown and Charles Wagley, Christian saw in Holy Week processions, Lenten events, and certain other occasional rituals the enactment of a public drama of provoked weeping. Taking weeping as a learned behavior that expressed feeling at the same time that it prompted it, Christian observed how the spectacle of weeping was framed by local beliefs about the importance of emotional display before God. Weeping, moreover, was required as a sign to neighbors that a person was invested in the public dramas that defined membership in the religious collective. Holy Week worship, among other ritual enactments, was important because it effectively staged the collective weeping that signaled to others— and to oneself—the state of one's "heart," itself a sociotheological construction. Such occasions evidenced that "a science for provoking public tears and compassion existed, with specialized, artists, sculptors, choreographers, and actors."[10] The significance of such emotional religious performances was multifaceted, but crucial was the fostering of a sense of collective identity among participants. What individuals found "meaningful"—or, perhaps more precisely, how they felt their place before God—in their personal pursuit of salvation was inseparable from their sense of belonging to an emotional community. Their commitment to vigilance in maintaining the interrelationships that formed that community, or, as could be the case, multiple communities each of which could have different styles of material religion, was of crucial importance for historical inquiry. Historians, even while focusing on local or narrowly conceptualized communities, embedded those communities in larger social and cultural contexts, and especially in broadly defined religious traditions (e.g., Catholicism, Zen Buddhism, Judaism, etc.). That approach has made it possible to understand something more of the emotional aspect in religion through the observation of differences or similarities (or both) between official and popular religion. Carlos M. N. Eire, in his study of early modern Spanish piety, called attention specifically to the linkage between feeling and the material culture of Catholic devotionalism both inside and outside the church. Eire details a highly emotional religious milieu in which the official power of crucifixes and representations of the Virgin Mary to stimulate feeling was matched by the power of bones, sinews, skin, and the garments of saints, among a great many other artifacts treasured by the ordinary people.

The boundary between formal religion and popular religion, as many historians of the late twentieth century were proposing, was porous and shifting so that emotional identities could be multidimensional and complex. While fear—of death and of judgment—was central to most emotional scenes, informing the weeping of the overwrought Philip II as well as the laborers who exhumed the body of St. Theresa, it was not the only emotion that mattered. Hope, especially as it was manifest in popular religious practice, could characterize membership in one group, while fear and other emotions, or combinations of them, could be found to predominate in other contexts.[11] In some instances, persons could be pulled in different directions by competing emotional cultures or drawn forcefully from one into the other. Susan Karant-Nunn's recent *The Reformation of Feeling: Shaping the Religious Emotions in Early Modern Germany* details the manner in which Protestant, Reformed, and Lutheran emotional "tenors" were created in the sixteenth century through the influence of emergent popular forms, the reemphasis of official tradition, and the negotiated blendings of components from each. Karant-Nunn demonstrates, for example, how sermons and material culture signaled to Lutheran churchgoers that late medieval "emotion-oriented piety was at an end." That piety was recast as a concentrated emphasis on masculinized demonstrations of faith that modeled composure and control, over against the recklessness of female emotionality. Pulpit messages were one way in which that shift was fostered, but so was the redecoration of Lutheran churches. The depictions of agonized bodies in the image of the crucifixion or in the torture of martyrs, which aroused the emotions of fear and terror among late medieval Christians, became less common in Lutheran churches in favor of art depicting outward tranquility as a marker of deep and careful reflection about sin, atonement, and salvation. Karant-Nunn suggests that the calm gaze of Jesus in the Wittenberg altarpiece represented that shift. Women, as emblems of loss of emotional control, all but disappeared from the inventories of holy art in Lutheran churches as those churches were readorned. Emotion, for Lutherans, did not disappear, however. It was remade in ways that fitted Lutheran theological interests and that represented the distancing of Lutheranism from some characteristic features of formal Catholic piety, as well as the selective embrace of aspects of popular religion that were manifest in art, stories and legends, ritual behaviors, and elsewhere.[12]

Although historians have found the give and take of official and popular religion a fruitful entry point into studying emotion, most research bearing on emotion still is undertaken with respect to specific religious groups. Sometimes those groups are identified in very general ways as Catholics, Protestants, Hindus, or Muslims, while at other times scholars have defined their investigations more narrowly by geography, period, or the size of the religious body, focusing for example on Sri Lankan monks, or mid-nineteenth-century Protestant Bostonians, or a small cluster of Egyptian bedouins.[13] The returns for emotions history so far have been strongest when the context is delimited but the breadth and depth of tradition are recognized. Part of the reason for that is that religious historians of the last several decades have cultivated a way of working back and forth between the analysis of individual lives, closely examined, and the broader social worlds in which those lives were lived, rather than seeking to characterize religious dynamics and religious change over very expansive geographical frames and sweeping chronologies. More to the point, there also has been an entrenched tendency of historians to prioritize community in their investigations of religion for historical reasons having to do with the residue of nineteenth-century attempts to demonstrate the superiority of one religion over another and the functionality of one religious community as superior to its competitors. Much religious history remains denomination-centric, focused on a religious group rather than a place or a period. Some of the best historical investigations of religion and emotion, then, represent a form of community studies, often along the lines suggested by medievalist Barbara Rosenwein, whose *Emotional Communities in the Early Middle Ages* articulated a way of doing emotions history that addressed "groups in which people adhere to the same norms of emotional expression and value—or devalue—the same or related emotions."[14]

Communities of religious persons can be of different sorts. Generally, adherence to a particular faith is made to define a group, but there are additional ways in which a community can be identified consistent with that designation. Carole Lansing's investigation of ritual mourning in the thirteenth-century commune of Orvieto takes civic activity alongside religious belief to be a key marker of official religious community. The study also represents something of the way in which much recent scholarship on religion and emotion moves thoughtfully between deep analysis of relatively small communities and a concern for wider backgrounds against which that community can be observed. In *Passion and Order: Restraint of Grief in the Medieval Italian Communes*, Lansing begins with an account involving 220 males (including 43 who were titled) who were fined for mourning the dead—a breach of the laws that they themselves had enacted. Moving from there to glimpses of broader religious and political contexts Lansing eventually returns to the Orvieto incident armed with a range of insights that enable her to make sense of the emotional lives of men who could not resist expressing their grief, with likewise appropriate comment on the roles of women. With emotional expression (and especially the gendering of emotion) at the center of her analysis, she demonstrates the interweaving of political experiences drawn from broadly shared cultural backgrounds with religious ideas and rituals in a small community of Christian mourners.[15] Phyllis Mack's study of men and women in early Methodism (which likewise stresses the gendering of emotion), treats religious community as a close-knit association of writers rather than as persons who practiced their daily lives together in a commune. Mack's approach is oriented toward understanding the shared aspects of the religious lives of Methodist writers such as Mary Fletcher, Samuel Bradburn, James Rogers, and John Pawson against the background of Puritan, pietist, and Enlightenment discourses about emotion. She moves between that larger canvas of intellectual influences and the shared agenda of the small-scale early Methodist community in describing how Methodists together conceptualized emotion and pursued it in religious practice. Her analysis of Methodists' everyday activities shows how men and women endeavored to cultivate emotion in their devotional lives by ascetical practices of varying intensity, believing that by experiencing even a small part of the suffering of Christ, they would be drawn into a deeper emotional connection with him. That ascetical impulse ran counter to an emerging Enlightenment view of the body that focused on its beauty and usefulness and stressed the importance of caring for it. The experience of emotional connection with God that came through denying the body food, drink, sleep, or other requirements for health had to be measured against the dangers of mistreating the body. So, for example, Mary Fletcher wrote that "I know that I have no right to hurt my body," but "on Mondays and Fridays I would omit butter in the morning, eating dry bread, and as usual rosemary tea without sugar. For dinner, water gruel, with salt and pepper, and, as on other days, teas for my supper. This cannot hurt my health."[16]

EMBODIMENT AND OBJECTIFICATION

Another way by which communities have been defined in studies of religion and emotion is as consuming communities, or in other words, as communities that objectify emotion in specific ways and share rules for handling it. June McDaniel, writing about emotion in Bengali *bhakti* traditions, has observed how *bhakti* promotes the cultivation of emotion as a means to union with God.

Emotion, however, like consciousness, is understood as substantial rather than conceptual and, as *rasa*, is a refined essence that is akin to "sap" or "juice." As substances, emotions have physical attributes. They can be hot or cold, collected and churned, flow like a river, taste like honey or clarified butter, and cooked from raw states into something aesthetic and religious. If emotion was intangible or invisible, it would be inaccessible. As substance it is available to play its key role in advancing one's spiritual state. Over time, such distinctive understandings of emotion have endured in Hinduism, clearly marking specific communities such as the Vaishnavites. A focus on a very specific and distinctive experience of emotion offers historians in this case the opportunity to track the development of a religious community over the *longue durée*, in the spirit of the "psychological" histories conceived by annalistes Marc Bloch and Julian Febvre.[17] Moreover, that kind of approach, as Paul M. Toomey has shown in his own study of *bhakti* traditions, can include a strongly constructivist aspect, as evidenced in his own research on the local construction of emotion as certain kinds of food in Hindu devotionalism at Mount Govardhan. Food there is prepared, shared, and consumed according to certain performance codes.[18]

The act of consumption more precisely is the topic of John Corrigan's inquiry into the emotional lives of mid-nineteenth-century Protestant Bostonians. Corrigan notes that while the mass performances of emotion in revivals issued from centuries-old conceptions of emotion as a crucial component of religious experience, the Boston revivals were contextualized by immediate events that made the performances modern. Bostonians' reflections on the financial panic of 1857, the changing nature of the relationship between parents and children and between spouses, shifting gender codes, and the powerful emergence of ideas about the free market all contributed to a rethinking of emotion as a commodity that was traded to God in exchange for spiritual and material benefits. In the emotional community of Boston Protestants, emotion increasingly was objectified and traded as a commodity between persons, and to God, according to performance rules that were coded in church teachings, marriage contracts, public media, and elsewhere. A revival-goer, for example, made a request on a slip of paper prior to the service—asking for spiritual succor but also for a better job, the cure of a sick child, a spouse, a new roof—and then during the service "gave the heart" to God in exchange for that favor. Prayer manuals and religious magazines referred frequently to the "business of religion," organizers issued "stock certificates" for "mansions in the sky" to those who pledged to "give the heart" to God, and newspaper articles explained that the emotionally expressive "business men's *prayer meetings* are simply prayer meetings, on *business principles.*"[19] There are some precedents to notice in such a scheme—such as in earlier Roman Catholic devotionalism—but the upshot for historians is that modern communities can find their way into being modern in different ways. In some cases (such as this one), modern conceptualizations and performances of emotion spread outward from the communities in which they coalesced and spurred broader reconceptualizations across regional or national populations. The emotional culture of revivals in Boston and New York, which took shape within an urban environment keenly aware of the pervasiveness of formal commodities markets, spread across most of the eastern half of the nation.

Interpretation emphasizing materiality and the objectification of emotion generally has been undertaken most effectively in studies that stress the cultural construction of emotion in religion. Researchers have for several decades experimented with strategies for identifying local codes of emotional life and their linkages to religion. Researchers also have been attentive to the risk of steering analysis too far into constructionist interpretation that might miss emotional expression that challenges culturally derived standards for feeling or that undermines human inventiveness.[20] Some of the studies of religious weeping that followed upon work by Christian and Eire reflect those considerations. Eliot R. Wolfson's investigation of the weeping of sixteenth-century Jewish mystics framed ecstatic experience with reference to sleep, death, vision, human sexual anatomy, and gender. For Wolfson, the key to understanding that weeping (and the emotional programs relevant to Jewish mysticism more generally) was to consider how the act of weeping was framed by a complex symbolic system that served both to elicit tears and to explain them. Such an approach enriched the argument for the scripting of emotion in religious settings at the same time that it suggested how weeping as a devotional exercise was involved in the invention of religious ideas and the alteration of a symbolic system.[21] Gary L. Ebersole took the analysis of ritual weeping further in that direction by stressing that historical actors are not automatons who respond passively to what custom requires. He argued that certain ritual weeping, far from being reducible to cultural scripts, could take place in protest against perceived unfairness in the social order. He explained how emotional display at the Shi-ite Muslim festival of Muharram, as a "symbolic currency in a moral economy," is understandable as an expression of minority identity, unfolding against the grain of cultural expectations.[22] Such scholarship has played an important role in demonstrating the necessity of considering local context and the power of what Peter N. Stearns and Carol Z. Stearns have called "emotionology"—the social and cultural standards for emotional display—alongside embodied emotion understood at least in part as biologically driven behaviors that occur across cultures.[23] Emphasis on the body, both as a canvas for portraying cultural mores and as a source of creativity that can subvert those mores, has increased as scholars have learned to frame their inquiries about emotion with respect to the body. Some research, such as Helene Basu's investigation of Sufi saints in India, has argued that emotional performances in religious life in fact contribute in key ways to the construction of counter discourses that reverse status orders (i.e., caste ranking) and invent alternative taxonomies of values.[24]

The approach to religious history that is most ambitious in its attention to the biological substrata of emotional life is the current work of historian Robert C. Fuller, who has argued for the role of hard-wired emotional programs in religious history.[25] Dealing with emotions in religious history though emphasizing biological considerations is especially challenging however and involves more than the usual amount of guesswork as researchers find themselves having to estimate the endocrinology, genetic makeup, neural functioning, and brain activity of religious persons long dead. Like the emergence of psychohistory in the mid–twentieth century, an emotions history that attempts to integrate the material body into a narrative about religion has to rely on theory—some of which is barely coalesced in science journals—to explain the behaviors of historical actors for whom there is little biological evidence. Just as psychohistory blanketed the lives of persons such as Martin Luther and Rabelais with psychoanalytic theory, so also does a radically materialistic approach to the history of religion and emotion require the investigator to step out onto a high wire of interpretation. Nevertheless, it is clear that historians increasingly find the prospect of shifting from a focus on the culturally constructed body to the raw biology of religious life to offer intriguing opportunities for framing new understandings of religious history. This is especially noticeable as a ripple effect of the strong recent interest in cognitive science among those who work in religious studies more generally. A strongly evolutionary approach to emotion characterizes much of this scholarship.[26]

WORDS, KNOWLEDGE, AND FEELING

Modern histories of religion typically have turned to religious texts, and related textual materials, to build interpretations of emotion in religion. Here we touch on new ways to use intellectual materials of the sort discussed at the outset of the essay. Some research has tracked specific tropes through scriptures, theological writings, prayer books, sermons, and other writings in the interest of clarifying how people conceived of specific emotions and how they understood the relation of a certain emotional state to their spiritual status. Typical in this regard is Charles Lloyd Cohen's analysis of Puritan piety, which he assesses not with ongoing reference to modern psychological theories but through analysis of the intellectual assumptions—such as Renaissance faculty-humoral psychology—that framed thinking about emotion in the sixteenth and seventeenth centuries. Drawing largely upon sermons and doctrinal statements, and asserting that "historical actors knew more about themselves than we ever will," Cohen describes how an emotional complex made up of love, anger, and fear was central to the religious lives of Puritans. He demonstrates how certain written and spoken words or phrases—"fear of God" for example—described and sometimes elicited emotional states but also how such words joined everyday Puritan piety to a well-developed theological system that informed official statements about ethics and salvation. His analysis, while confined to explicit textual references to specific emotions, nevertheless succeeds in indicating something of the ambiguity and fluidity of emotions in religious life because of his willingness to work back and forth between official clerical pronouncements about feeling in religion and the popular appropriation and partial reshaping of official emotional guidelines.[27]

The importance of emotional words embedded in religious texts is evidenced as well in Catherine Peyroux's historical study of the seventh-century Frankish figure of St. Gertrude. Working from the hagiographic *Life of St. Gertrude*, Peyroux offers interpretation that is narrow in one sense—it is an inquiry into the meaning of one word, *furor*—but that is fruitfully expansive in its attempt to build from the significations of that word a view of a shared culture of emotion, the "affective world of Frankish nobility." While exploring various medieval linguistic idioms indicating anger, she pointedly asks why Gertrude flew into such a rage when her parents proposed a candidate for marriage. Exploring where previous historians had failed to detect a lead, Peyroux shows how Gertrude's emotional state, as reported by the *Life*, is the key to understanding her vocation, which she conceived as a marriage to God. In the process, Peyroux implies how even a narrow focus on text can disclose a complex emotional world.[28]

In her emotional portrait of Gertude, Peyroux remarks on the relationship between cognition and feeling and how moral judgment was related to *furor*. That theme, especially in studies that favor close readings of classic texts, has continued to inform historical studies of religion and emotion. The intertwining of emotion and cognition in Western philosophical discourses (and especially those before Descartes), as we have seen, suggests such an approach. But text-centered historical study of religion and emotion has for the most part done a good job of attending to the slipperiness of the categories of "knowledge," "passion," and "reason" that typically organize this kind of scholarship. That awareness has been elevated by recent philosophical writing such as that of Robert

Solomon, which has advanced the case for cognitive emotions.[29] A willingness to play on the boundary of feeling and knowledge is evident, for example, in Debra K. Shuger's study of Renaissance sacred writings about morals and metaphysics. Shuger demonstrates how appeals to emotion worked hand-in-glove with literary designs that were geared to persuade through references to knowledge. Knowledge in that respect was itself "passionate," and the emotional power of sacred rhetoric was marshaled to present truth in a "nonliteral, nontransparent language."[30] A similar sort of sensitivity to the ambiguity of emotions language in classic religious texts is visible in Anna M. Gade's writing about emotions in Sufism, which shows an "affective understanding of the moral order." The Qur'an and *hadith*, alongside a cluster of Muslim hagiographies, served in early Islam as bases for the coalescence in Sufism of a process whereby emotions became aestheticized. Emotive experience was conceptually joined with the didactic power of the message of the Qur'an, and that interplay of affect and cognition was practiced through the cultivation of sentiment in the musical recitation of poetry. Emotion was understood neither as merely cognition nor embodied experience but as a technique of joining the individual with the social, the body with thought.[31]

That description of emotion as an experience that is present through the medium of public practice (e.g., Qur'an recitation) and that is neither strictly constructionist nor entirely the product of free agency also has been central to the writing of historian William Reddy. For Reddy, emotion arises "from interaction between our emotional capacities and the unfolding of historical circumstances." His conceptualization of the relationship between what individuals feel and cultural commands for the performance of feeling shapes his analysis of the emotional culture of Revolutionary France. Reddy points to the rise of sentimentalism in Europe in the eighteenth century and its replacement in France by "reason" after 1795 (with its vast consequences for religion). Sentimentalism as the official emotional style of the Revolution soon proved its flaws, however, because of "its naturalism, the doctrine that emotional sensitivity constituted an inborn moral sense." The sentimental heart was too private a conceptualization of emotion for the purposes of the modern state, where a new kind of public life that theoretically was organized around the principles of reason and liberty promised a greater range of freedom in emotional life. For Reddy, historical circumstances proved too much for the survival of sentimentalism as a dominant "emotive," but history also drew emotional life in a new direction by allowing the individual a greater range of emotional expression. Like Shuger and Gade, Reddy offers an approach to the historical study of emotion that steps away from inflexible dyadic categories of body and mind, cultural constructedness and human agency, and private initiative and public action. In that space, as Reddy writes, "'emotions' come to life, to vex, enlighten, guide, encumber, to reveal goal conflicts we have overlooked, to aid us in overlooking others. When we speak of such matters, we inevitably alter their configuration."[32]

It is that space, again, that Buddhologist Jeffrey Samuels explores in his analysis of the roots of Buddhist community among monks in Sri Lanka. Shying from approaches that build emotional histories by stressing either, on the one hand, constructedness, relativity, and cognitive attributes or, on the other hand, universality, embodiment, and agency, Samuels proposes a linkage between emotion and aesthetics. He treats aesthetics as a set of standards that prompt and guide emotion at the same time that they serve as cultural judgments that continuously influence aesthetic sensibilities. In short, Samuels, like some others who have studied religion and emotion, proposes that the writing of histories of religious texts, communities, and persons must proceed with an eye to the emotional actor as agent as much as to the processes that pull the individual's behavior into line with cultural standards for feeling.[33]

RELIGIOUS MEANING

To speak of the search for middle ground in historical studies of religion and emotion is to rehearse what already is known by scholars in most areas of the study of emotion. After a late-twentieth-century rally of enthusiasms about cultural construction, biology, radical locality, and so forth, historical researchers have sought ways to demonstrate the centrality of political, economic, and social factors and the power of culture to make selves, while seeking to avoid the flattening of subjectivities in historical narratives. A related issue, and one that arises especially in the context of the study of religion, has to do with the relation of emotion to religious meaning. Scholarship in religion, including the history of religion, long has been focused on what certain words, texts, rituals, dress, foods, and feelings *mean* to persons. In that project, they have disclosed their collaboration with the presumption—underlying most Western scholarship about religion—that persons engage in religious activities because such activities are meaningful. But meaning, like emotion, is an ambiguous term, and especially so for modernity. Its invocation might have less to do with its adequacy as a category for sorting the experience of modernity than its reflection of religiously grounded bias. Specifically, some scholars wonder whether the preoccupation with meaning is an artifact of Christianity and whether there are instances when we ought to set it aside as a prime criterion—as a central element of a hermeneutics—in our analysis of belief and action. Clifford Geertz, mentioned earlier, has been important for his influence on the history of emotion generally and especially for his emphases upon the constructed self, context, and human drive to build meaningful lives within meaningful cultures.

In the historical study of religion and emotion, however, we must consider that a way of doing emotions history that is preoccupied with meaning can fail to make lives, behaviors, and events understandable. Geertzian framings of interpretation, as Talal Asad has noticed, can overvalue meaning and continue to seek for it when it is elusive, opaque, or illegible.[34] In studies by Shuger, Gade, Reddy, and Samuels, we have seen how scholars stretch categories of feeling and thought, body and mind, public and private, among others, to arrive at interpretative standpoints that enable them to finesse the question of how emotion is understood and practiced "meaningfully" within religious or parareligious communities. Those interpretations hinge on the translation of emotion into morality, aesthetic standards, beliefs, and rituals, all characteristic features of culture rationally structured and meaningfully arrayed. Such an approach is useful, and in some cases leads to important beachfronts in the exploration of religion as an emotional phenomenon. But, like Reddy's French who were constrained in their emotional lives by a social discipline that rendered emotion as sentimentalism, scholarship in this area risks missing potentially key aspects of emotion in religion by construing the emotional lives of people as inherently meaningful simply because they are lived within recognizable communities in historically definable milieus.

In historical analysis of religious events and behaviors we have to accept that emotion does not always represent religious meaning and that religion can provoke emotionality that is insusceptible to analysis according to what we might identify as shared codes of feeling. We need to keep in mind that the practice of religion, like all cultural practice, is about "webs of mystification as well as signification."[35] We should recognize with Matthew Engelke that there are "moments in ritual where ambiguity is central to the unfolding of events"[36] and that emotion often is crucial to those moments. Emotion should not be construed a priori as linked to doctrine, ethics, judgment, or individual agency, and should not be presumed, when scrutinized, to lay bare in its performance the architecture of the complex social ordering of communes. The historical study of religion and emotion, as it has demystified emotion, has taken major steps toward identifying how feeling is manifest in religious cultures and how religious identity is constructed in and through emotional life. We nevertheless should not forget that previous depictions of emotion—as in the cases of Schleiermacher and Otto, whose ideas were the subject of the beginning of this essay—are not so hopelessly parochial that nothing of their approach can be salvaged. While we should continue to resist the view of emotion in religion as an irreducible datum and as such a potential signifier of the supernatural or divine, we should retain as a working theory the insight that human experience and collective identity are sometimes ambiguous, that meanings are not always clear, that clarity is not always useful to religious life, and that we should not habitually demand meaning from emotional performances in the interest of enabling rapprochement with other historical discursives.

In short, there is a danger of overinterpretation of which we should remain aware. As we "re-launch a discussion" of emotions history, as Peter N. Stearns has proposed in the first chapter, we should keep in view the two ends of a spectrum as they have come into focus in the study of religion and emotion: the role of ambiguity and mystery at one end and the importance of clarity and meaning at the other. That naming of the spectrum, while appearing general and broadly applicable to other areas of emotions history, has much relevance specifically for religion. Religious history will have to continue to develop ways to address the ambiguous in religious life, and the history of emotions will have to devise ways to identify data that will allow us to navigate there.

The recent study of emotion in religion has developed through attention to several themes, some of which occasionally are interlocked in interpretation. Much scholarship has focused on local religion and the details about individual lives that are discernible in small, relatively close-knit communities. Such research, however, has been framed to various extents by consideration of broader contexts of extralocal clerical leadership, state political power, and orthodox belief/practice. Historians generally have moved between different scales of community in studying emotion in religious life, and that movement has proven useful in as much as it has allowed for consideration of the ways in which innovations in the conception or performance of emotion take place locally even as emotional codes are disciplined by broader cultural authorities. There also has been much attention to the body and to religious ideas about emotion as substance. Studies in that vein, like some work that is focused on local religion, sometimes stress the ways in which emotion is constructed in culture. There is debate, however, about the role of biology in the emotional aspects of religious life, with some arguing that interpretation must take seriously biological states that are not conditioned by culture. Another kind of approach to emotion emphasizes the relation between emotion and cognition, with a particular focus on language and its relationship to feeling and to knowing. Much work in all of these areas has been concerned to some extent with the "meaning" of emotions, an orientation that runs the risk of too easily fitting emotional religion into interpretative grids that have been built to understand meaningfulness in other parts of culture. The emotional lives of religious subjects can get lost in such an enterprise.

PROSPECTS

How we do emotions history then, as far as religion is concerned, has much to do with continuing to explore in territories where currently there are beach-heads, including everyday practice, embodiment, locality, and the constructed self, among others. Biology can and should be integrated into that enterprise, though how and to what extent that will permit an integrated interpretation is still an open question. I propose three additional areas in which I foresee potentially strong returns on scholarly investment. First, by taking the recent "spatial turn" seriously and engaging the growing interdisciplinary scholarship about space and place, historians of religion and emotion can move beyond deadlocked debates—and outmoded language—about "sacred space" and "holy place." The investigation of space and place as it has been broached in recent books such as *Emotional Geographies* and *Emotion, Place and Culture* would help to alter the current approach, which too often takes space as an empty receptacle that is filled by culture, where "geography often presents us with an emotionally barren terrain, a world devoid of passion, spaces ordered solely by rational principles."[37] The experience of space and the process of place-making are central elements of how communities develop codes that order emotional life. It is debatable whether the emotional experience of being in the desert at night, as the French historian Ernst Renan argued, defines the origins of mono-theistic religious belief.[38] But the critical consideration of space can broaden the field of investigation for those already focused on embodiment, permit-ting analysis that embeds the physical body in physical space, and in so doing, enabling fuller interpretation of emotion in the religion that is practiced there.

Second, the historical study of religion and emotion has much to gain from collaboration with the emergent digital humanities. The algorithmic querying of massive digital corpora, such as the *Early American Imprints* and *Early English Books*, can lead to the construction of large linguistic datasets of emotions terms that potentially can be correlated with linguistic markers of religion. Forays in this direction have suggested that work with datasets of scale can yield insights that are not obtainable from analysis of small communities.[39] By advancing on this front, studies of emotion and religion that already are designed as linguistic analyses potentially can establish much broader databases for investigating the relation of emotional cultures to cognitive regimes, including ideologies and epistemologies. A study of Puritan emotional life, for example, might develop from the focus on "fear of God" as expressed in a limited sample of Puritan writings to a very broad consideration of all of the uses of "fear" within English and American writing from the sixteenth–eighteenth centuries and the religious and political ideas associated with those usages.

Third, researchers can learn from the surge of scholarship on religious violence since 9/11. That violence typically has strong emotional components and identifies the often self-destructive nature of religious violence—a window into the ambiguity of feeling and its complicated relationship to cognitive aspects of religious life. Investigation of emotion with an eye to religion and violence would steer emotions histories away from the convenient focus on rational strategies of emotional expression and concealment into waters where persons sometimes act against their self-interest, "rational choice" is a less compelling interpretive option, and questions about finality spar with concerns about historical contingency and relativism. More of a focus on violence would help to correct the preoccupation with rational "meanings" that can flaw work in this area. Religion is sometimes rational and sometimes it is not. Emotions in religion are sometimes understandable as part of a broader system of meaning and sometimes they are not. When we examine cases of religious frictions and especially religious violence—undertaken by groups against their own members as well as against other groups—we see more of the ways in which emotions are less predictable and less systematically arranged in religious life than we might otherwise.

NOTES

1. See John Corrigan, Eric Crump, and John Kloos, *Emotion and Religion: An Annotated Bibliography and Critical Assessment* (Westport, Conn.: Greenwood Press, 2000).

2. Part 3 of Corrigan, Crump, and Kloos, *Emotion and Religion*, is replete with examples of such writing; see pp. 212–218.

3. See the essays in John Corrigan, ed., *The Oxford Handbook of Religion and Emotion* (New York: Oxford University Press, 2008), Part 4, 349–473; Freidrich Schleiermacher, *On Religion: Speeches to Its Cultured Despisers*, trans. and ed. Richard Crouter (New York: Cambridge University Press, 1996); and Schleiermacher, *The Christian Faith*, trans. H. R. Mackintosh and J. S. Stewart (London: T&T Clark, 1999).

4. Rudolf Otto, *The Idea of the Holy*, trans. John W. Harvey (New York: Oxford, 1958).

5. Andrew S. Jacobs "What Has Rome to Do with Bethlehem? Cultural Capital(s) and Religious Imperialism in Late Ancient Christianity," *Classical Receptions Journal* 3 (2011), 29–45.

6. Diana Fritz Cates, "The Religious Dimension of Ordinary Human Emotions," *Jour-

nal of the Society of Christian Ethics 25 (2005), 35–53; Martha C. Nussbaum, Upheavals of Thought: The Intelligence of Emotions (Cambridge: Cambridge University Press, 2001).

7. For criticisms of Western attempts to narrate Asian histories of emotion, see Owen M. Lynch, ed., Divine Passions: The Social Construction of Emotion in India (Berkeley: University of California Press, 1990).

8. Emile Durkheim, Suicide, trans. John A. Spalding (New York: Free Press, 1997); and Durkheim, The Elementary Forms of the Religious Life, trans. Carol Cosman (New York: Oxford, 2001).

9. Clifford Geertz, The Interpretation of Cultures (New York: Basic Books, 1977); Robert Darnton, The Great Cat Massacre and Other Episodes in French Cultural History (New York: Vintage, 1985); Richard A. Schweder and Robert A. Levine, eds., Culture Theory: Essays on Mind, Self, and Emotion (New York: Cambridge University Press, 1984).

10. William A. Christian Jr., "Provoked Religious Weeping in Early Modern Spain," in Religious Organization and Religious Experience, ed. J. Davis (London: Academic Press, 1982), 97–114. Quote is from page 112. See also Timothy Mitchell, Passional Culture: Emotion, Religion, and Society in Southern Spain (Philadelphia: University of Pennsylvania Press, 1984).

11. Carlos M. N. Eire, From Madrid to Purgatory: The Art and Craft of Dying in Sixteenth-Century Spain (New York: Cambridge University Press, 1995).

12. Susan Karant-Nunn, The Reformation of Feeling: Shaping the Religious Emotions in Early Modern Germany (New York: Oxford University Press, 2010), 65.

13. Lila Aba-Lughod, Veiled Sentiments: Honor and Poetry in a Bedouin Society (Berkeley: University of California Press, 2000) focuses on a community of Muslims in western Egypt but also notices the divisions in that community and how they are manifest in emotional life.

14. Barbara Rosenwein, Emotional Communities in the Early Middle Ages (Ithaca, N.Y.: Cornell University Press, 2006), 2.

15. Carole Lansing, Passion and Order: Restraint of Grief in Medieval Italian Communes, in the book series Conjunctions of Religion and Power in the Medieval Past (Ithaca, N.Y.: Cornell University Press, 2008), 10.

16. Phyllis Mack, Heart Religion in the British Enlightenment: Gender and Emotion in Early Methodism (New York: Cambridge University Press, 2008), 202.

17. June McDaniel, "Emotion in Bengali Religious Thought: Substance and Metaphor," in Religion and Emotion: Approaches and Interpretations, ed. John Corrigan (New York: Oxford University Press, 2004), 249–270. Lucien Febvre's well-known "Histoire et psychologie" (1938) and "Comment reconstituer la vie affective d'autrefois? La sensibilite et l'histoire" (1941) are seminal. Marc Bloch's early contributions likewise are important. See John Corrigan, "History, Religion, and Emotion: An Historiographical Survey," in Business of the Heart: Religion and Emotion in the Nineteenth Century (Berkeley: University of California Press, 2002), "Appendix A," 269–280.

18. Paul M. Toomey, "Krishna's Consuming Passions: Food as Metaphor and Metonym for Emotion at Mount Govardhan," in Corrigan, Religion and Emotion, 223–248.

19. Corrigan, *Business of the Heart*, 220–221.

20. William R. Reddy, *The Navigation of Feeling: A Framework for the History of Emotions* (New York: Cambridge University Press, 2001). See also chapter 8, "Emotion and Political Change," by Nicole Eustace in this volume.

21. Eliot R. Wolfson, "Weeping, Death, and Spiritual Ascent in Sixteenth-century Jewish Mysticism," in *Ecstasy and Other Worldly Journeys*, ed. John J. Collins and Michael A. Fishburne (Albany: SUNY Press, 1995), 209–247.

22. Gary R. Ebersole, "The Function of Ritual Weeping Revisited: Affective Expression and Moral Discourse," *History of Religions* 39 (2000), 211–246.

23. Peter N. Stearns with Carol Z. Stearns, "Emotionology: Clarifying the History of Emotions and Emotional Standards," *American Historical Review* 90 (1985), 813–836.

24. Helene Basu, "Hierarchy and Emotion: Love, Joy, and Sorrow in a Cult of Black Saints in Gujarat, India," in *Embodying Charisma: Modernity, Loyalty, and the Performance of Emotion in Sufi Cults*, ed. Pnina Werbner and Helene Basu (New York: Routledge, 1998), 117–139.

25. Robert C. Fuller, *Theology in the Flesh: Bodily Sources of Religious Experience* (New York: Oxford University Press, 2008); Fuller, and *The Body of Faith: A Biological History of Religion in America* (Chicago: University of Chicago Press, 2013); Fuller, "Wonder and Religious Sensibility: A Study in Religion and Emotion," *Journal of Religion* 86 (2006), 364–384.

26. Stewart E. Guthrie, *Faces in the Clouds: A New Theory of Religion* (New York: Oxford University Press, 1995); Pascal Boyer, *Religion Explained: The Evolutionary Origins of Religious Thought* (New York: Basic Books, 2001); Ilkka Pyysiäinen, *How Religion Works: Towards a New Cognitive Science of Religion* (The Hague: Brill, 2001); Harvey Whitehouse, *Modes of Religiosity: A Cognitive Theory of Religious Transmission* (Walnut Creek, Calif.: AltaMira Press, 2004).

27. Charles Lloyd Cohen, *God's Caress: The Psychology of Puritan Religious Experience* (New York: Oxford University Press, 1986), 20.

28. Catherine Peyroux, "Gertrude's *furor*: Reading Anger in an Early Medieval Saint's Life," in *Anger's Past: The Social Uses of Emotion in the Middle Ages*, ed. Barbara H. Rosenwein (Ithaca, N.Y.: Cornell University Press, 1998), 26–55.

29. Robert C. Solomon, *Thinking about Feeling: Contemporary Philosophers on Emotions* (New York: Oxford University Press, 2004); Solomon, *What Is an Emotion? Classic and Contemporary Readings* (New York: Oxford University Press, 2003).

30. Debra K. Shuger, "The Philosophical Foundations of Sacred Rhetoric," in *Rhetorical Invention and Religious Inquiry*, ed. Walter Jost and Wendy Olmstead (New Haven: Yale University Press, 2000), 47–64. Quote is from p. 61.

31. Anna M. Gade, *Perfection Makes Practice: Learning, Emotion, and the Recitation of the Qur-an in Indonesia* (Honolulu: University of Hawai'i Press, 2004); Gade, "Islam" in Corrigan, *Oxford Handbook of Religion and Emotion*, 43.

32. Reddy, *Navigation of Feeling*, 45, 332.

33. Jeffrey Samuels, *Attracting the Heart: Social Relations and the Aesthetics of Emotion in Sri Lankan Monastic Culture* (Honolulu: University of Hawaii Press, 2010).

34. Talal Asad, *Genealogies of Religion: Discipline and Reasons of Power in Christianity and Islam* (Baltimore: The Johns Hopkins University Press, 1993); Matthew Engelke and Matt Tomlinson, *The Limits of Meaning: Case Studies in the Anthropology of Christianity* (Oxford: Berghahn Books, 2006).

35. Roger Keesing, "Anthropology as Interpretive Quest," *Current Anthropology* 28 (1987), 161–176.

36. Matthew Engelke, "Clarity and Charisma: On the Uses of Ambiguity in Ritual Life," in Engelke and Tomlinson, *Limits of Meaning*, 64.

37. Joyce Davidson, Liz Bondi, and Mick Smith, eds., *Emotional Geographies*, (Farnham, U.K.: Ashgate, 2005), 1; Mick Smith, Joyce Davidson, Laura Cameron, and Liz Bondi, eds., *Emotion, Place, and Culture* (Farnham, U.K.: Ashgate, 2009).

38. John Corrigan, "Spatiality and Religion," in *The Spatial Turn: Interdisciplinary Perspectives*, ed. Barney Warf and Santa Arias (New York: Routledge, 2009), 158.

39. John Corrigan, "Words in Space: GIS, Data Mining, and the Visual Display of Religion," Conference on New Technologies and the Interdisciplinary Study of Religion, Harvard University, Kennedy School of Government and Center for Geographic Analysis, Institute for Quantitative Science, March 12, 2010: http://isites.harvard.edu/fs/docs/icb.topic544785.files/Religion_Workshop_Program_4.pdf and https://cga-download.hmdc.harvard.edu/publish_web/Annual_Spring_Workshops/2010_Religion/2_John_Corrigan.pdf (accessed March 30, 2013).

CHAPTER 8

EMOTION AND
POLITICAL CHANGE

NICOLE EUSTACE

From Henry St. John, Lord Bolingbroke, to Jürgen Habermas, social theorists
have long argued that political transformations rest on a foundation of reasoned public critiques. Habermas contended that widespread public debate
about—and criticism of—official government policies first developed in the
seventeenth and eighteenth centuries through a process of rational disputation
conducted via the press. For Habermas, emotion had no part to play in this
idealized political process. Instead, he applauded "the critical judgment of the
public making use of its reason." From his contemporary eighteenth-century
vantage point, Bolingbroke too saw little efficacy in emotion. He famously urged
readers to "contemplate ourselves, and others, and all things of this world . . .
through the medium of pure, and if I may say so, of undefiled reason." But, he
also lamented that "reason has so little, and ignorance, passion, interest and
custom, so much to do in forming our opinions." He was thus not entirely san-
guine in his assessment of the common people's capacity for rational objection.[1]

Taking Bolingbroke's prescription as description, Habermas staked the claim
that "Bolingbroke . . . propounded the relationship of private and public interests as the relationship of court and country, of 'in power' and 'out of power,'
of pleasure and happiness, passion and reason." For Habermas, this list of contrasting pairs made clear that reason was *the* critical weapon of choice for those
"out of power" who sought to promote the true "public interest." If Bolingbroke
had posited a certain correlation between political corruption at court and the

indulgence of luxury and passion, Habermas ultimately interpreted this to mean that effective political opposition rested on reason alone.[2]

Nevertheless, the revolutionary transformations that swept the eighteenth-century Atlantic in the decades after Bolingbroke's death gave lie to both his predictions and to Habermas's later reflections on the course of events. In fact, from the American Revolution to the French Revolution to the Haitian Revolution, from the rise of eighteenth-century republicanism to the emergence of nineteenth-century nationalism, emotion would prove pivotal to political change. Whether animating the spirit of freedom or sparking action on behalf of the nation, emotion was, by definition, central to patriotism in all its dynamic forms.

EMOTION AND REASON IN THEORY AND PRACTICE: THE EIGHTEENTH CENTURY

One of the first and most dramatic political changes of the eighteenth century, the American Revolution, did *not* rely on the rational to the exclusion of the emotional. Instead, as a number of historians have recently stressed, the upheavals of the revolutionary era grew from a carefully calibrated blend of emotion and reason. In her work *Sensibility and the American Revolution*, historian Sarah Knott affirms that for revolutionary Americans, "cognition and emotion were understood as necessarily intertwined and bound together." Indeed, while emphasizing the crucial role of print in the spread of political ideas and alliances, Knott rejects the notion that print was the exclusive realm of reason, insisting to the contrary on the importance of "sentimental print." She explains that "the story of sensibility and the world of print in the turmoil of imperial crisis and independence is primarily one of popularization." In Knott's well-documented account, sentimental print culture was a key conduit for the formation of public opinion. In responding to Habermas's claims about the centrality of reason to the rise of public opposition, it is essential to measure his assertions against the revolutionary ideas and events of the enlightenment era.[3]

In *Passion Is the Gale: Emotion, Power and the Coming of the American Revolution*, I demonstrate that American revolutionaries explicitly rejected the traditional associations between passion and sin propounded by theorists like Bolingbroke. Instead, eighteenth-century British Americans relied on the assurances of writers like Alexander Pope, who offered them the rhyme "On life's vast ocean, diversely we sail / Reason the card [compass], but passion is the gale." The force of emotion gave power to the human will, put wind in people's sails. Contradicting the widespread notion that passions were private and useful only in advancing personal interests at the expense of the common good, Pope asserted that "reason and passion answer one great aim." With reason to guide people's ideas, emotion could propel them to implement them. Nor would indulgence of emotion lead people to luxuriate in sin for, Pope insisted, "true self-love and social [love] are the same." Individual ambition brought the promise of collective progress. For revolutionary Americans, these proved to be inspiring words.[4]

Up and down the social spectrum, eighteenth-century British Americans came to see emotion as an essential animating force for social and political change. As emotion's moral valence changed, social attitudes were likewise transformed. So long as individualistic passion was associated primarily with sin, it remained linked to servility. Faced with any rebellion on the part of members of subordinate groups, from runaway servant women to restive backcountry vigilantes, leading colonial men were likely to ridicule their protests as the product of unbridled passion rather than respect them as the legitimate response to injustice. Those who were slaves to their own passions deserved to inhabit subservient roles in society. Yet in the socially unsettled atmosphere of eighteenth-century British America, the attractions of individualism, of opportunities to follow one's passions and rise in the world, proved irresistible to all.

Even members of the putative local elite (who should have been most interested in maintaining a fixed communal order) could not deny the efficacy of emotion for social communication and political negotiation. And as they sought to recalibrate their status in relation to English aristocrats, members of the colonial leading class too embraced an ethos of ambitious advancement. Meanwhile, in the ordinary course of daily life, wives and children, bound servants and enslaved laborers, disenfranchised whites and embattled Indians all drew on the power of emotion in mounting new challenges to the status quo. If expressions of cheerfulness conveyed social compliance and declarations of love papered over conflicts of interest, displays of grief demanded sympathetic redress and eruptions of anger threatened violent confrontation. In a fluid Atlantic system of social and economic volatility, in which everyone wanted to advance, no one was prepared to forgo the promptings of passion.

These transatlantic trends were reinforced in the North American context by imperial rivalries between European powers (especially France) that played out in the midst of frequent conflict and competition with Native American nations. As members of Northeastern Indian groups, from the Algonquin to the Iroquois, fought to retain their traditional land rights, they triangulated their strategy by playing British colonists against each other and against the French. Indians had their own emotional standards, and their negotiators at treaty conferences did not hesitate to point out Anglo-American shortcomings. Indians expected that all deaths among their people should be met by formal colonial condolences, and they reproached any diplomat who failed to follow this ritual protocol. If they solicited Anglo-American tears, Indians also demanded Anglo-American anger. They regarded their own shows of anger as a source of strength and upbraided colonial allies as "unmanly" if they failed to display angry resolve in opposition to common foes.

With the crisis of the Seven Years War, from 1754 to 1763, British colonists began to adopt some Indian attitudes toward the links between anger and might. Eager to defeat the French and their Indian allies, British Americans undertook a radical revision of old ideas linking passionate anger to servility and instead began to view anger as a prime source of strength. At the same time, Indian demands that treaty negotiators convey respect through displays of sympathy and grief for Indian dead only confirmed existing colonial emphasis on these emotions. British colonists responded to these multiple challenges by claiming to epitomize both emotional civility (as evidenced by deep sympathy) and masculinity (as demonstrated by aggressive anger). Their ultimate victory over the French in the Seven Years War allowed British Americans to portray themselves as the most successful practitioners of emotional moderation, combining European standards of sympathetic feeling with Native American powers of angry passion.

Another factor compounding the American embrace of passion was the rising impact of slavery. As the eighteenth century wore on and British North America took on more and more characteristics of a slave society, the intensity of links between emotion and politics only increased. Contemporaries connected strong emotion to freedom and apathy to slavery. Eighteenth-century slaveholding whites routinely claimed that the enslaved Africans and African Americans in their midst displayed little affect. In private correspondence and in public newspapers, whites made strikingly few records of emotional expression by the enslaved, even in areas where blacks made up a substantial and growing proportion of the population. Instead, whites repeatedly and routinely claimed that blacks tended to walk about with "down looks," their reportedly habitually downcast aspect reflecting a sort of insensate lethargy.

Such stereotypes about blank affect among enslaved people served a significant and specific political purpose. They marked colonists' resurgent belief in the Aristotelian idea that naturally free people had qualities of both *thumos* and *logos* (of emotion and reason) that set them apart from natural slaves. Some people enjoyed the inherent propensity to love liberty, whereas the naturally slavish lacked this level of sensitivity. According to such logic, those without the inborn ability to feel strong emotion could hardly be said to love—or de- serve—freedom. Thus, the emotional emphasis of early abolitionist literature, so often dismissed as merely the evidence of mawkish sentimental culture, ac- tually advanced the radical counterclaim that Africans and African Americans had every bit as much emotional sensitivity—and the attendant natural right to liberty—as did Europeans.

Meanwhile, the renewal of popular ideas linking emotional sensitivity and love of freedom amplified the political content of colonial British Americans' positive attitudes toward the passions. Rejection of stoical standards of emo- tional containment became a key element of the rhetoric of revolution. When American patriots proclaimed their passions in arguing for independence, they were deliberately demonstrating to the British their innate love of liberty.

EMOTIONAL EXPRESSION AND POLITICAL PROTEST: THE REVOLUTIONARY ERA

By the revolutionary era, British Americans took quite literally the idea that there was such a thing as a "spirit of freedom." As objections to British policies mounted, American patriots came to rely on emotional expression as a key element of political protest. They loudly declared their love of liberty while parading through the streets in massive shows of public mourning over the supposed death of freedom. They first demanded that the British provide a compassionate response to their political tears and then eventually declared that they would unite with each other against the British through bonds of sympathy. Throughout the years of protests leading to the outbreak of war, revolutionary Americans determined to advance their own claims to liberty against the strictures of British imperial rule by emphasizing their full posses- sion of the spirit of freedom.

The British too shared in this eighteenth-century culture of emotion. But whereas royal advocates in Parliament clung to the fiction that there were dis- tinct differences in kind as well as in degree between the refined feelings of the elite and the rude passions of the masses, the most radical leaders of the patriot protest movement took a novel progressive stand. They argued that all people were capable of the same range of emotions, indeed that this shared human attribute was the very basis of natural equality. When Thomas Paine issued his famous call to arms by appealing to the common "passions and feelings of mankind," he not only traded on the motivational power of emotion in politics but also argued that all people everywhere shared the same basic emotions and thus had an equal natural right to political liberty.[5]

Wherever revolutionaries cast emotion as the common inheritance of all humankind, they laid the groundwork for theories of universal rights. True as this proved in my research on the American Revolution, there are strong hints that the same can be said of the Haitian Revolution as well. Although little work has yet been done on emotion and politics in eighteenth-century Haiti, the topic is ripe for investigation. In a recent thought-provoking essay, "Neoclassicism and the Haitian Revolution," Carlos Célius observes briefly that when Haitians took their land from the French, they both created "a community bound together by emotion" and advanced new principles that "emphasiz[ed] the humanity of all men." No matter where we look in the revolutionary Atlantic, it seems we will find emotion playing a pivotal part in political change.[6]

FIRST PRINCIPLES FOR THE ANALYSIS OF EMOTION AND POWER

In arguing that emotion played a central role in the revolutionary transformation of the eighteenth-century Atlantic, I advance a number of points with broad applicability to studies of emotion and political change more generally. Achieving a true understanding of "political change" requires defining politics in the broadest possible sense to include power relations in the private as well as the public realm. For example, the dynamics of negotiation and contestation that played out in colonial British America among courting couples as they decided when and whether to declare their love for each other were organically related to efforts to cast potential settler-Indian alliances in terms of mutual affection, which were in turn connected to the broad struggles of colonists over the question of how strong were the bonds of love that bound them to the British king.

In all cases, the exchange of affection was meant to assure the seamless melding of interests. What was good for the gander was supposed to be good for the goose. Yet everyone knew that the supposed identity of interests achieved by mutual declarations of love was at best a useful fiction and at worst a coercive lie. As a result, anxieties about the possibilities of the alienation of affection remained endemic at all levels of colonial life. Threats to withdraw love had real implications everywhere from the marriage chamber to the treaty council to the halls of Parliament. Achieving a true understanding of the role of emotion in political change requires recognizing that emotional expression defined negotiations of power at all levels of society and interlinked them continuously.

Even as we use the hybrid histories of emotion and politics to interpret the affective dimensions of power relations at all levels of life, we also need to consider emotion from the broadest possible array of theoretical and practical angles. Because politics itself is always a blend of competing theories of governance and practical maneuvers for power, effective analysis of the role of emotion in politics must take equal account of theory and practice.

What good does it do us to recite Thomas Paine's call to the "feelings and passions of mankind" without knowing of the contemporaneous debates of eighteenth-century moral philosophers, poets, and theologians that gave weight to his words? We won't advance far in our inquiries if we simply accumulate examples of emotion in the historical record without regard for the culturally specific ideas and attitudes that gave concrete significance to emotional expression. On the other hand, can we really understand Paine's impact unless we also explore the reverberations of his words in the daily conversations of ordinary colonists? If what we are trying to understand is the place of emotion in shaping real-world political events, we can't look at theoretical debates in isolation.

Opinion has diverged about whether scholars ought to be more focused on evidence of external emotional expression or more determined to uncover the interior experience of emotion. Pioneering work in the history of emotion undertaken by William Reddy helps to resolve this seeming dilemma. Reddy sought to analyze the action of emotion in yet another major popular political upheaval of the eighteenth century, the French Revolution. Considering the deep chasm between theorists who focused on emotion as a physical, biological phenomenon and those who emphasized its social construction through language, he urged scholars to incorporate both approaches. He argued in essence that there is a gap between the physical experience of emotion and the expression of that emotion in words. The sensations of feeling lie in the realm of nature, but the linguistic identification and communication of emotion lies in the realm of culture. And in the work of bridging that gap rests the exercise of power.[7]

Histories of emotion and politics are intrinsically linked to histories of language and power. As Reddy first explained it, in an article titled "Against Constructionism: Toward a Historical Ethnography of Emotion," scholars must recognize that "emotional control is the real site of the exercise of power: politics is just a process of determining who must repress as illegitimate, who must foreground as valuable, the feelings that come up for them in given contexts and relationships." If all people have the same potential to feel emotion, then variations in historical records of emotional expression can serve as a sort of map of the state of political asymmetries in any given time and place.[8]

To make meaning from emotion, scholars need to delineate patterns of actual expression and repression in myriad realms. Understanding the contributions of emotion to political change requires taking into account a wide range of elements—ideas *and* actions, abstract rhetoric *and* concrete expression. We must chart how emotions were expressed and when and by whom; we must tally how emotions were attributed and defined; and we must set this data against the kaleidoscopic cultural context that gave historically specific meaning to emotional utterances issued at particular moments of conflict.

Nevertheless, when Reddy recommends departing from strict construction-ism, he asks us to recognize that while there may be no escape from language itself, there is also no totalizing power by which emotion can ever be wholly controlled, no single cultural repository by which its meanings can ever be completely standardized. There are always multiple contexts and ideas against which expression can be measured.

As Barbara Rosenwein has so usefully demonstrated in her book *Emotional Communities in the Early Middle Ages*, multiple "emotional communities" always exist simultaneously, serving as alternate, overlapping, or competing sources of subjectivity. Her study of the varied emotional "repertories" available to Europeans of the early middle ages has wide applicability. In the case of revolutionary America, colonial contact created a teaming terrain for emotional encounter, featuring religiously diverse, polyglot European colonists; forced African migrants of many different ethnic origins; and Native Americans of multiple linguistic traditions and tribal affiliations. These varied emotional streams together formed the wellspring of political change.[9]

Ultimately, historical analysis of emotional theories, emotional experience, and emotional expression yields more than the sum of its parts. Across the eigh-teenth-century Atlantic, when people accepted the fundamental commonality of emotion across groups, they took a key step in admitting the natural equality of all people and thus in making the case for universal human rights. Yet, the very universality of emotional potential is what in turn made marked variance in the social expression and cultural definition of emotion politically signifi-cant. Emotional expression inevitably conveys social messages, the meaning of which is defined by cultural context. Thus, any show of personal feeling also amounts to a salvo in power negotiations. No "pure" realm of politics excised of emotion exists, nor can emotion ever be free of power.

PRINT POLITICS AND EMOTIONAL ARGUMENT
IN EARLY NATIONALISM

Setting aside Habermas's contention that emotion played little part in the emer-gence of critical public opinion in the Enlightenment era, where can we turn for help in understanding the role of emotion in public life? For many historians considering eighteenth-century revolutions as the outgrowth of nascent nationalism, the formulations provided in Benedict Anderson's *Imagined Communities* have proven useful. Like Habermas, Anderson stresses the efficacy of print for producing political movements. Yet unlike Habermas, Anderson's theory of nationalism places affect at the center of analysis, making emotion crucial for political change, arguing that "nations inspire love." He emphasizes that this love of country is transmitted through language: "what the eye is to the lover . . . language is to the patriot." Ultimately, the rise of print culture was far from being an exclusively rational phenomenon. On the contrary, print has always facilitated the emotional exchanges that allow people to envision the invisible bonds of nationhood.[10]

Yet Anderson, like Habermas, mistrusts the role of emotion in public life. His particular emphasis is on the destruction unleashed when love is invoked in the service of domination and death. Although many associate nationalism primarily with hatred and fear of the "other," Anderson contends that ideals of brotherly love were far more influential in the emergence of nationalism. He explains, "ultimately, it is this fraternity that makes it possible, over the past two centuries, for so many millions of people, not so much to kill, as willingly to die for such limited imaginings." He contends repeatedly that love is both fundamental to the nation and detrimental in its effects.[11]

NATIONALISM AND THE QUESTION OF EMOTIONAL AND POLITICAL UNITY

As Anderson describes it, the love that binds person to nation can be said to function by promoting identity in two senses. Love supposedly works first by advancing identification: a vision of the self as seamlessly united with other selves. Often this unity is said to proceed from ties of birth so that national love is thought to be literally natal in origin. Anderson explains, "the nature of this political love can be deciphered from the ways in which languages describe its object: either in the vocabulary of kinship (motherland, *Vaterland*, *patria*) or that of home." Second, love is supposed to work by promoting belief in the identicalness of interest between disparate people. Anderson observes, "regardless of the actual inequality and exploitation that may prevail in each, the nation is always conceived as a deep, horizontal comradeship." Having identified with each other, the members of a nation can then proceed in the unified pursuit of identical interests. Though Anderson himself critiques the "naturalness" of patriotism, he asserts that nationalists themselves do not. On the contrary, Anderson's nationalists bask in the supposedly organic nature of their lineal emotional bonds: "precisely because such ties are not chosen they have about them a halo."[12]

The idea that emotional identification is central to patriotism has been so widely accepted that scholars tend to assert that such feelings must have emerged even in nations—like the new United States—in which prior ties of birth did not exist. Surveying the American situation, Joyce Appleby, Lynn Hunt, and Margaret Jacob declare in *Telling the Truth about History*, for example:

> Americans at the time of independence ... had to create the sentiments of nationhood which other countries took for granted. There was no uniform ethnic stock ... only a shared act of rebellion. Americans had to invent what Europeans inherited: a sense of solidarity, a repertoire of national symbols, a quickening of political passions.

The authors make easy reference to common foundational assumptions about patriotism when they stress that key to nation-making are quickened "political passions," the "sentiments of nationhood."[13]

These scholars mark an important departure when they point out that in the United States, nationalistic emotions had to be "created." Because unity through birth was unavailable to Americans, nationalists in the era of the early republic had to develop modes of patriotism deliberately, rather than inherit them naturally. Yet Appleby et al. remain committed to the basic proposition that nationalism requires the formation of a communal sense of self. As they explain the American problem: "what a successful War for Independence could not supply were the shared sentiments, symbols, and social explanations necessary for an integrative national identity. Since the "shared sentiments" essential to the formation of the nation did not arise spontaneously, they had to be produced. As they describe the American difficulty: "the fighting of the War for Independence had not turned Americans into a united people. Rather it had created the problem of nationalism—that imperative to form a more perfect union." Though Americans were not born with a "natural" common identity, according to Appleby et al., the exigencies of patriotic nationalism required that they create one. According to these scholars, Americans faced a veritable "imperative to form a more perfect union."[14]

The resonance of phrases like "a more perfect union"—first trumpeted in the preamble to the U.S. constitution—can deafen us to the fact that the unity celebrated was far from literal. American nationalists not only failed to achieve unity, they did not even pursue it as an ideal. The Federalists who penned the U.S. constitution sought primarily the consolidation of their own power, that of a specific class of white men. Insofar as they did seek unity, they were troubled most by geographic sectionalism. For generations, it was the rare American indeed who sought to achieve a wide collective capable of encompassing women as well as men, the poor as well as the rich, African Americans and their descendents as well as Euro-Americans and theirs, Native American peoples and new European immigrants as well as "native born" white Americans. In fact, the constitution's signal achievement in the realm of inclusivity was its commitment to the toleration of religious pluralism, itself an admission of the fractured nature of American culture.

Appleby et al. posit that "shared sentiments" were "necessary for an integrative national identity." But, given that an "integrative identity" did not exist, indeed manifestly was not desired by the few who might have had the hegemonic power to try to impose one, we must question what the so-called "sentiments of nationhood" really felt like in early America. There can be no question of the emergence of American nationalism, of the creation of a functioning state, of the formation of a nation. But the notion that political union arose out of unified identity is hard to defend. Indeed, as genuinely useful as Anderson's central idea, "the imagined community," has been for scholars of nationalism (and Appleby et al. invoke it directly), the concept has heretofore unacknowledged constraints. Anderson-influenced models depend on ideals of "integrative identity" that were seldom invoked in American practice.[15]

Recent work by American literary critics like Christopher Looby and Trish Loughran has questioned the very idea that such a thing as American national identity emerged at any time before the Civil War. Loughran's reflections on the applicability of Anderson's ideas on identity to the early United States are especially apposite. In accord with the observations of Appleby et al., Loughran notes that "one promise of independence was undoubtedly the much sought-after sense of self-identicality that had long been denied colonial populations." But she then adds a crucial qualification to this observation: "though we frequently forget it, the Revolution did not produce this kind of integration on a national scale—nor was it meant to. The later fetishization of July 4 notwithstanding, 1776 produced not a nation but a confederation." For Americans of the early republic, Loughran argues, "affective affiliation" occurred far more at the local than national level.[16]

Earlier studies also emphasized the prominence of discord over comity in early American national life. Joanne Freeman's work on violence in politics, detailed in *Affairs of Honor: National Politics in the New Republic*, explores how policy debates often devolved into interpersonal conflicts, as slights to honor became the emotional provocation that led to physical blows and even fatal duels. Investigating public festive culture in his book, *In the Midst of Perpetual*

NICOLE EUSTACE

Fetes: The Making of American Nationalism, 1776–1820, David Waldstreicher stressed that even the apparently unifying work of communal celebrations could ultimately serve as a mechanism of alienation. When noncitizens tried to carve themselves a place in politics by taking part in patriotic parades and public demonstrations celebrating the nation, they only helped affirm the legitimacy of the very structures that enforced their own political exclusion.[17]

Together, these studies indicate that while analysis of emotion is important to understanding early American nationalism, we cannot fully apprehend emotion's place in American political change by focusing only on its (failed) potential to produce unity. We need, instead, a theory of political participation that makes discord and disagreement central to the political process. This brings us almost, but not quite, full circle back to Habermas.

EMOTION, STATE, AND SOCIETY

A workable model of emotion in politics would combine Habermas with Anderson, analysis of reasoned debate with that of emotional persuasion. Leora Auslander's survey of eighteenth-century revolutions offers one potential creative solution to the problem of reconciling Habermas's claims regarding the centrality of rationality to the rise of democratic argument with Anderson's claims concerning the fundamentality of emotion to nationalism. Her proposal relies on the notion of a gendered division of political labor. She asks that we take seriously the nineteenth-century notion of separate spheres and distinguish the masculine rational realm of the formal state from the feminine emotional realm of the nation at large. She argues that "although women's supposedly essential emotional character[s] made them dangerous to the state, they made them essential to the nation." Auslander elaborates that "transforming the heart as well as the mind, the home as well as the legislature, were as necessary to the difficult task of turning monarchists into republicans and subjects into citizens as was creating new systems of governance and taxation." Although there are a couple of significant conceptual drawbacks in this formulation, there are also some highly productive suggestions.[18]

One drawback lies in Auslander's claim that emotion had no role to play in the state, in formal structures of governance. Neither the claim that emotion was gendered feminine nor the assertion that it was excluded from the formal realms of government turns out to hold up well for the American case. Sarah Knott has placed particular emphasis on the point that the eighteenth-century culture of "sensibility comfortably embraced both men and women." Work by other scholars, such as Brendan McConville's findings on the political significance of American revolutionaries' interrupted love for their king, confirms this position. And my own research in *Passion Is the Gale* makes clear that eighteenth-century men made skillful and explicit use of emotion even in the most highly formalized political situations, such as in crafting official correspondence between colonial legislators and their governors.[19]

A second significant drawback to Auslander's formulation comes with her contention that the emotional work of nationalism turned "subjects into citizens." In fact, as just established at length, one of the signal features of early American nationalism was that it did *not* succeed in transforming all subjects into citizens, nor did it seek to do so. Subjecthood to the crown was a general status that applied to all inhabitants of the royal realm—man, woman or child; freeholder, servant, or slave; English or otherwise—throughout the British Empire. But the status of citizen, as it evolved in the early United States and elsewhere, was *not* a universal category. On the contrary, citizens enjoyed special legal standing and particular political rights unavailable to many simple inhabitants of the nation.

Yet, despite the problems with elements of Auslander's formulation, she is absolutely right to insist that the emotional work of nationalism is fundamentally related to the rise of a critical public sphere. It is in considering both of these activities in tandem that we can best meld Anderson's emphasis on collective emotion with Habermas's focus on reasoned debate. Auslander's reminder that the cultural work of nationalism relies simultaneously on the emotional contributions of women as well as men—indeed benefits from effusions of feeling on the part of all noncitizens who dwell within the nation—provides an important point of departure. The issue we must address is how patriotism—love of country or national attachment as it is variously called—develops among individuals who not only share no common origins but also can't claim comparable civic status.

PATRIOTISM AND POPULATION THEORY
IN THE ENLIGHTENMENT ERA

A useful alternative starting point for considering the question of how patriotism functions among those not fully admitted to the nation can be found in a recently translated series of essays by Michel Foucault, *Security, Territory, Population* (first published in English in 2007). Can all those who inhabit the nation feel love of country whether or not they also enjoy national rights? To begin, we need a collective term to describe the many whose lives are defined by the nation. For the early United States, we seek a single term to demarcate both the white men who could be full citizens and the women, immigrants, and people of color who faced varied levels of exclusion. Foucault proposes that we use the term *population* as the catchall category to describe all who live within the nation, no matter the terms of their emotional and legal affiliation.

Foucault explains that in the eighteenth century, "the population as a political subject, as a new collective subject absolutely foreign to the juridical and political thought of earlier centuries [was] appearing." Before the age of Atlantic revolutions, Europeans, regardless of status, lived and died as natural-born subjects of their kings. Within each royal realm, subjecthood was not optional; it was total and perpetual. By contrast, in the age of the emerging nation-state, citizenship became volitional. Membership in the nation did not require being born on its soil. At least for white men, the only requirement was that they take a voluntary oath of allegiance after living in the nation for a period of time.[20]

Scholars often characterize this transition in people's relation to the state as the shift from subject to citizen. In this schema, noncitizens who inhabited the nation were anomalies whose status was ultimately destined to be resolved by the extension of universal citizenship to all. The problem with this teleology is that these "anomalous" people made up the majority of the inhabitants of the United States for the better part of the country's first century. Could all these "anomalous" people be patriots? What did love of country mean among those who could not fully call the country home?

Foucault argues that "the population as a collective subject is very different from the collective subject constituted and created by the social contract." Members of the population do not consent to government so much as they submit to management. In many new nations, members of "the population" were neither royal subjects nor democratic citizens, but a new category entirely. All those who interacted with state institutions (through tax collection, public health, or the penal system, to cite several of Foucault's examples) were members of the population regardless of whether or not they could also claim status as members of the political citizenry.[21]

Foucault's notion of "population" describes well how white male citizens imagined that many noncitizens would be incorporated into the nation in the early United States. Linked neither to lineal descent nor to legal consent, population afforded a universal category in which affiliation could be achieved through joint participation. A small portion of the population held the additional distinction of being "citizens," persons with recognized political and civil rights. But everyone, male or female, young or old, black or white, native-born or new immigrant, who inhabited the nation constituted its population—everyone that is except the one class of people that remained in but not of the nation—Native Americans.

While Native Americans were denizens of North America, they were not residents of the United States in any meaningful sense. Foucault's theory of "population" accounts for this extranational category with the term *the people*. In this special sense, "the people . . . are those who resist regulation of the population, who try to elude the apparatus by which the population exists." In the nineteenth-century United States, Native Americans (who shared space within the territorial claims of the nation without constituting part of the U.S. population without accepting government regulation) constituted "the people."[22]

In my work on the War of 1812, *1812: War and the Passions of Patriotism*, I have applied Foucault's insights on population to try to understand the work of emotion in the new United States. If we stop trying to discover the elusive emotions that created putative unity and instead interrogate the emotions that helped to motivate action and coordinate contributions among a diverse and divided population, we will advance much further in the effort to effectively analyze patriotism.

PATRIOTIC EMOTION IN A DEMOCRACY AT WAR: THE NINETEENTH-CENTURY UNITED STATES

By focusing on the first constitutionally declared war in a modern democratic republic—one in which politicians both had to earn the approval of a critical electorate and elicit contributions of men and material from broad swaths of the population that did not enjoy voting rights—we can begin to understand what it meant to evoke national devotion in all members of the populace, both those who could and those who could not claim official standing as citizens. In the United States in 1812, almost anyone who could bear arms or bear children counted as a member of the patriotic "population." For contemporaries, the problem of population in the early United States came to a crisis point with the coming of military conflict.

Anderson's notion of community, in the sense of unified national identity, may have precluded us from considering how nationalism can also proceed from a more easily achieved—and more readily restricted—commitment to joint action. In *1812: War and the Passions of Patriotism*, I argue that emotion served as a source of political motivation in the early United States, as a spur to collective action, but not necessarily or inherently as a means of union. There can be common cause without singular identity. In searching for the emotions of early American nationalism, then, we might do well to focus less on those supposed to advance the formation of "identity" and more on those that might enhance instrumentality.[23]

While Anderson's theory of patriotism rested primarily on the homosocial bonds of brotherhood, American nationalists of the 1812 era centered their emotional efforts on heterosexual romance. In the course of researching the impact of emotion on politics in the era of 1812, I found that efforts to stir up patriotism relied far more frequently on romantic love than on fraternal affection. Again and again, I found prowar commentary, from the pronouncements of politicians to the rhymes of popular songbooks, conveying the idea that there were essential links between American love and American liberty. Public prints continually reaffirmed that the freely chosen love of romantic partners served well as the model for loyalty to country and that the heat of romantic passion could spark patriotic feats.

By 1812, American expansionists sought above all to foment military action: to force Indians to relinquish lingering territorial rights to the lands of the Great Lakes and the Mississippi basin and to compel the British to abandon all diplomatic and trading ties to American Indians. They needed, ultimately, to fuel lust for geographic gains. Quite conversant with the notion that there is an inherent connection between passion and action, Americans at the turn of the nineteenth century knew that they had to stoke longing before they could stake claim to new lands. It was no accident, then, that the love that underlay early American nationalism was an explicitly yearning kind, one that grew out of ordinary desires to expand families and acquire farms. Patriotism encouraged members of the population to enact sexual and territorial desires, to seek to produce children and populate the land, without creating a sense of "horizontal comradeship."

Moving the population to action on behalf of the nation presented a critical emotional challenge. In the United States in 1812, the nation needed to draw strength from the actions of its entire population, but its leaders neither needed nor desired to grant every member of the populace the same kind of status. All Americans were not citizens; in this way, their unity was sharply limited. Yet by acting cooperatively to support the country in an hour of crisis, they could coordinate their interests. Patriotism may as often arise from joint pursuits as from shared personhood.

Foucault's observations on the importance of population as an analytic category, separate from that of both subject and citizen, grew directly out of his empirical study of eighteenth-century states. In fact, as I discovered in working on the War of 1812, many political economists in Europe and the United States were also highly focused on the issue of population. American and French physiocrats theorized openly that population was the chief source of strength for nations. National progress required population growth. Far less significant than the expansion of citizenship was the simple increase in the number of able-bodied men and women who could serve the nation.

Nothing could bring such facts into sharper relief than the emergency of war. In the United States in 1812, focus on the links between love, liberty, and progeny was further intensified by the fact that the leading political economist in Great Britain, Thomas Malthus, argued the opposite, claiming that unfettered reproduction inevitably led to imperialistic encroachments on the subsistence rights of rival populations. Malthus minced no words in singling out the United States for its incursions on Indian territory. In what many Euro-Americans saw as a virtuous cycle, but many Native Americans and their British and Canadian allies viewed as a vicious circle, the continent's wide-open grounds supported demographic expansion even as the increasing U.S. population enabled the seizure and settlement of new land. Bearing arms and bearing children both advanced the nation.[24]

As the war unfolded, a romantically defined love of country was invoked time and again as a way of defining events. When Commodore Perry won a great victory on Lake Erie, he was commended in Congress and in the public prints as a courtly suitor much to be admired for the way he had "enticed victory into his arms." After Andrew Jackson saved New Orleans, everything from his authorized biography to broadside ballads claimed that by his romantic gallantry he had preserved "American Beauty" and averted a supposed British plot to rape and pillage the city.

More generally, while war opponents complained about the "false love" that led soldiers and their supporters to equate war with romance, militant nationalists claimed that for Americans, choosing a sweetheart and choosing a nation, two means of enjoying love, were closely related forms of liberty. Ultimately, the end of the war was celebrated as an opportunity for American men and women, black and white alike, to realize their romantic dreams by acquiring the land on which to raise large families. Only Indians, the "people" outside the "population," were left out of this circle of love.

Ultimately, the U.S. war effort in 1812 accomplished next to nothing with respect to Great Britain, the declared opponent in the war. The peace treaty signed into law in 1815 returned all relations with Britain to the status quo antebellum. Meanwhile, the national debt had nearly tripled and the nation's capital had been burned to the ground. None of these facts stopped the war from becoming an enormous popular success. President James Madison won reelection in the midst of the war and his Secretary of State, James Monroe, succeeded him in 1816.

People had taken great pleasure in the rise of patriotism and warmed to the idea that breaking new farms on which to raise families was the first and best enactment of freedom. In the years after formal peace with Britain was achieved, a parade of new states in former Indian territory entered the union: Indiana in 1816, Mississippi in 1817, Illinois in 1818, Alabama in 1819, Maine in 1820, and Missouri in 1821. The real legacy of the war was a renewed commitment to territorial expansion and a certainty that the nation had earned the right to enjoy what the newspapers quickly dubbed an "era of good feelings."[25]

While I wholly reject the idea that emotion played little role in the emergence of a critical public sphere and likewise want to jettison the notion that love of country inevitably springs from unified identity, I do think that emotionally energized political debates in the early United States helped mobilize the nation for war. In a perfect blend of form and function, U.S. polemicists argued that romance and reproduction were both the requirement and the reward of patriotism, the root and the fruit of political liberty. Though formal civic rights remained a special flourish allowed only to few, all could claim freedom in its most fundamental form.

In the United States in 1812, contributing to the population allowed personal love and patriotic contributions to be one and the same. Americans at the turn of the nineteenth century were well familiar with the notion that there was an intrinsic link between passion and action. The emotional content of public prints in the era of 1812 worked to rouse the population of the United States for war.

EMOTION AS A SUBJECT OF HISTORICAL ANALYSIS

In conclusion, I want to state clearly that emotion itself is value-neutral in politics. This point is easy to miss given that emotional language is so often used to lend moral coloration to ideas and actions. But we need to remember that although emotion is intimately tied to motivation, to decisions about whether or not to act, it is not in itself inherently good or bad any more than action itself is. Even as Anderson emphasizes the role of love (generally considered a positive and enjoyable emotion) in the work of death, there are also studies like that of Rachel Hope Cleaves on the moral power of fear (generally considered a negative and repugnant emotion) to advance progressive aims from antiwar activism to antislavery projects. The point is not that love is really wrong or that fear is actually fun. The point is that, as scholars, we need to serve as analysts of how the pleasurable or uncomfortable sensations of a given emotion have been used throughout history to shift public judgments about the legitimacy of political movements.[26]

As neuropsychologists have recently sought to alert us, our emotional systems are fundamentally very simple. Just as the decimal system in mathematics can ultimately be reduced to the binary system of zeros and ones, so all emotions can ultimately be boiled down to those that produce approach behaviors and those that produce avoidance, those that promote affiliation and those that provoke dissociation. When a new stimulus of undetermined value is introduced by a prior stimulus with strongly positive or negative appeal, a person's reaction can be artificially shifted toward approach or avoidance. Powerful snap judgments about the practical and moral worth of a given course of action can result from the emotional reaction a person has to otherwise unrelated ideas and events.[27]

Political manipulations of the emotions become potentially problematic when the emotions evoked by a particular stimulus are deliberately used to induce revulsion or attraction toward a second unrelated stimulus. It's easy to regard these tactics as nefarious when analyzing how love can be invoked in support of war, as in the case of the United States in 1812. Objection to this sort of "bait and switch" tactic accounts for much of the tendency to either deny or deplore the role of emotion in politics. Yet, there are also plenty of instances in which we appreciate and even applaud the process by which emotional identification leads to political motivation. Emotional universalism provided a key support for theories of natural rights across the revolutionary Atlantic. Demagogues draw on emotion, but so do democratic reformers.

As human beings, we can no more eliminate the interrelationship of emotion and cognition than we can erase the part that moral judgments play in political calculations. But, as historians, we can and should trace the processes by which invocations of emotion are used to provoke political actions. The ideas that give contextual meaning to emotion and the language in which emotion is expressed will vary almost infinitely across time and place. Yet the personal impact and political charge of emotion always endure. It is in accepting and then analyzing the role of emotion in political change that scholars can gain strength from the power of feeling.

Both revolutionary support and early-nineteenth-century nationalism in the United States derived in part from the reconsideration of emotion's validity, from the mid–eighteenth century onward, and particularly the new validation of love. This is one important instance of the interaction between reevaluations of emotions, of political loyalties, and of behavior. The connection invites other inquiries, for other times and places, of points where emotional and political changes intersected; it can also apply to points (for example: the contemporary United States) where different political sides diverge not only in expressed political goals but also in degree of acceptance or rejection of emotional investment. There is rich potential for further explorations in political and emotions history alike.

NOTES

1. Jürgen Habermas, *The Structural Transformation of the Public Sphere: An Inquiry into a Category of Bourgeois Society*, trans. Thomas Burger (Cambridge: MIT Press, 1991), 24; Henry St. John, Lord Viscount Bolingbroke, *The Works of the Late Right Honorable Henry St. John, Lord Viscount Bolingbroke*, vol. 4 (London: J. Johnson, 1809), 167.

2. Habermas, *Structural Transformation*, 64.

3. Sarah Knott, *Sensibility and the American Revolution* (Chapel Hill: University of North Carolina Press, 2009), 5, 27, 68.

4. Nicole Eustace, *Passion Is the Gale: Emotion, Power and the Coming of the American Revolution* (Chapel Hill: University of North Carolina Press, 2008), 56, 54.

5. Eustace, *Passion Is the Gale*, 3.

6. Carlos Célius, "Neoclassicism and the French Revolution," in *The World of the Haitian Revolution*, ed. David Patrick Geggus and Norman Fiering (Bloomington: Indiana University Press, 2009), 352–392, quotations on 360 and 361.

7. William Reddy, "Against Constructionism: The Historical Ethnography of Emotion," *Current Anthropology* 38 (1997): 327–351; Reddy, *The Navigation of Feeling: A Framework for the History of Emotions* (New York: Cambridge University Press, 2001).

8. Reddy, "Against Constructionism," 35.

9. Barbara H. Rosenwein, *Emotional Communities in the Early Middle Ages* (Ithaca, N.Y.: Cornell University Press, 2006).

10. Benedict Anderson, *Imagined Communities: Reflections on the Origin and Spread of Nationalism*, rev. ed. (London: Verso, 1991), 145, 158.

11. Ibid., 7.

12. Ibid., 143, 147.

13. Joyce Oldham Appleby, Lynn Avery Hunt, Margaret C. Jacob, *Telling the Truth about History* (New York: Norton, 1995), 93.

14. Ibid., 94.

15. Ibid., 92.

16. Christopher Looby, *Voicing America: Language, Literary Form, and the Origins of the United States* (Chicago: University of Chicago Press, 1996); Trish Loughran, *The Republic in Print: Print Culture in the Age of U.S. Nation Building, 1770–1870* (New York: Columbia University Press, 2009), 12.

17. Joanne Freeman, *Affairs of Honor: National Politics in the New Republic* (New Haven, Conn.: Yale University Press, 2002); David Waldstreicher, *In the Midst of Perpetual Fetes: The Making of American Nationalism, 1776–1820* (Chapel Hill: University of North Carolina Press, 1997), esp. 231.

18. Leora Auslander, *Cultural Revolutions* (Berkeley: University of California Press, 2009), 8.

19. See Knott, *Sensibility*, 189; and see Brendan McConville, *The King's Three Faces: The Rise and Fall of Royal America* (Chapel Hill: University of North Carolina Press, 2006).

20. Michel Foucault, *Security, Territory, Population: Lectures at the College de France, 1977–1978*, ed. Michel Senellart, trans. Graham Burchell (New York: Picador, 2007), 42–44.

21. Foucalt, *Security, Territory, Population*, 44.

22. Nicole Eustace, *1812: War and the Passions of Patriotism* (Philadelphia: University of Pennsylvania Press, 2012); Foucalt, *Security, Territory, Population*, 44.

23. For more on identity as a theoretical problem, see Rogers Brubaker and Frederick Cooper, "Beyond 'Identity,'" *Theory and Society* 29 (2000): 1–47, discussion on 4.

24. See Donald Winch, ed., *Malthus: An Essay on the Principle of Population*, Cambridge Texts in the History of Political Thought (Cambridge: Cambridge University Press, 1992). I discuss Malthusian debates at length in *1812: War and the Passions of Patriotism*.

25. For statistics, see Donald R. Hickey, *The War of 1812: A Forgotten Conflict* (Urbana: University of Illinois Press, 1989), 303.

26. See Rachel Hope Cleaves, *The Reign of Terror in America: Visions of Violence from Anti-Jacobinism to Antislavery* (Cambridge: Cambridge University Press, 2009).

27. See Jonathan Haidt, "The New Synthesis in Moral Psychology," *Science* 18 (May 2007): 998–1002; and see Piercarlo Valdesolo and David DeSteno, "Short Report: Manipulations of Emotional Context Shape Moral Judgment," *Psychological Science* 17, no. 6 (2006): 476–477, quotation on 476.

CHAPTER 9

MEDIA, MESSAGES, AND EMOTIONS

BRENTON J. MALIN

Communication media inevitably raise questions about emotion. In Plato's *Phaedrus*, Socrates worries about the emotional effects of writing—the new medium of his time. Talking with Phaedrus, a young man who brings a written speech to him, Socrates expresses concern for the "frenzied enthusiasm" he believes it is likely to produce in those who read it. Among the faults that Socrates finds with writing is that it "doesn't know how to address the right people, and not to address the wrong."[1] Because a written script, unlike a live speech, does not require a person to deliver it, it cannot make choices about where and when *not* to communicate and cannot answer questions that interlocutors might pose to it. How Socrates addresses the speech is telling in these regards as well. It is a *pharmakon*—a drug, or charm; it is the original source for the English word pharmacy. Divorced from a speaker, Socrates argues, writing has a powerful and intoxicating affect over the emotions of its reader.[2]

This chapter considers links between media and emotion in a modern American context. Like Socrates, the people I discuss are concerned with media's capacity to stimulate and transmit emotions. While many worry about the negative effects of frenzied enthusiasm, however, others celebrate the emotional unification they presume to be created by the new media of their age. These often conflicted discussions illustrate what Leo Marx, David Nye, and James Carey describe as the rhetoric of the technological or electrical sublime—an idea that they argue has dominated the American experience of technology.

New technologies have consistently been celebrated as saint and condemned as Satan, often for precisely the same technological power.

I will argue that this rhetoric makes the most sense when viewed within the framework of a broader history of emotion. At the same time that Americans became increasingly concerned about how to manage their emotions, film, radio, and the phonograph found a place both in American homes and in the research practices of a range of social scientists. Among the most interesting and conflicted of these are those media technologies used by scientists to study the emotional effects of the media themselves. Psychologists and others undertook such experiments as hooking people up to motion picture recorders to capture the impact of motion pictures on their emotions, attempting to use the presumed emotional power of motion picture technology against itself.

This chapter traces some of these understandings of emotion in order to tell a story about how American media critics have wrestled with questions of the affective life. I begin by showing some thinking about emotion and media that preceded the explosion of mass media and mass media criticism in the early twentieth century. I then lay out some key popular and academic understandings of media from the early twentieth century. For the thinkers I discuss, emotions were predominantly individual sensations stored in human bodies in the same way they were presumed to be stored in phonograph records and motion pictures. From here, I move to late-twentieth-century modifications and extensions of these ideas and then discuss their continued relevance at the dawn of the twenty-first century. The approach to media established in the early twentieth century was largely an ahistoric, decontextualized one. While this opened up the study of particular physiological and emotional effects, it also made it difficult to explore a number of other areas of the emotional life. The early twenty-first century has seen the emergence of a more contextual approach to mediated emotion, even as a more narrowly physiological approach is gaining strong footing in the larger culture.

ELECTRIC FEELINGS

Soon after its discovery, electricity began an important relationship to the emotions in Western culture. In the eighteenth century, Italian scientist Luigi Galvani discovered that he could make a frog's leg contract by applying electricity to it. This demonstrated to Galvani and other scientists that electricity was a fundamental part of animal and human bodies; scientists practicing Galvanism suggested that electric currents could cure everything from sciatica and rheumatism to herpes and constipation.[3] The eighteenth-century science of Mesmerism, or animal magnetism, as its inventor Franz Mesmer called it, held that it was electrical forces that were responsible for the attraction of both physical and social bodies. Lovers were drawn to each other with no less electrical force than positively and negatively charged magnets.[4] Electricity was a vital force with an important role in people's physical and emotional health.

Because it harnessed electricity for communication, Morse's nineteenth-century telegraph struck many as an especially strong conveyor of emotion. A range of critics worried about the overstimulation of the high-speed telegraph even as others celebrated its ability to create a global village of shared feelings. "The magnetic telegraph searches every nook and corner of the world every day, dragging into light, not only every crime that is committed, but every disagreeable feature of human society," wrote one nineteenth-century commentator.[5] A letter in the *Philadelphia Medical Times* from 1883 similarly noted that "when a man only got his letters in the morning he was pretty safe from surprises for the rest of the day; but with the telegraph he has no remission from anxiety and is on the tenterhooks all day long." Because of this excessive excitement, the writer continued, "what chance have the assimilative organs, so intimately related with the emotions, of preserving their even way amid such tumult and disturbance?"[6]

In contrast, a poem entitled "The Atlantic Telegraph" by Elizabeth Barnard celebrated the telegraph as a great emotional unifier:

Peerless theme of glad emotion
Linking national hearts in one;
Through this nerve across the ocean
Thrills the triumph newly won![7]

Noting a similar linking of national hearts following the assassination of U.S. President James Garfield, Massachusetts Governor George Hoar wrote that "science, the telegraph and the press enabled the emotion of human sorrow, at the time of Garfield's funeral, to be felt over the entire civilized world." As a result, Hoar continued, "a poor, feeble fiend shot off his feeble bolt; a single human life was stricken down; and, lo, a throb of Divine love thrills a planet!"[8] The same emotional power that worried the writer for the *Philadelphia Medical Times* was precisely what Hoar and Barnard were celebrating.

This powerful and conflicted rhetoric had some very concrete manifestations. For instance, the telegraph's status as national nerve resulted in some heated court cases. As the newest, most rapid form of communication, the telegraph assumed a special status for emotionally urgent messages. Deathbed requests could now be sent with great speed, allowing people to see their loved ones before they passed away—at least when the messages were transmitted.

In the late nineteenth century, a series of people successfully sued telegraph companies for emotional distress when they failed to deliver such messages. The assumption of the courts who found on behalf of these emotionally distraught customers was that as operators of a rapid form of communication, telegraph companies had a great responsibility for their customers' emotional well being.[9]

In some important ways, these discussions surrounding the telegraph illustrate the earlier American ideas about emotion addressed by historian Peter Stearns. According to Stearns, the emotional history of the United States can be understood as a kind of movement from a more expressive and public Victorian conception of *the passions* to a more controlled, private idea of *emotion* that he calls "American Cool."[10] On the one hand, eighteenth- and nineteenth-century Americans had been comfortable with an extremely wide range of powerful emotional expressions—including, for instance, intentionally terrifying children, as some earlier Christmas traditions had done.[11] At the same time, it was common for earlier Americans to convey their intimate emotions quite publicly, as Nicole Eustace has nicely demonstrated in her research on love letters and further explains in her chapter for this volume. When expressing one's love, a person would address a letter not to the beloved, but to one of her or his relatives. This practice aimed to demonstrate a commitment to the larger social relations in which a romantic relationship took place.[12] Here, love was assumed to be a public and social good.

The celebrations of the emotional unification of the telegraph championed just this public understanding of emotion. Courts that found that telegraph companies violated their responsibilities by not delivering emotionally urgent messages would do so as well. Emotions were not confined to individuals but were shared collectively across a whole network of connections—including technological ones. Of course, this public and expressive understanding of emotion had never been completely dominant. Concerns about the telegraph's impact on the "assimilative organs" of the body demonstrated a clear anxiety about individual emotional control. Still, moving into the twentieth century and the age of phonograph records, film, and radio, discussions of the media put still more emphasis on emotional control, even as emotions and the media themselves would be seen as increasingly private entities.

MASS EMOTIONS AND MASS TECHNOLOGIES

As had been the case with the telegraph in the nineteenth century, the new media of the twentieth century were not immediately or exclusively decried for their emotional effects. In one of the earliest studies of movies, American psychologist Hugo Münsterberg celebrated the emotional possibilities of this new media. At the beginning of his book, published in 1916, Münsterberg said directly that "to picture emotions must be the central aim of the photoplay."[13] He would go on to celebrate the aesthetic possibilities of motion picture cameras to create a range of emotions, including "a feeling of dizziness" and "an uncanny, ghastly unnaturalness."[14] Far from decrying the motion picture's new technological possibilities, as Socrates might have, Münsterberg worried that the standard practices of the stage theater would likely prevent filmmakers from taking advantage of the motion camera's emotional possibilities. Münsterberg regretted that the emotionally powerful cinema he imagined "still belongs entirely to the future."[15]

Even as Münsterberg was writing, other academics were beginning to take a stronger position against the emotional stimulation of the new media. The English psychologist Graham Wallas's criticisms of "the Great Society" had a strong impact in the United States. According to Wallas, a variety of cultural and technological developments, including changes in "communication by written and spoken words," were creating new global attachments that resulted in additional psychological and emotional stress.[16] The American journalist and social critic Walter Lippmann, who had studied with Wallas, and to whom Wallas addressed the preface of *The Great Society*, echoed much of this concern about information overload. "What," Lippmann asked, "do eight or twelve hours of noise, odor, and heat in a factory, or day upon day among chattering typewriters and telephone bells and slamming doors, do to the political judgments formed on the basis of newspapers read in street-cars and subways?"[17]

Lippmann was not alone in his concern about information overload or emotional overstimulation, and neither was this purely a concern among academics. One writer railed against the "communistic emotions" being developed by the mainstream media, arguing that "several hundred thousand listen to the same speeches every night and the same jazz bands, then at breakfast heave communistic sighs and shed communistic tears over the same calamities, at the bidding of the press."[18] Indeed, much of the anxiety about media and emotion had to do with the larger political climate of the period. In the wake of WWI, Americans got a new sense of their emotional connections with the rest of the world, as well as how the media could be used to foster nationalism and other forms of sentiment. In a book on propaganda use during the war, American political scientist Harold Lasswell wrote that "we live among more people than ever, who are puzzled, uneasy, or vexed at the unknown cunning which seems to have duped and degraded them."[19] The cacophony of voices raised by the new media was presumed to have a range of effects on the minds and emotions of the American public.

These concerns about technology and emotion both reflected and amplified changes taking place in the social sciences themselves. At the same time that the emotional stimulations of the new media were becoming troubling for certain critics, a number of the scientists who took up media research were attempting to distance themselves from their own presumably hyperemotional pasts. In the 1910s and 1920s, psychologists, who were among some of the most active early media researchers,[20] were seeking to end their connections to philosophy, and sociologists were working to separate themselves from social work. For both, these earlier connections tied them to questions about feeling, mind, and spiritualism (which had close connections to Galvanism and Mesmerism[21]) that many felt stood in the way of their recognition as legitimate sciences. In response, a great number of sociologists and psychologists would employ more presumably quantitative, scientific approaches, including scientific recording and measurement of the emotions.[22] Given the broad cultural concern about their emotional impact, the mass media made an especially strong target for these new studies, presumably allowing scientists to demonstrate their own emotional detachment from the new media age.

Among the most well-known of this early-twentieth-century media research were the highly influential Payne Fund Motion Picture Studies, which attempted to detail the impact of movies on American children. The Payne Fund had been created by Frances Payne Bolton, a philanthropist with interests in child literacy and a range of other social issues. The fund's motion picture studies had begun in the 1920s under the leadership of William Short. The resulting studies were published as a set of thirteen monographs in 1933. Similarly to Socrates, the Payne Fund viewed motion pictures as a kind of drug (in fact, opium use was one of the other subjects explored by the organization). In *Content of Motion Pictures*, Edgar Dale compares using drugs to watching romance and crime films. Because they offer a form of escape, Dale argues, both drugs and movies can provide a social good. However, just as drugs should be used only "when nothing can be done for the patient except to relieve him of pain," the dangerously stimulating crime and romance films should not be provided to children when other forms of recreation are available.[23]

Of the Payne Fund monographs, the most specific study of the emotions came in Wendell Dysinger and Christian Ruckmick's *Emotional Responses of Children to the Motion Picture Situation*. Ruckmick was a professor and Dysinger a graduate student in the Department of Psychology at the University of Iowa. Capturing the era's concerns about emotional stimulation, in a letter to William Short, Ruckmick wrote that "continuous or frequently repeated high emotional stress leads to a neurotic condition of the human organism."[24] Dysinger and

Ruckmick's study sought to detail the emotional dangers of movies, both for children and the population more generally. They took aim at the technological sophistication of "the talkies" in particular, whose "illusion of reality in the theater is so great that to most of the spectators and auditors the presentations carry with them a deep emotional tone, especially in the case of children."[25] Watching movies created "profound mental and physiological effects of an emotional order," which resulted in "unnatural sophistication and premature bodily stimulation."[26] The aim of Dysinger and Ruckmick's study was to offer proof of this unnatural stimulation in the hopes that it could be combated.

Although much of Dysinger and Ruckmick's criticisms of movies had to do with their presumed technological sophistication, as was the general trend in psychology at the time, these scientists employed advanced technologies in their own research. For their study, Dysinger and Ruckmick had children watch a selection of movies while monitoring their emotions through a psycho-galvanometer—an instrument named for Luigi Galvani that captured a subject's "galvanic skin response." The electrical conductivity of a person's skin changes when a person perspires, and scientists using psycho-galvanometers assumed that these changes provided a measurement of a subject's emotional stimulation. But the psycho-galvanometer used by Dysinger and Ruckmick not only provided measurements of subject's responses; it recorded these responses on film.[27] The same technological power that made movies dangerous to people's emotions apparently made them the ideal technology for the psychological laboratory. In the new mass media, psychologists found both their sinner and saint.

The Payne Fund Studies, and Dysinger and Ruckmick's monograph in particular, resonated strongly with the general culture. A headline from a *New York Times* article from 1933 that summarized the studies cut directly to Dysinger and Ruckmick's primary apprehension. "OVEREXCITEMENT IS SEEN," the article proclaimed.[28] But the general approach to media suggested by this and similar studies had a still wider influence. Indeed, research such as Dysinger and Ruckmick's grew from, and helped to establish the dominance of, what media scholar James Carey would eventually label a *transmission model* of communication. As Carey explained it, the transmission model understands communication as a linear process of information transmission; this contrasts to a ritual model, which Carey favored, that sees communication as a matter of sharing and community, but which Carey argued has been a minority perspective in American thought.[29] When thinking about communication, American scholars, and to a great extent the wider public, has tended to imagine a single sender transmitting a message to a more or less passive receiver—much as Dysinger and Ruckmick imagined emotions to be flowing from movie to audience to the electrical scribbling of the psycho-galvanometer.

This transmission model of communication had several important implications for thinking about media and emotion. In Dysinger and Ruckmick's study, emotions were electrical and physiological processes that adhered in both bodies and communication technologies, below the surface of individual perception. Given the technological power of motion pictures and the overwhelming emotions of the new media age, Dysinger and Ruckmick assumed that audiences were oblivious to just how movies influenced them. Asking people about their own emotional reactions would thus never achieve an authentic response. By going directly to the physiological changes of the body, however, the high-tech psycho-galvanometer presumably got below peoples' perceptions to a deeper emotion truth. For Dysinger and Ruckmick, "real emotions" lay beyond human consciousness, in the intimate physiological details only the psycho-galvanometer could know. The new media did not simply overload people with information, Dysinger and Ruckmick suggested. It separated them from their own feelings, bodies, and experiences. Everyday people required technology-wielding scientists in order to understand their own emotional lives.

In isolating people from their own emotions, this perspective also separated emotion from a range of larger social and cultural matters. The nineteenth-century courts that had held telegraph companies responsible for the emotional distress of their customers had seen emotion as a largely public good. In line with larger thinking about the passions—an idea that was even then beginning to lose its dominance—these courts assumed that emotions were not simply the property of individuals but jointly constructed by, and jointly the responsibility of, a range of people. The implications of the movement to the early-twentieth-century's more private conception of emotion is clear from looking at the *Communications Act of 1934*, the chief legislation governing the American broadcast media until the 1990s. The *Communications Act of 1934*, which created the FCC, largely dismissed the sense of emotional responsibility championed in nineteenth-century telegraph cases. Rather, it defined telecommunications companies' responsibilities as technical matters of transmission. Telecommunications companies served the public by simply maintaining their technical facilities. When emotions were addressed by the FCC, it would largely focus on questions of "decency"—on whether individuals or groups had been or could be offended by particular messages. This relatively private conception of emotions ignored a whole host of other ways that they are implicated in the communication process.

Finally, and no doubt against the intentions of a number of early media re-searchers, this transmission view framed emotion in the terms most amenable to the corporate media of the day. Dysinger and Ruckmick had imagined the interaction between media and audiences as a kind of *exchange* relationship; emotions were a product that could be packaged and delivered from movie to audience and from audience to psycho-galvanometer. The research paradigm they helped to establish—with its emphasis on the emotional effects of me-dia—raised precisely the questions that media producers wanted to answer. What kinds of scenes had the biggest emotional impact on audiences? How long would this emotional stimulation remain after viewing some particular media? From the transmission perspective, emotions were one isolatable vari-able in the media process—something that could be measured, recorded, and manipulated by social scientists and media producers alike.

This understanding of emotion played into a variety of other movements taking place at this time. Dale Carnegie's claims that he could teach people how to *Win Friends and Influence People* rested on a similar conception of emotion.[30] If emotions were physiological processes percolating below people's percep-tions, then if someone learned to trigger them, they would presumably have a great power to get what they wanted. Edward Bernays, who founded the field of public relations in the 1920s and 1930s, attributed a similar power to the communication of emotion. Bernays celebrated the cacophony of voices and enhanced connections that Lippmann and others decried. The "organization of communication in the United States enables practically any person or any group or any movement to be brought almost immediately into the closest juxtaposi-tion with people almost anywhere," he wrote in 1935.[31] Bernays believed that these connections allowed people to win favor to various causes by the same sort of emotional manipulation that Carnegie celebrated. A view of emotions as isolatable, manipulable, and private, thus served the aims of psychologists attempting to redefine themselves as natural scientists, as well as corporate and self-help gurus working to use communication to advance particular marketing or individual agendas. These ideas would have important effects on how late-twentieth-century American academics, and the broader culture, conceived of media and emotion.

TRANSMITTING AND TRANSFORMING
AN EMOTIONAL LEGACY

If psychologists performed some of the earliest media research, the next phase of studies was dominated by sociologists. This shift saw emotion become less of a central focus; however, it remained, often as an implied category, within many other kinds of research. Although this later research modified many of the perspectives put forward in the early part of the century, much of these earlier ideas continued as well. Among the most prominent centers for sociological media research was the Office of Radio Research established by Hadley Cantril and Paul Lazarsfeld at Princeton University in 1937 and then moved to Columbia University in 1939. One of the first studies to be published by the center was Cantril's *Invasion from Mars: A Study in the Psychology of Panic*.[32] This book attempted to analyze public reactions to Orson Welles famous *War of the Worlds* broadcast, which frightened audiences with the tale of a supposedly real Martian invasion on October 30, 1938.

Unlike the experimental psychologists Dysinger and Ruckmick, the Columbia School of media research—as it came to be called—favored in-depth interviews as a research method. For *Invasion from Mars*, Cantril and his colleagues interviewed a large sample of people who had listened to Welles's broadcast. Their goal was to assess the number of people who believed that the fictional invasion was real and then to evaluate those people's reaction to it. One Newark housewife reported that after listening to the broadcast, "My knees were shaking so, I could hardly walk up the stairs." Resolved that the world would soon end, she explains, "I looked in the icebox and saw some chicken from Sunday dinner that I was saving for Monday night dinner. I said to my nephew, 'We may as well eat this chicken—we won't be here in the morning.'"[33] By including such personal reports—something that Dysinger and Ruckmick had planned to do, but discarded because they saw them as not objective enough[34]—Cantril indicated a deeper faith in people's sense of their own emotions. Likewise, in his attempts to understand why various listeners were panicked by the program, Cantril offered some broader discussion of the cultural prestige attributed to radio announcers as well as about listeners' perceptions of the authenticity of radio itself. Cantril placed listeners' emotional reactions within a much larger cultural context than was offered by Dysinger and Ruckmick's experimental approach.

At the same time, Cantril reiterated a number of early-twentieth-century ideas about emotion. Despite the fact that he had found that even highly educated listeners felt panicked by the broadcast, Cantril attributed much of listeners' emotional reactions to a lack of education or lower-class status. In order to be critical listeners of radio, Cantril said in the book's closing sentences, these lower-class listeners "must be less harassed by the emotional insecurities which stem from underprivileged environments."[35] Although Cantril did not pay special attention to radio as a technology, he also reinforced important elements of the earlier transmission model, especially its conception of emotion as a kind of exchange relationship. By focusing on whether or not the Welles broadcast created panic in individual listeners, Cantril ignored a range of other ways that audiences might have responded to the program. The view of emotion here remained largely pharmacological—either the broadcast did or did not evoke "panic" in a listener.[36]

Moving forward, Columbia continued to conceive of emotion within a complex cultural process that nonetheless seemed to reduce to a set of individual characteristics. Herta Herzog's essay "On Borrowed Experience: An Analysis of Listening to Daytime Sketches," explored the pleasures women derived from radio soap operas by interviewing a group of listeners.[37] One of Herzog's central arguments was that these programs satisfied listener's desires for emotional release by, among other things, giving them "a chance to cry" and allowing them to both escape from and magnify their own suffering. In *Personal Influence: The Part Played by People in the Flow of Mass Communications*, Paul Lazarsfeld and Elihu Katz made similar claims about how someone's emotions could account for their particular media use. For example, they claimed that the more anxious a woman was, the greater the frequency of her consumption of such media as radio soap operas and confessional magazines.[38]

Although there were external factors influencing people's emotional dispositions—such as their interactions with others—these later studies tended to view emotions as fairly discreet entities, separated from larger social and cultural processes. In "On Borrowed Experience," Herzog offers very little information as far as the social or cultural backgrounds of the women she interviews, focusing instead on their particular emotional responses. The implications of this focus can be seen by looking at a model that developed from Herzog's work to become one of Columbia's most influential contributions to media research: *uses and gratifications theory*.[39] This approach focuses on the kinds of gratifications people derive from media use, seeing them as active participants in their own media pleasure. This perspective challenged the kind of passive audience imagined by Dysinger and Ruckmick. Similar to them, however, it viewed the emotions of gratification as largely private impulses belonging to individual audience members. From a uses and gratifications perspective, emotions are the particular needs that different audience members satisfy with particular kinds of media use. In putting forward these ideas, Herzog and, especially, those who built on her work, would reiterate the individualized, decontextual, exchange understanding of emotion suggested in Dysinger and Ruckmick's research. Indeed, today uses and gratifications research tends to be much more quantitative and survey-based, losing even the context that was provided by Herzog's more in-depth interviews.

Similarly to uses and gratifications theorists, the technologically focused work of Marshall McLuhan, which found wide popularity in the 1960s, reversed some of the criticisms that had been leveled by previous media theorists. Rather than decrying the world created by the electronic media, McLuhan argued that the speed and simultaneity of radio and television had, in fact, liberated people from the more oppressive world of writing, the printing press, and books. McLuhan based his arguments on changes in what he called "sense ratios." The written world created a culture of "the eye," which, McLuhan argued, worked to separate the senses through a problematic stress on rationality and abstraction that aimed to put everything into a category. In contrast, the oral culture that was displaced by writing, like the new electronic media of McLuhan's age, emphasized "the ear," drawing synesthetic and other connections between various kinds of sensory experiences. Auditory culture united rather than divided human experience.[40]

Although McLuhan often wrote of media within a larger historical frame, his discussion of sense ratios nonetheless recalled the physiological emphasis of early-twentieth-century media research. In his 1962 book *Gutenberg Galaxy*, he claimed that "literacy affects the physiology as well as the psychic life of the African," referencing research by J. C. Carothers on how writing impacted oral cultures in Africa.[41] Still more directly, in *Laws of Media*, coauthored by his son and published after his death, McLuhan connected the sense ratios of ear and eye to the right and left hemispheres of the brain. Citing neurological research and even including a brain scan, McLuhan's take on the sensations of media looked more and more like Dysinger and Ruckmick's physiological approach.[42] Although McLuhan would celebrate the electronic media that Dysinger and Ruckmick criticized, he would not free media studies from the view of emotion that their writing had helped to advance.

As McLuhan was writing, another perspective was gaining a strong presence in American media studies: the *cultural studies* tradition. In the American context, this general approach took several distinct forms. One perspective developed within Ray Browne's Popular Culture Association, centered at Bowling Green State University.[43] If McLuhan and the uses and gratifications tradition had rescued the electronic media and audience pleasure from various kinds of criticism, Browne's approach would do so still more vehemently. The association took one of its primary goals to be documenting a whole range of even the most presumably mundane popular culture artifacts. BGSU would eventually have a library collection devoted to mass market books, popular magazines, and similar ephemera.

Despite the value of this archival work, the association's general approach remained relatively atheoretical and apolitical. One of Browne's early essays focused on the Southern "holler"—a vocal expression that he ties to folk culture and agricultural life in particular. While acknowledging that hollers were performed by poor Southern Whites and African Americans engaged in lonely, isolating forms of work, Browne ultimately deemphasizes this cultural context. "The 'holler' was as natural a call as the song of the bird, a spontaneous overflow of the poetic urge," he writes.[44] Highlighting the spontaneity of these emotional expressions, rather than their place in a series of tensions over race and class, Browne would ignore a more deeply political reading of the holler. In fact, by celebrating the supposed authenticity of the holler's emotions, Browne reiterated a common stereotype about the emotional expressions of racial and class minorities—who are often presented as more emotional than the presumably rational dominant classes. Browne's and the larger popular culture movement's attempt to democratize pleasure had come at the expense of a wider, more critically informed theory of emotion.

A more theoretically and politically sophisticated cultural studies tradition would develop from the American incorporation of British Cultural Studies— the tradition of work developing at the University of Birmingham under the direction of Richard Hoggart, Raymond Williams, Stuart Hall, and others. Perhaps this tradition's most prominent theorization of emotion came in the form of Williams's concept of "structures of feeling." As Williams explained, he chose the term "feeling" in order "to emphasize a distinction from more formal concepts of 'worldview' or 'ideology.'" When exploring structures of feeling, scholars were to concern themselves "with meanings and values as they are actively lived and felt." Williams elaborated that the relationship between individual feelings and "more formal and systematic beliefs are in practice variable (including historically variable)."[45] Williams's aim was to explore the complex relationships between feelings and social and historical structures.

As Stuart Hall has suggested, Williams's "culturalist" approach—which took seriously such categories of experience as "feeling"—would be largely supplanted by what he calls a "structuralist" paradigm:

> Whereas the "culturalist" paradigm can be defined without requiring a conceptual reference to the term "ideology" (the word, of course, does appear: but it is not a key concept), the "structuralist" interventions have been largely

articulated around the concept of "ideology": in keeping with its more impeccably Marxist lineage, "culture" does not figure so prominently.[46]

As *ideology* became a central term, emotion and experience more generally would largely fall out of focus for cultural studies scholars. As long as emotion was simply subsumed within ideology, the more politically and contextually informed understanding of the emotional life that might have developed from the cultural studies project would not come to fruition.

TWO AFFECTIVE TURNS

If the perspectives of late-twentieth-century media studies largely pushed emotions from view, at the turn of the twenty-first century, the emotional life has seen a dramatic increase in attention. One version of this has largely returned to the perspective of Dysinger and Ruckmick and the culture of thinking out of which their research grew. Just as the new media of the early twentieth century created an interest in emotion, the growth of the internet, social networking, and so forth has done so for the early twenty-first century. Likewise, just as a belief in the power of these media technologies led Dysinger and Ruckmick to use them to study themselves, contemporary media researchers are employing digital technologies to analyze the emotional effects of digital technologies. Today, Magnetic Resonance Imaging (MRI) and Functional Magnetic Resonance Imaging (fMRI) are taking a central place in certain areas of media research. Extending the ideas of McLuhan and Dysinger and Ruckmick, these studies attempt to isolate emotional responses to the media within the physiology of the brain. According to one group of researchers, the "ability to watch the brain and its responses to various media material in real time," opened up by these new brain imaging technologies, "promises the potential of finding biological bases for the behavioral changes from media exposure that have been observed for decades."[47] Presumably, this new research has finally delivered on the physiological perspective that Dysinger and Ruckmick believed they had established.

As would Dysinger and Ruckmick's work, this renewed physiological approach has gained wide publicity in the general culture. Two recent best-selling books have used the evidence from MRI research to support claims about the emotional and intellectual effects of our age's digital media. Steven Johnson's *Everything Bad Is Good for You: How Today's Popular Culture Is Actually Making Us Smarter*, purports to show the positive effects of the hyperstimulation he argues characterizes contemporary media. Video games, reality television, and various forms of interactive media, Johnson asserts, create powerful brain activities that enhance people's intellectual and emotional intelligence.[48] Nicholas Carr's book, *The Shallows: What the Internet Is Doing to Our Brains*, a Pulitzer Prize finalist, uses the same evidence as Johnson to make an apparently opposite argument. The ways that digital media stimulate our brains, he argues, are intellectually and emotionally shallow, creating digital-age citizens who can only establish superficial relationships to both information and each other.[49]

Despite these apparent disagreements, both Johnson and Carr are confident that emotions are physiological processes and that the best way to understand them is via high-tech emotion-measuring equipment. Early in his book, Carr argues that "media work their magic, or their mischief, *on the nervous system itself*,"[50] later making explicit his belief that "thoughts, memories, emotions, all emerge from the electrochemical interactions of neurons, mediated by synapses."[51] Johnson similarly argues that if someone is to understand the emotional effects of video games, "you need to look at game culture through the lens of neuroscience."[52] As did Dysinger and Ruckmick's research, this contemporary physiological perspective—particularly as popularized by Carr and Johnson—explicitly cuts off questions about emotion from the larger social context in which it takes place, assuming that the neurological responses to the medium itself are the entire picture when understanding digital media. Looking at only this brain/technology relationship, Carr and Johnson make a number of highly problematic assumptions about the differences between more and less technologically advanced societies, suggesting that the brains and emotions of societies with more developed technologies will be more advanced—for both good and ill—than those without them. These ideas re-create many of the biases about both technological and emotional advancement that many critics have worked to discredit.

The turn of the twenty-first century has also seen a movement toward a more critical, contextual analysis of emotions. Communication scholar Lawrence Grossberg had begun theorizing affect in the 1980s and 1990s, as would Brian Massumi.[53] By the beginning of the twenty-first century, it was possible to speak of an "affective turn"[54] in media and cultural studies scholarship. Writers such as Melissa Gregg, Greg Seigworth, and Sara Ahmed offered theories of the public and political aspects of emotion, and Jennifer Harding and Deidra Pribram reconceptualized the work of Raymond Williams for addressing a contemporary politics of emotion.[55] In reinvigorating Williams's more political understanding of emotion, this work has offered a more explicit analysis of the contextual issues—especially questions of power—that were occluded by the approaches of traditional media research.

This cultural studies work on emotion also offers an important response to the more traditional conception of mediated emotion being promoted by Johnson and Carr, as well as in much mainstream experimental media research. However, these two takes on the emotions are hardly on equal footing. The traditional physiological account of emotion and media is an extremely seductive one that draws on a modern American faith in science and technology itself. The Payne Fund Studies resonated with a public that wanted concrete evidence—however simplified—of the effects of the new media of motion pictures. Arguments about physiological overexcitement reinforce a common-sense feeling that new media speed up the world and overload people with information—an idea as powerful in the early-twenty-first-century internet age as it was for the early-twentieth-century broadcasting one. Unfortunately, scholars or critics putting forward these physiological perspectives seldom think so deliberately about the place of these responses in a larger media and emotional history, seeing the present moment simply as a scientific fact induced by the new media environment.

CONCLUSIONS AND IMPLICATIONS

The history of the interaction between contemporary media and emotional standards and experience offers many avenues for further research. If a technology as bare bones as the telegraph affected emotion—in ways both real and imagined—what of the new media that offers extensive impact and invasive presence? Have the emotional results been as revolutionary as the technologies themselves? In addressing such questions, an interdisciplinary approach remains essential.

Historians of emotion have a lot to offer to this conversation, and media theorists and media historians would do well to make emotion a central component of their own analyses. Until contemporary media research is more reflexively situated within the emotional climate of its time, it will be extremely difficult to evaluate the strengths of claims about the emotional impact of various media. How are we—as researchers and as a wider culture—to separate assertions about the emotional impact of Facebook from the ongoing concerns that characterize the rhetoric of the technological sublime, or from our own moment's anxieties about emotion? Telling the longer history of media and emotion should demonstrate the extent to which particular arguments and criticisms repeat at different moments in time, challenging the uniqueness people tend to attribute to their own media moment. This should run in parallel with another approach: offering historical analyses of claims about media and emotion at particular moments in time—including our own.

The way that Dysinger and Ruckmick approached the motion picture was influenced by changes in social science during the time they were writing, including a general emphasis on emotional control. What sorts of values and anxieties are influencing thought on media and emotion today, not only in the general culture but in the research practices of academics? What does it mean when we—as scholars, critics, or everyday media users—suggest that new technologies are making us more emotionally stimulated? How do these claims relate to similar claims about earlier communication technologies offered at other moments in time? Asking such questions is a first step toward understanding our complex emotional relationships to the media.

NOTE

1. Plato, "The Phaedrus," in *The Collected Dialogues of Plato*, ed. Edith Hamilton and Huntington Cairns (Princeton, N.J.: Princeton University Press, 1989).

2. On the significance of the use of the term *pharmakon* in this dialog, see Jacques Derrida, "Plato's Pharmacy," in *Dissemination* (Chicago: University of Chicago Press, 1981). On the larger issue of the transformation from oral to written culture, and Plato's place in it, see Eric Alfred Havelock, *Preface to Plato* (Cambridge, Mass.: Harvard University Press, 1963); Walter J. Ong, *Orality and Literacy: The Technologizing of the Word* (London: Methuen, 1982); John Durham Peters, *Speaking into the Air: A History of the Idea of Communication* (Chicago: University of Chicago Press, 1999).

3. Marcello Pera, *The Ambiguous Frog: The Galvani-Volta Controversy on Animal Electricity* (Princeton, N.J.: Princeton University Press, 1992).

4. Anne Harrington, *The Cure Within: A History of Mind-Body Medicine*, 1st ed. (New York: W. W. Norton, 2008); Peters, *Speaking into the Air*.

5. "Not So Dark as It Seems," *Christian Union*, November 4, 1874, 350.

6. "Correspondence," *Philadelphia Medical Times*, April 7, 1883, 480.

7. Elizabeth Barnard, "The Atlantic Telegraph," in *Heart Offerings* (Chatfield, Minn.: Elizabeth Barnard, 1883), 87.

8. George F. Hoar, "Address of Senator George F. Hoar," *American Missionary* 35, no. 11 (1881): 372.

9. Brenton J. Malin, "Failed Transmissions and Broken Hearts: The Telegraph, Communications Law, and the Emotional Responsibility of New Technologies," *Media History* 17, no. 4 (2011): 331–344.

10. Peter Stearns, *American Cool: Constructing a Twentieth-Century Emotional Style* (New York: New York University Press, 1994). On the movement from passions to emotion, see also Daniel M. Gross, *The Secret History of Emotion: From Aristotle's Rhetoric to Modern Brain Science* (Chicago: University of Chicago Press, 2006). On the relevance of Stearns arguments to theories of communication, see Brent Malin, "Communication with Feeling: Emotion, Publicness, and Embodiment," *Quarterly Journal of Speech* 87 (2001): 216–235.

11. Peter Stearns, *American Fear: The Causes and Consequences of High Anxiety* (New York: Routledge, 2006), 104.

12. Nicole Eustace, *Passion Is the Gale: Emotion, Power, and the Coming of the American Revolution* (Chapel Hill, N.C.: University of North Carolina Press, 2008).

13. Hugo Münsterberg, *The Photoplay: A Psychological Study* (New York: D. Appleton and Company, 1916), 112.

14. Ibid., 130.

15. Ibid.

16. Graham Wallas, *The Great Society: A Psychological Analysis* (New York: Macmillan, 1914), 3.

17. Walter Lippmann, *Public Opinion* (New York: Harcourt Brace, 1922), 46.

18. Carl Dreher, "Communized Emotion," *Forum* 74, no. 6 (1925): 844. On anxieties about speech and emotion as connected to radio, see Brenton J. Malin, "Electrifying Speeches: Emotional Control and the Technological Aesthetic of the Voice in the Early 20th Century U.S.," *Journal of Social History* 45, no. 1 (2011): 1–19.

19. Harold D. Lasswell, *Propaganda Technique in the World War* (New York: A. A. Knopf, 1927), 2–3.

20. Brenton J. Malin, "Mediating Emotion: Technology, Social Science, and Emotion in the Payne Fund Motion Picture Studies," *Technology & Culture* 50, no. 2 (2009): 366–390; Brenton J. Malin, "Not Just Your Average Beauty: Carl Seashore and the History of Communication Research in the United States," *Communication Theory* 21, no. 3 (2011): 299–316.

21. Peters, *Speaking into the Air*.

22. Charles Camic, "On Edge: Sociology during the Great Depression and the New Deal," in *Sociology in America: A History*, ed. Craig J. Calhoun (Chicago: University of Chicago Press, 2007); Robert C. Bannister, *Sociology and Scientism: The American Quest for Objectivity, 1880–1940* (Chapel Hill: University of North Carolina Press, 1987); Mark C. Smith, *Social Science in the Crucible: The American Debate over Objectivity and Purpose, 1918–1941* (Durham, N.C.: Duke University Press, 1994); Ernest Keen, *A History of Ideas in American Psychology* (Westport, Conn.: Praeger, 2001); Deborah Coon, "Standardizing the Subject: Experimental Psychologists, Introspection, and the Quest for a Technoscientific Ideal," *Technology & Culture* 34, no. 4 (1993); Otniel Dror, "The Scientific Image of Emotion: Experience and Technologies of Inscription," *Configurations* 7, no. 3 (1999); Malin, "Mediating Emotion."

23. Edgar Dale, *The Content of Motion Pictures* (New York: Macmillan, 1933), 225–226. Only twelve of the thirteen monographs actually made it to press. The thirteenth manuscript, Paul Cressey's *Boys, Movies, and City Streets*, never made it into publication. See Garth Jowett, I. C. Jarvie, and Kathryn H. Fuller, *Children and the Movies: Media Influence and the Payne Fund Controversy* (Cambridge, U.K.: Cambridge University Press, 1996); and Garth Jowett, Ian Jarvie, and Kathryn H. Fuller, "The Thirteenth Manuscript: The Case of the Missing Payne Fund Study," *Historical Journal of Film, Radio and Television* 13, no. 4 (1993): 387–402.

24. Christian Ruckmick to William Short, September 26, 1930, Container 28, Folder 560, The Payne Fund, Inc., Records (MSS. No. 4315), The Western Reserve Historical Society Manuscript Collections, Cleveland, Ohio.

25. Wendell Dysinger and Christian Ruckmick, *The Emotional Responses of Children to the Motion Picture Situation* (New York: Macmillan, 1933), 6.

26. Ibid., 119.

27. Christian A. Ruckmick, "How Do Motion Pictures Affect the Attitudes and Emotions of Children?: The Galvanic Technique Applied to the Motion Picture Situation," *Journal of Educational Psychology* 6, no. 4 (1932): 210–219; Dysinger and Ruckmick, *Emotional Responses of Children*.

28. "Child's Reactions to Movies Is Shown," *New York Times*, May 28, 1933, E7.

29. James W. Carey, *Communication as Culture: Essays on Media and Society* (Boston: Unwim Hyman, 1989). On the wider history of this perspective, see also Peters, *Speaking into the Air*.

30. Dale Carnegie, *How to Win Friends and Influence People* (New York: Simon and Schuster, 1936).

31. Edward L. Bernays, "Molding Public Opinion," *Annals of the American Academy of Political and Social Science* 179 (1935): 85.

32. Hadley Cantril, *The Invasion from Mars: A Study in the Psychology of Panic* (Princeton, N.J.: Princeton University Press, 1940).

33. Ibid., 54.

34. Dysinger and Ruckmick, *Emotional Responses of Children*, 59.

35. Cantril, *Invasion from Mars*, 205.

36. Such questions about effects and exchange were well suited to the Columbia perspective. If the approach of Dysinger and Ruckmick had, however unintentionally, created the sorts of research sought by the media industry, the Columbia School would quite explicitly undertake what Lazarsfeld called an "administrative approach" to communication. Paul Lazarsfeld, "Remarks on Administrative and Critical Research," *Studies in Philosophy and Social Science* 9, no. 1 (1941): 2–16. They aimed to create media research that was amenable to the aims of corporations and the government. In fact, CBS executive Frank Stanton would serve the Office of Radio Research in an advisory capacity and would be intimately involved in the research for *Invasion from Mars*.

37. Herta Herzog, "On Borrowed Experience: An Analysis of Listening to Daytime Sketches," *Studies in Philosophy and Social Science* 9, no. 1 (1941).

38. Elihu Katz and Paul Felix Lazarsfeld, *Personal Influence: The Part Played by People in the Flow of Mass Communications* (Glencoe, Ill.: Free Press, 1955), 378.

39. Jay G. Blumler and Elihu Katz, *The Uses of Mass Communications: Current Perspectives on Gratifications Research* (Beverly Hills, Calif.: Sage Publishing Company, 1974); Elihu Katz, Jay G. Blumler, and Michael Gurevitch, "Uses and Gratifications Research," *The Public Opinion Quarterly* 37, no. 4 (1974); Elihu Katz and David Foulkes, "On the Use of the Mass Media as 'Escape': Clarification of a Concept," *Public Opinion Quarterly* 26, no. 3 (1962).

40. Marshall McLuhan, *The Gutenberg Galaxy: The Making of Typographic Man* (Toronto: University of Toronto Press, 1962); Marshall McLuhan, *Understanding Media: The Extensions of Man* (New York: McGraw-Hill, 1964).

41. McLuhan, *Gutenberg Galaxy*, 33; J. C. Carothers, "Culture, Psychiatry, and the Written Word," *Psychiatry* 22 (1959): 307–320.

42. Marshall McLuhan and Eric McLuhan, *Laws of Media: The New Science* (Toronto: University of Toronto Press, 1988), 69.

43. Ray Browne, *Mission Underway: The History of the Popular Culture Association/ American Culture Association and the Popular Culture Movement 1967–2001* (Bowling Green, Ohio: Popular Culture Association, 2002).

44. Ray Browne, "Some Notes on the Southern 'Holler,'" *Journal of American Folklore* 67, no. 263 (1954): 74.

45. Raymond Williams, *Marxism and Literature* (Oxford, U.K.: Oxford University Press, 1977), 132.

46. Stuart Hall, "Cultural Studies: Two Paradigms," *Media Culture Society* 2, no. 1 (1980): 64.

47. Daniel R. Anderson et al., "Brain Imaging—An Introduction to a New Approach to Studying Media Processes and Effects," *Media Psychology* 8, no. 1 (2006): 6.

48. Steven Johnson, *Everything Bad Is Good for You: How Today's Popular Culture Is Actually Making Us Smarter* (New York: Riverhead Books, 2006).

49. Nicholas G. Carr, *The Shallows: What the Internet Is Doing to Our Brains* (New York: W. W. Norton, 2011).

50. Ibid., 3. Emphasis added.

51. Ibid., 20.

52. Johnson, *Everything Bad Is Good for You*, 33.

53. Lawrence Grossberg, *Dancing in Spite of Myself: Essays on Popular Culture* (Durham, N.C.: Duke University Press, 1997); Lawrence Grossberg, *It's a Sin: Essays on .Postmodernism, Politics & Culture* (Sydney, N.S.W.: Power Publications, 1988); Lawrence Grossberg, *We Gotta Get out of This Place: Popular Conservatism and Postmodern Culture* (New York: Routledge, 1992); Brian Massumi, *The Politics of Everyday Fear* (Minneapolis: University of Minnesota Press, 1993).

54. Patricia Ticineto Clough and Jean O'Malley Halley, *The Affective Turn: Theorizing the Social* (Durham, N.C.: Duke University Press, 2007); Melissa Gregg, "Learning to (Love) Labour: Production Cultures and the Affective Turn," *Communication and Critical/Cultural Studies* 6, no. 2 (2009); Melissa Gregg and Gregory J. Seigworth, *The Affect Theory Reader* (Durham, N.C.: Duke University Press, 2010).

55. Gregg and Seigworth, *Affect Theory Reader*; Sara Ahmed, *The Cultural Politics of Emotion* (New York: Routledge, 2004); Jennifer Harding and E. Deidre Pribram, "Losing Our Cool?" *Cultural Studies* 18, no. 6 (2004): 863–883; Jennifer Harding and E. Deidre Pribram, "The Power of Feeling: Locating Emotions in Culture," *European Journal of Cultural Studies* 5, no. 4 (2002): 407–426.

AFTERWORD

SUSAN J. MATT AND
PETER N. STEARNS

The momentum for research in the history of emotions is truly impressive, after the somewhat tentative launch of the field several decades back. Major centers in the United Kingdom, Australia, and Germany as well as periodic conferences in many other countries demonstrate the growing institutional interest in emotions history. Individual scholars and writers contribute additional vigor, under the emotions history label or more indirectly. A recent study of the modern history of sincerity, calling attention to the important emotional alignments involved, is an intriguing case in point.[1] Emotions history is gaining recognition as an innovative way to improve understanding of how the human animal operates. As noted in the introduction, it is turning from duckling to academic swan.

This book has been intended to capture existing strengths, without pretending to comprehensive coverage, but above all to suggest examples and directions for the future. The essays certainly address a number of crucial points, vital to the field as it moves forward. Several chapters, for example, explicitly deal with causation, highlighting the possibility of understanding why emotional change occurs rather than simply recording it. Even such simple technological innovations as the telegraph can factor into emotional change (or perceptions of change). Likewise, urbanization and industrialization have significant effects on emotional life.

Dealing with the consequences of emotional change is a close twin to causation. Emotional shifts, even around specific feelings such as joy, help explain important developments in politics. They're crucial to understanding patterns of legal change. John Corrigan reminds us of the opportunity to use emotions history to help explain surges in violence, and surely more work on this connection will pay dividends in the future. The chapters on religion, politics, and the media are deliberately designed to show how emotions history interconnects with historical inquiry into other facets of society, and connections of this sort will be expanded in the future—for example, to link to analyses of economic change or innovations in health and medicine.

Historical analysis thus deals both with how emotions respond to discrete developments in other domains and with how emotions help to translate change not only into personal and family life but into wider areas of social behavior. These connections provide abundant spurs to further research.

The essays in the volume, particularly of course in chapters 3 and 4, show the great potential in expanding emotions history beyond Western confines. It's obvious that a number of important regions are still largely left out of emotions history, unavailable for comment. But glass half full: at least we're gaining important examples of how a more ambitious geography can be tackled and what the benefits are in terms of both better regional and better emotional understandings.

We can hope as well that future efforts will push more directly into comparative work, something that emotions historians have thus far largely avoided.

Additional innovations are already on the horizon. The steady development of research in neuroscience cries out for imaginative combination with history. John Corrigan reminds us of the difficulties of using data on emotional biology to understand developments in religion, but we will surely see some further efforts in the future. Tentative conversations between neuroscientists and historians are already generating new projects—for example, around the emotional experiences of witches seen through a combination of neuroscience categories and historical materials—and we can expect more.

As more cultural materials are digitized, we can also expect the techniques of data mining to contribute directly to emotions history. By allowing historians to determine the incidence of key words and combinations, data mining can establish some analytical parameters in ways heretofore impossible, though the results still will require qualitative work. An example: the word *sulky*—an intriguing emotional term—entered the English language in 1744. Data mining on published materials in the nineteenth-century United States shows that the word was almost never actually used until the 1840s but then surged forward steadily in the early twentieth century, after which it declined rapidly and leveled off once more.[2] Why did emotional sulkiness draw new interest? Why did concern drop? The answers depend on further work, but the questions, which can be clearly posed only through quantitative assessments, are already intriguing. Stay tuned: this aspect of emotions history is just getting going.

Finally, as noted in the Introduction, the emotions historians of the future need to continue to ponder their relevant audiences. There are two angles here. First, potentially at least, emotions history could win significant attention from that elusive animal, the wider reading public. Expansion in this direction could facilitate better understanding of history and of emotion alike. As with most research fields, emotions historians to date have been pretty busy dealing with other problems—like sources and methods—and writing for other researchers, but down the line there might be opportunities to develop a broader readership. Further expansion to student audiences is already possible and would constitute a step in the right direction.

Fruitful popularization aside, emotions historians must also keep in mind their mutual connections with other fields engaged in similar research. There's an audience here for good emotions history, as long as it is not too bogged down in historical minutiae. A key reason to pay renewed attention to the relationships between modernity and emotion is to improve dialogue with disciplines like sociology that look to historical big pictures in areas like emotions study. But interdisciplinarity involves openness to findings and methods from other disciplines beyond the ranks of historians alone. The essays in this volume reflect enough interdisciplinary links to remind us of the wider possibilities, but both challenge and opportunity will persist as we move forward.

Above all, emotions historians in the future must remain actively aware of the two kinds of basic questions they are trying to answer, or help to answer. They owe it to their discipline to deal with issues about emotions in the past and how their explorations improve our understanding of historical developments in various times and places. But at least some of them must also deal with questions about how their work improves our grasp of emotions and emotional concerns in the present. There are a number of paths here, ranging from exploring continuities in regional emotional cultures to explicit analysis of past changes that lead directly to current standards. The study of emotion is an expanding enterprise, and the historical component, itself growing rapidly, promises its own contributions to understanding why contemporary emotional patterns are what they are. The history of emotions allows us to see more clearly both these contemporary patterns and their relationship to past modes of experiencing and expressing feelings.

NOTES

1. R. J. Magill, *Sincerity* (New York: W. W. Norton and Company, 2012).
2. googlebooks.byu.edu/x.asp (accessed March 16, 2013).

CONTRIBUTORS

JOHN CORRIGAN is the Lucius Moody Bristol Distinguished Professor of Religion and History at Florida State University. His recent work on emotion and religion includes *The Oxford Handbook of Religion and Emotion* (Oxford University Press, 2008), *Religion and Emotion: Approaches and Interpretations* (Oxford University Press, 2004), and *Business of the Heart: Religion and Emotion in the Nineteenth Century* (Berkeley: University of California Press, 2002). His current research is on the feeling of emptiness in America.

PAMELA EPSTEIN received a BA in American culture from Vassar College in 1999 and a PhD in history from Rutgers University in 2010. She has been published in *Media History* and the *New York Times*. She currently works at the New York City Department of Cultural Affairs.

NICOLE EUSTACE is associate professor of history at New York University. She received a BA in history from Yale University in 1994 and a PhD in history from the University of Pennsylvania in 2001. She is the author of *Passion Is the Gale: Emotion, Power and the Coming of the American Revolution* (Chapel Hill, 2008) and *1812: War and the Passions of Patriotism* (Philadelphia, 2012).

NORMAN KUTCHER is associate professor of history and Laura J. and L. Douglas Meredith Professor for Teaching Excellence at Syracuse University. He is the author of *Mourning in Late Imperial China: Filial Piety and the State* (Cambridge University Press, 1999). His articles have appeared in the *Harvard Journal of Asiatic Studies*, the *Journal of Asian Studies*, and the *American Historical Review*. He is currently at work on a study of eunuchs in seventeenth- and eighteenth-century China.

BRENTON J. MALIN is an associate professor of communication at the University of Pittsburgh with a focus on media theory, history, and criticism. His essays have appeared in *Media History, Technology and Culture, Communication Theory*, and the *Journal of Social History*. He is the author of *American Masculinity under Clinton: Popular Media and the '90s "Crisis of Masculinity."*

SUSAN J. MATT is Presidential Distinguished Professor of History and chair of the history department at Weber State University in Ogden, Utah. She is author of *Homesickness: An American History* (Oxford University Press, 2011) and *Keeping Up with the Joneses: Envy in American Consumer Society, 1890–1930* (University of Pennsylvania Press, 2003). With Peter Stearns she is editor of the History of the Emotions Series for the University of Illinois Press.

DARRIN M. McMAHON is the Ben Weider Professor of History at Florida State University. He is the author of *Enemies of the Enlightenment* (Oxford, 2001), *Happiness: A History* (Atlantic Monthly, 2006), and *Divine Fury: A History of Genius* (Basic Books, 2013), and the editor, with Samuel Moyn, of *Rethinking Modern European Intellectual History* (Oxford, 2013).

PETER N. STEARNS is provost, university professor, and executive vice president at George Mason University in Fairfax, Virginia. He has published widely in modern social history, including the history of emotions, and in world history. Representative recent works include *Satisfaction Not Guaranteed: Dilemmas of Progress in Modern Society; Human Rights in World History* and *Demilitarization in the Contemporary World* (forthcoming). Since 1967 he has served as editor in chief of the *Journal of Social History*.

MARK D. STEINBERG is professor of history at the University of Illinois at Urbana-Champaign. His publications include *Petersburg Fin de Siècle* (Yale University Press, 2011); *Interpreting Emotions in Russia and Eastern Europe*, coedited with Valeria Sobol (Northern Illinois University Press, 2011); *A History of Russia*, 8th ed., with Nicholas Riasanovsky (Oxford University Press, 2010); and *Proletarian Imagination: Self, Modernity, and the Sacred in Russia, 1910–1925* (Cornell University Press, 2002).

INDEX

advertisements, matrimonial, 120–137; computer and online dating and, 134–135; consumerism and, 127–128; growing middle class and, 122–123, 126; letters in response to, 126–127, 129–132; loneliness as a theme in, 126; newspaper personal columns and, 133–134; nineteenth century, 120–121; opponents of, 128–129, 133–134; purpose of, 121–122; urban migration and, 124–125. *See also* marriage

Affairs of Honor: National Politics in the New Republic, 173

African Americans, 46–47, 173, 196

"Against Constructionism: Toward a Historical Ethnography of Emotion," 169

Akenside, Mark, 111

American Revolution, the, 164–165, 167–168; emotion, state, and society in, 174–175; nationalism and emotional/political unity in, 171–174; patriotism and population theory in, 175–177. *See also* politics

Analects, 59–60

Anderson, Benedict, 171–172, 174, 178, 180

anger, 36, 105; murder and, 50; restraint, 27–28

Anna Karenina, 107

Annales School, 3–4

Appleby, Joyce, 172, 173

argument, emotional, 170–171

Ariès, Philippe, 3, 18

Aristotle, 47, 104, 110, 114

Armenian genocide, 78

arranged marriages, 26

artistic representations of emotions, 48

Asad, Talal, 156

audience, 7

Augustine, 143, 144

Auslander, Leora, 174, 175

Austen, Jane, 48–49

Ba Jin, 58

Bakunin, Mikhail, 80

Barnard, Elizabeth, 186

Basch, Norma, 132

Baumeister, Roy, 104

Belinsky, Vissarion, 80

Benjamin, Walter, 107

Bernays, Edward, 192

Beyreuther, Erich, 112

Bian Gong, 65

The University of Illinois Press
is a founding member of the
Association of American University Presses.

University of Illinois Press
1325 South Oak Street
Champaign, IL 61820-6903
www.press.uillinois.edu